"This book is the perfect buddy read by every student teacher has an uncanny ability to support new teachers while simultaneously sparking in their mentors!"

—**Melissa Emler**, *chief learning officer, Modern Learners*

"*Always a Lesson* by Gretchen serves as an indispensable guide for instructional coaches and mentors, articulating the Teacher Success Pathway with precision. It lays out a strategic framework for coaches and mentors to identify and focus on key areas for teacher development, ensuring efforts directly amplify teacher proficiency and student success. Gretchen's insightful approach equips coaches with the tools to effectively prioritize and advance teaching excellence."

—**Nicole S. Turner**, *author and CEO of Simply Instructional Coaching Inc.*

"Teachers of all experience levels will benefit from reading *Always a Lesson* as Gretchen Bridgers expertly outlines a pathway of success as though she is your personal teacher mentor. Readers will walk away with actionable insights and an abundance of bonus content in downloadable resources."

—**Linda Rhyne**, *owner of Linda Rhyne Consulting, North Carolina*

"Classroom teachers along with those who mentor them would greatly benefit from the insights shared in this book. Gretchen helps shift the perspective of readers to realize more tools do not equal more success, but it's the implementation of the tools that make the difference while providing a clear pathway that will enable readers to know which tools to use when."

—**Jamal Maxsam,** *MEd, CEO of Lead Like a Champion L.L.C.*

Always a Lesson

Teacher Essentials for Classroom and Career Success

Gretchen Bridgers

JOSSEY-BASS

A Wiley Brand

Library of Congress Cataloging-in-Publication Data:

Names: Bridgers, Gretchen, author.
Title: Always a lesson : teacher essentials for classroom and career success / Gretchen Bridgers.
Description: First edition. | San Francisco, CA : Jossey-Bass, [2024] | Includes bibliographical references and index.
Identifiers: LCCN 2023055090 (print) | LCCN 2023055091 (ebook) | ISBN 9781394158805 (paperback) | ISBN 9781394158812 (adobe pdf) | ISBN 9781394158829 (epub)
Subjects: LCSH: Effective teaching. | Mentoring in education. | Classroom management. | Teacher effectiveness.
Classification: LCC LB1025.3 .B752 2024 (print) | LCC LB1025.3 (ebook) | DDC 371.102—dc23/eng/20231206
LC record available at https://lccn.loc.gov/2023055090
LC ebook record available at https://lccn.loc.gov/2023055091

COVER DESIGN: PAUL MCCARTHY
COVER ART: © GETTY IMAGES / IMAGE SOURCE

Arrow image from Flaticon.com.
SKY10066910_020924

CONTENTS

Part Four | Brick 3: Student Engagement   145

Part Five | Brick 4: Student Choice and Ownership   179

Part Six | Implementing Your New Learning   215

FOREWORD

Effective teachers in today's classrooms must understand that learning outcomes can no longer be solely intended for the students. Today's effective teachers recognize that she or he must also attain new levels of learning in order to move students forward in instruction.

In this book, Gretchen Bridgers presents reciprocal outcomes for instructional growth. Her work emphasizes how well-planned lessons deepen the learning of the students as well as the teachers who designed them. This architecture for teaching and learning ensures that there is **always a lesson.**

Gretchen's poignant message for what effective teachers should know and certainly be able to do in the classrooms, whether in person or online, is a foundation for school improvement. School leaders who apply her strategies will experience what happens when teachers assess not only students, growth and development, but also their own.

Gretchen addresses three critical components of effective teaching for today. Her work includes the design of appropriate and thoughtful lesson design, the need for effective classroom management, and the value of honoring student choice.

All three aspects of Gretchen's approach to elevating instruction in this book are equally critical to moving beyond "sit and get" or "click and watch" to whole-class engagement and schoolwide change. Implementation of the educational changes the current learning landscape demands is not easy. But it starts with intentional planning and powerful delivery of instruction. It's **always a lesson!**

—Dr. Cathy Owens-Oliver

PART ONE

THE BEGINNING, THE PATHWAY, AND THE FORMULA

The information provided in this book is based on my personal experience as an elementary school teacher, a K–12 new teacher coach, an educational speaker, and a professional learning developer. I have learned what works, what doesn't work, and—most important—why the essentials in this book make all the difference regarding who gets better and stays better. But don't worry—I'll also share relevant research to support my claims.

There is no reason strategies for effective instruction should remain a secret. Every teacher deserves to operate at their potential, and every kid deserves to be taught by the best version of the teacher in front of them. Our future depends on it.

Throughout this book I include moments of my personal story that offer segments of my own journey as an educator. But I don't share these "Lessons from the Trenches" just because I hope you'll enjoy them; I want to provide an analogy of sorts to help you see how each lesson could apply to you and your particular circumstances.

So, before diving into the teacher essentials, I'd like to share with you the trail that led me to what would later become the Teacher Success Pathway. After that I'll share how to use this book, and how this book can help you.

PROLOGUE: WHERE IT ALL BEGAN

Lessons from the Trenches

I always knew I wanted to be a teacher. That might not be the reality for many educators out there, but for me I fell in love hard and fast. I played school with my stuffed animals in the front hallway, wearing my dad's oversized T-shirts and my mom's high heels.

As I grew older, I was able to convince my two older brothers and even my parents to play along. I gave up pretty quickly on including my brothers in my playtime because they argued, misbehaved, and made a mess of all my papers. (I think they did it on purpose so I wouldn't invite them back—it worked.) I'd invited my parents to play along as well, but they weren't any more helpful. My dad cheated off my mom's papers, flirted with her during class, and never raised his hand to speak. He would tell me, "I'm just helping prepare you for the reality of the classroom." Sadly, he was right. My mom was my star student, completed all assignments and listened to every direction. In all my years of teaching, I had more students like my brothers and Dad than I did my mom. Thankfully, I was well prepared for that!

Every Christmas, Santa would bring me items for my classroom—a wall-sized world map, stickers, pens, teaching books, comfy shoes, and so on. I was well equipped to enter the profession. We turned a bay of our garage into my classroom. I had a shelf to store all of my teaching materials, including my own school papers I used as student work to pass out to imaginary students. I referenced the wall map more than necessary, gleaming with pride as I pretended I was in my own classroom with the pull-down map.

It was a no brainer that I would go to college for elementary education. My fourth-grade teacher, Ms. Lofy, made learning fun and easy. I wanted to do that for kids, too. Although she handed me a job prediction certificate at the end of the year that said "Most likely to work at JCPenney," she knew my love of teaching. My parents had gone out of town a handful of times and she babysat for us. I was star struck having my favorite teacher ever in my home. I showed her all of my supplies and one day she told me to stop by her classroom. She handed me all of her old teacher manuals (with the red answers on the pages!) and said I could add them to my collection because she was going to be getting new ones. I carried those teaching manuals around everywhere I went. The power I felt having the answers in front of me was enough to make me feel 10 feet tall.

I was pretty bored in most of my college classes because I had been learning about teaching for decades prior. I was a psychology/special education major, only because that is what the college offered. My psychology classes were pretty interesting, but I knew right away special education [SPED] wasn't my forte. I didn't have the patience, and that paperwork is a nightmare! (Shout out to all SPED teachers: you are saints!)

One of my adjunct professors taught in a school during the day and came to teach our class at night. I leaned into every word she spoke. She was actively in the classroom, with amazing stories to tell, giving us practical examples of what we were learning. Excitement poured out of me. I arrived early and stayed late. I wanted more classes like that one—practical and relevant.

In my college courses, I learned a lot of theory and stories of famous dead guys. I had a "how to teach math and literacy" class for one semester. Out of four years of undergrad, you'd think more of my classes would be focused on the art of teaching (strategies, techniques, psychology, etc.). By senior year, I had a quick stint of student teaching at two nearby elementary schools—one regular ed class and one SPED. I guess four years of learning about teaching (not how) and six months practicing in real classrooms meant I suddenly was capable to do it on my own. (What a joke!) Although that equation didn't seem to add up, I absolutely loved every moment of being in a school and teaching children.

specific niche of teaching teachers. I now knew how I wanted to help them. No longer would I provide generic help, but I would provide intensive support, homing in on their weak areas and developing systems to strengthen those areas. Over time, I knew with a targeted approach, I could really have an impact on teaching performance.

Around this same time of my "aha," my new principal saw my own classroom management strength and asked for help. The fifth grade had no veteran teachers on the roster, and the student misbehaviors were out of control. These students had to pass the end-of-grade test in reading, math, and science (a test heavy in vocabulary). I agreed to help teach science to the entire fifth-grade class the following year by departmentalizing across the grade level. I had to freshen up on fifth-grade science, especially vocabulary, and design my best lessons to ensure every student in this entire grade level could be successful.

It didn't take long for me to realize this age of student was not my favorite. They were stinky (literally) and sarcastic. Although I love sarcasm, it didn't belong in the classroom and quickly turned into apathy and disinterest. My third-grade approach wasn't going to work with fifth graders. I was going to have to learn some new tricks. Many attempts failed, but my skill in managing a classroom with many moving pieces (like four classes of fifth graders rotating in and out all day) enabled things to run fairly smoothly.

I got to teach my previous class of third graders as fifth graders. That was a cool experience. They adored me and our bond is what inspired them to get back into the love of learning. Their peers noticed this bond and they too started to build strong relationships with me, translating to higher participation and a decrease in absences. I'll call that one a major win. I survived that year (and so did they). It was a long one, but memorable nonetheless.

My principal promised me that I could choose any grade I wanted to teach after that. She knew I disliked the grade level, but appreciated my leadership among my fifth-grade colleagues. She also knew what type of teacher needed to be in my place and quickly interviewed some options. I requested to move to second grade the following year because being in two testing grades (third and fifth) the last few years had stressed and worn me out. She told me I deserved it and to enjoy the break.

I fell in love with teaching again with my second graders. They loved to learn, aimed to please, and were cute as a button. I had the freedom to teach how I wanted, without the stress of strictly following the pacing guide due to the testing schedule. The second-grade curriculum was interesting (I loved the life cycle unit in science—a nod to my new fifth-grade repertoire of knowledge!) and foundational to all the work my third graders had been doing. I used my knowledge of where these second graders needed to go and worked backwards to design rigorous enough instruction paired with flexibility and fun appropriate for the age of students. The jump from second grade to third is huge in terms of responsibility of assignment completion, acquisition of knowledge, participating in a long testing event, and so on. Many students struggle because second grade is set up so differently that the adjustments prove to be too much. I was able to collaborate with my second-grade colleagues to inform them of what these students would have to be able to do the following year. We then discussed that fourth quarter would be a practice run for third grade so that they truly would be ready before the stakes were high. This method worked tremendously. I highly suggest every grade level meet with their colleagues a grade level below and above to ensure we are all doing our part to ensure the transition among grade levels is made with ease.

At this point, I had taught three grades at one school, under four different leaders. I was ready to try a different environment. Working with title-one students was so rewarding because they desperately needed life lessons in addition to content lessons. That was fulfilling to inspire and encourage children in a way that their parents working multiple jobs couldn't do. However, I was emotionally exhausted. I decided a school with high parental involvement would be so polar opposite of my experiences that I would sharpen my craft in a whole new way. I'd be able to solely focus on teaching kids content and learn how to manage parent expectations and involvement.

I applied at our district's transfer fair and only interviewed at one school. I knew what I wanted. This principal reminded me of my first leader. She was laid back, confident, personable, and a dang good principal. The school culture was inviting like one big family. The school building was brand-new like my old school. My colleagues were welcoming and I fit right in. I even got to teach my favorite grade again, third.

One steamy North Carolina afternoon, I was in my classroom hanging the alphabet letters above the white board. My messy bun, athletic shorts, and oversized t-shirt seemed appropriate for all the physical labor I would be doing moving furniture and hanging posters. I heard a knock at the door and turned around to see two smiling adults.

"Hi, we are your room moms. How can we help?"

I barely got out an "excuse me," as I was so stunned at the presence of parents already, before school even started! My brain also wasn't translating "room moms." I never had one before. My students' parents at my previous school worked around the clock to make ends meet so that many times I only caught them on the phone for a brief conference. I literally had no idea how to use a room mom.

Nonetheless, we sat down at the back table and planned out some options. I apologized for my attire, they apologized for arriving without notice. When they received the teacher assignment, they immediately Googled me. Thankfully, my social media accounts were private and cleaned up from containing anything unprofessional (a task the head of student teaching placements at my college assigned to us before graduation.) They said they didn't know who I was and they had to come see for themselves. Looking back, I guess they self-appointed themselves as room moms! Either way, it doesn't matter. It was a wonderful year teaching third graders. Parents communicated in every type of way every day of the year. It was overwhelming but heart-warming. They made sure I performed my best for their child. These two room moms were saints, making learning fun in a way I didn't have time for—mystery readers, holiday parties, teacher gifts, and all sorts of crafts. I still keep up with these room moms to this day and with their sweet precious girls who have grown to be successful women in college!

I was ready for the next year when I received devastating news from my principal. She was retiring. I cornered her and said, "No! You can't leave. I came to this school because of you!" She knew that and appreciated it. She was glad I was there and assured me I would be just fine. And then she said something I have never forgotten, "The good ones always leave." She saw the desires of my heart and my natural talent that, with time and honing, could really make an impact on the profession. She knew someone like me would continue to move on to new experiences to further my skill and knowledge while continuing to help students and teachers at higher levels. How she saw that in me at that point, I have no idea. But she was certain.

Following blogs had been my hobby for a few years now to ensure I kept current on what was happening in other teachers' classrooms across the nation. I felt like I should start chronicling my classroom experiences. I was teaching all sorts of curriculum and life lessons while also learning a lot of lessons about great teaching along the way.

I brainstormed a few blog names and even had my family vote. Always a Lesson *was born. I didn't care if anyone read my blog, I just felt compelled to write down what was happening. I had no idea what was to come with this little old blog!*

I served on the interview panel to handpick our next principal. She was young, and only interviewed for our school. Just like I had, she knew what she wanted. She also knew our performance data forwards and backwards. She knew how she planned to keep the school moving forward and was a breath of fresh air after the very serious candidates we had been interviewing thus far. I loved handpicking interview questions, watching her process and respond, and even hearing the rest of the panel share their perspective of her afterwards. I didn't know hiring would become one way I'd love to support teachers, but I was bit by another bug—finding teaching talent.

She was hired and after a few months, this principal also saw my leadership potential. She spent a significant amount of time 1:1 with every staff member in the building. She truly wanted to know who she was working with but also how to leverage their strengths. As a leader she knew the success of the school wasn't going to be on her shoulders alone; we all had a part to play. I loved our 1:1 conversation together where I got to dream out loud like I had done numerous times before with mentors. I shared my past, present, and trajectory for the future. We had numerous conversations about what I wanted to do next in my career, such as leading professional development for staff members and mentoring colleagues and future teachers. She even invited me to shadow her for a day to see if becoming a principal was what I wanted to do. The short answer was "no" and the long answer was "not ever." She had an entire day scheduled out for us to showcase all of the different tasks she completed in her role. Sadly, we never got to do much of that list because within 5 minutes an angry parent came flying through the door, a food fight broke out in the cafeteria, followed by an impromptu visit from the district. I quickly realized this was not the way I wanted to work with teachers. It was too distant. I wanted to be in classrooms with teachers. I didn't even finish shadowing her that day, and she understood why. Even though that experience could be categorized as a "flop," it was monumental in directing my path. I am forever grateful for that closed door.

During this time, I heard about the National Board Certification process for teachers. It was another way to learn and grow my craft while also giving me a differentiating factor in comparison to my colleagues if I ever needed to stand out among them for a future position. The process required me to videotape my own teaching, reflect on its effectiveness, implement current best practices, track student performance over time, and demonstrate that I am a highly qualified teacher. This process was more beneficial than my master's degree because it was applying what I was learning in the present with the kids I was teaching right now. It was extremely relevant, timely, and purposeful. It wasn't just learning about the average kid and the research behind a teaching technique. It was me learning, applying, reflecting, revising, analyzing, and so on in the moment. What a powerful professional development opportunity. The process was hard. I wanted to quit, convinced myself I wasn't good enough, and wanted to crawl into a hole imagining the embarrassment of not earning certification after all this effort and time. I missed my first try by ¼ of a point. I was so shocked you could lose by such minimal margins. It was almost so unbelievable I didn't feel sad or embarrassed. I got mad and I went even harder the next round. I only had to redo my lowest scoring entry (thank goodness!) My literacy facilitator was able to help me pinpoint some areas that made that entry weak and write in a way that showcased all that I was doing. She was confident I was worthy of being certified because she had seen me teach numerous times. I didn't toot my horn enough the first time and it did not showcase my strength in performance as an educator. I passed the second time by leaps and bounds. I was finally nationally board certified! (Later, in 2022, I maintained that certification by completing a mini version of the process to demonstrate I still was highly qualified.) This process helped me gain clarity on what decisions I was making in the classroom that had the biggest effect on student achievement. I believe this is the moment when I started to formulate the four bricks that I write about in this book.

As a nationally board certified teacher, more leadership opportunities came my way. One day after school, I sat down at my computer to email parents about our upcoming field trip. I received an email from The New Teacher Project (TNTP). They were wanting to know if I would apply to coach new teachers in grades K through 12 in our district. It was a summer position, and I was ready to take a break from working with children directly (tutoring, babysitting, etc.). I had never heard of TNTP but working with new teachers was my passion and this felt like the perfect opportunity to lead, like I had always dreamed of.

I thoroughly planned a segment of a professional development session on teaching strategies from Doug Lemov's book Teach Like a Champion. This was the book TNTP used to teach new teachers strong instructional classroom practices. I also participated in an interview where I had to explain how I have a passion and gift for leading teachers while also being an effective teacher myself. Although I hate talking about myself, I was able to convey my teaching success in the classroom while also highlighting how I continued to mentor colleagues and because of that . . . I got the job!

I was bit again by the ed leadership love bug. I never knew coaching teachers was a job and I wanted it more than ever. I thoroughly enjoyed teaching teachers about effective teaching practices. Modeling teaching techniques, breaking down the science behind why a technique is most effective to reach students, building relationships with colleagues, and watching educators grow their skill set in real time were a few of the things I fell in love with in my new role as an instructional coach.

I started taking on other roles at TNTP such as reviewing candidate applications, placing them in cohorts nationwide, interviewing them, and of course, coaching them at the TEACH Charlotte location. I eventually left the classroom to work these multiple roles on a full-time basis. I loved giving back to my profession by handpicking future teachers who would go on to positively affect our neediest population of students in underperforming schools across the nation. I was able to teach, mentor, and coach teachers on a much larger scale than if I had stayed in my own classroom.

Around this time I heard of a website called Teachers Pay Teachers [TpT]. It was an online marketplace where teachers could upload their lesson plan materials for sale and other teachers in need of those items could purchase and download them. I decided to upload many activities I was using in my classroom. This was yet another way to share what I was doing in my classroom that was working—and make extra income! Helping teachers save time and increase the effectiveness of their instruction enabled me to affect students around the world. As my store on TpT grew over the next few years, I started uploading professional development (PD) pdfs for teachers and teacher leaders to download and implement their learning at their school sites. This was a great option for teachers who liked to read but didn't have time for an entire book. It was also used by teacher leaders creating PD sessions for their staff members and they could reference my topic, examples, and implementation guidelines to create personalized learning opportunities.

For years, I had been collecting teaching ideas and strategies on notecards and keeping them in a recipe box since I was a teenager, sharing them with every student teacher and new colleague. Someone suggested I type them up so I could easily share them with more teachers. So, I finally took those cards and turned them into my first self-published book, Elementary EDUC 101: What They Didn't Teach You in College. I felt proud to be able to pass on secrets of the trade that I painfully figured out over the years. I knew I would have been glad to have read the nitty-gritty details of the job before landing my first role in education. I hoped readers would feel the same. Again, I was able to give back to my profession, helping teachers become more effective in their classrooms—and this time, worldwide!

Over the next few years, my personal life got super busy. I got married, my husband and I built a home, and we had three beautiful children (two girls and one boy). I eventually had to give up my roles with TNTP as my mommy duties increased with each new baby. I knew I wanted to still work with teachers, but I didn't have the capacity to commute to a school every day nor work the long hours I had been accustomed to. Plus, I knew I wanted to stay home with my children while they were young if we could handle it financially.

In 2015, I officially launched my consulting business, Always a Lesson. ("Whether you're teaching a lesson, or learning one yourself, there's Always a Lesson.") This was a natural expansion of the blog I started so many years earlier, but now it was an all-encompassing website. Teachers could still read my blog, but I knew many were busy and didn't have time to read. I heard about podcasts being similar to an audio blog for busy teachers on the go. I had never listened to a podcast before and had no idea how to even make one, but I knew it was something I needed to do to continue sharing lessons with educators. I invested in a podcasting course and the Empowering Educators podcast was invented. Teachers had always told me how encouraging I was so I figured creating a safe place where they could get filled up mind and soul would be beneficial. Over the years, I learned how to deliver content in an engaging story with actionable tips. Honing my craft is my goal no matter how long I have been contributing to the educational field. When I hit the one million downloads milestone, I knew this was the avenue teachers needed and wanted help. I am so thankful to reach teachers and teacher leaders across the globe.

I perfected my speaking craft beyond the podcast by presenting and speaking at conferences. I realized this was another way I could share the lessons I had learned about great teaching practices from years teaching myself and observing other great teachers in action. When COVID-19 entered the education scene, virtual PD became the rage. Luckily, I had been offering bite-sized PD sessions on my website for years. Teachers consumed virtual PD more than ever and some even preferred the convenience of it over in-person versions. This alerted me to continue to develop my virtual sessions so that the content was timely and applicable to how classrooms were changing due to social distancing and hybrid instruction—teaching students online while some attended in person at a safe distance.

Teacher leaders, like instructional coaches, started to invest in a more guided virtual PD option I created called the Teacher Leader Mastermind. I designed this option when I realized teacher leaders were struggling to implement what I was teaching them. They needed help translating a strategy or technique I was teaching them into their particular situation. They also needed accountability to continue growing their skill set, especially when things got stressful and they wanted to stop engaging in PD. This Teacher Leader Mastermind was available to teacher leaders nationwide, meeting twice a month for one hour. I placed them in cohorts so no more than 10 teacher leaders engaged in the learning opportunity each semester. I determined this number based on my first cohort in 2018. I had eight members and felt I was able to provide 1:1 assistance while also facilitating strong collaboration among the virtual colleagues. I knew any more than 10 and I wouldn't be able to dive in as personally as I needed to in order to find out roots of obstacles rather than surface-level fires. At our virtual meetings, we would discuss monthly topics relevant to that time of the school year (e.g., establishing coaching protocols in September or increasing student ownership in March). I also incorporated a "hot seat" element so that each cohort member had a chance to share their biggest question, obstacle, or upcoming event they wanted help talking through. All members listened and contributed, as did I. When we were not meeting, teacher leaders had access to micro PD sessions related to leadership and instruction as well as hundreds of downloadable coaching forms. Cohort members have returned semester after semester because of the accountability piece. They know they have grown immensely from receiving help with their unique situation and applying their learning in that setting. PD is a start but aiding educators in applying their learning is how we can ensure what they learn enters into practice, positively affecting those they support (teachers and students).

Whether it is virtual or in-person PD, the Teacher Leader Mastermind, or downloadable resources, I was supporting the growth of teachers. Having a variety of ways to guide them, I was able to meet educators where they were in the way they needed help. Every position I held as an educator enabled me to do what I do today. It prepared my knowledge and skill level so that I could help develop and grow the knowledge and skills in others. And I believe that everything I continue to do will prepare me for what the future has in store. I know this to be true for you, too. Each position you hold will prepare you for your next role. Take advantage, go all in, and grow like a weed! Your future self will appreciate your hard work.

In 2020, during the pandemic, I was asked to cowrite a book with a dozen other educators called Educators Who Know What to Do: Experts in Education. *We each contributed a chapter based on our expertise in education. I wrote a chapter about supporting the growth and development of teachers—something I had unknowingly been doing my whole career. I highlighted the various ways teachers need support (e.g., mentorship, coaching, PD sessions, etc.) and outlined how to provide that effectively. It was a pleasure to collaborate on this book because I was able to meet teachers from all over the United States who had unique ideas and proven methods for how to revolutionize education. My professional learning network grew with even more powerful educators.*

In 2022, I started my speaking circuit. I keynoted at in-person and virtual conferences, led PD sessions, and sold my books at vendor tables. I learned I was affecting more than the people in attendance because these educators were going back to their campuses and sharing what they learned with their teams of colleagues. Multiplying learning and making a wave of more effective instruction in schools through speaking has been an absolute joy. I got to meet so many passionate educators at these events. Had I never taken the chance to forgo my own classroom to enter everyone else's classroom and school buildings, I would have limited whom I was able to help. What a joy it is to work with educators who love what they do!

The more I presented to teachers, wrote instructional technique blog posts, podcasted about teaching best practices, and coached teacher leaders, I came to realize a proven method for improving teacher talent. A year after the release of my second book, Jossey-Bass Publishers noticed my contributions in education and wanted to partner together on my third book. Their educational book division, Wiley, helped birth this book that you're reading right now into existence.

As a three-time author now, I can't even imagine what would have happened if I didn't type up those notecards full of tips for teachers or chronicle my teaching experience in a blog format. My journey in teacher leadership has enabled me to widen my net of impact, sharing what I know that best helps students and teachers become successful in the classroom and beyond. Doing so to meet educator needs and learning styles has allowed me to contribute in myriad ways I would have never thought possible when I started teaching.

What an opportunity we all have to give back to the profession! As you learn about the Teacher Success Pathway in this book, I hope you share it with others so they too can be effective in the classroom. If there are ideas, strategies, or principles that you've learned on your own journey that you'd like to share, I hope you do. Start with a single format (e.g., blog, podcast, downloadable materials, etc.). As you gain experience, consider trying additional formats to reach even more educators. Together, we can create positive change in our schools across the world.

INTRODUCTION

THE TEACHER SUCCESS PATHWAY

You have before you the book I wish I had been given when I was just starting my teaching career, because it contains a long-earned, proven method for improving teacher talent. I offer myself as your personal tour guide, illuminating the path forward to achieving stronger, more effective instructional practices for years to come.

I have come to realize a few things about teacher effectiveness over the years that I want to share with you. Being a great teacher calls for more than just standing in front of students and explaining a topic. Great teachers must possess and enact a number of skills while simultaneously delivering high-quality instruction that meets the unique needs of their students. It's an intricate mental and physical dance—thinking, planning, revising, creating, delivering, and adjusting.

This is why it can take years for teachers to get the "hang of teaching," meaning that they don't just have the skills and knowledge for teaching best practices—those skills have become ingrained in how they teach.

As a side note: It doesn't matter how many years of experience you have—implementing learning can be difficult. And then, to do it well repeatedly takes time, for all of us. Try to not get disheartened. Instead, get realistic and allow yourself repetitious practice for that learning to solidify.

What makes teaching even more difficult is that it is ever-changing. Curriculum, standards, subject area topics, school policies—to name just a few—change every couple of years or less, requiring teachers to acquire yet new skills and knowledge and adding yet more time to the learning trajectory of building new habits and showcasing them consistently.

The sheer truth is that we cannot remain effective without increasing our skills and knowledge. So, teachers battle numerous obstacles; they need to acquire skills and knowledge of best practices for teaching, sort through an abundance of information to develop stronger teaching practices, and navigate the ever-changing aspects surrounding their environment.

By choosing to read this book, you can accomplish the following:

- Acquire skills and knowledge of instructional best practices.
- Receive clear next steps to develop stronger teaching practices.
- Apply these core competencies no matter what changes are made in your teaching environment.

Know this: trends will come and go during your teaching career. Without a solid foundation in how you plan and deliver instruction, you will struggle to reach effectiveness no matter what trend you try to incorporate. However, if you follow the Teacher Success Pathway by implementing and solidifying your skill sets in the sequence as suggested, you will be able to enhance your planning and delivery of instruction with effectiveness while adding in the new trend flair. Essentials first, trends second. If you can do that, you will already be ahead of others trying to grow their craft.

How to Use This Book

Whether you are teaching a lesson or learning one yourself, there is Always a Lesson. I've built my business on that tagline because we never stop learning—and the lessons we acquire along our journey can also help others along their path. I share these lessons so that you can avoid the pitfalls I encountered and better navigate your terrain, so you too can experience classroom and career success.

I encourage you to pay close attention to what is happening around you. Be present. Reflect on what messages you receive; strive to be better personally and professionally. There's Always a Lesson to be learned!

I wrote this book to be foundational in helping teachers build and sustain proficiency in teaching, to strengthen your knowledge and skills so your teaching core is rock solid. This book can be your one-stop-shop go-to guide. It lays out a specific sequence of skills and knowledge to master, each in turn, before moving on to the next. If you take the time to consume and apply what you learn in this book, you will strengthen your teaching core competency.

This book serves as a tool for teachers of all experience levels to grow their craft. For more, see the following sidebar.

Which of the Following Applies to You and Your Situation?

NEW TEACHERS: You'll find this book helpful as a road map for sequentially growing your skill set. Be sure to do the following:

- Pay close attention to the "Getting Started" chapters.
- Take time for reflection and planning before moving on to the next section. The best way to strengthen your impact in the classroom—for generations to come!—is to take it slowly and strategically.

If you do the work, you'll see the reward. Mastering the Teacher Success Pathway calls for diligence and perseverance.

STRUGGLING OR TRANSITIONING TEACHERS: This book can help you home in on the area(s) where you face the most obstacles—leading to skyrocketing performance. To do this, I recommend the following:

- Pay close attention to the "Mastering" chapters. You might realize that a detail that trips you up comes in a brick you thought you'd already mastered.
- Overcome any temptations you have to skip chapters or speed-read through sections. This book shares instructional best practices that stand the test of

time. When you encounter points that are already familiar to you, accept the validation and celebrate what you're already doing.

- When you reach new ideas, go slow and deep, taking time to reflect and plan how you can best adjust your approach. Some skills take longer to master, so focus on results, not the time spent.

HIGH-ACHIEVING EDUCATORS: You can use this book as a resource to mentor and train student teachers and new colleagues. I offer some pointers to that end in Appendix 2: Using This Book to Mentor Others.

Regardless of where you fall in this mix, this book will provide clear directives to help you have the biggest impact on your students. Each chapter will reveal a brick of instructional practice that will lead to classroom and career success through the development of two things:

- **Teacher proficiency:** the ability level of a teacher based on a performance rubric
- **Student learning outcomes:** the data that showcases growth in student learning as a result of the teacher's instruction

It's crucial to note: *The sequence of the pathway is more important than the focus area itself.* The order in which I present the teacher essentials is the order in which I recommend you attack the obstacles you're facing in the classroom. And when you implement changes by following the subscribed sequence, you will notice long-lasting positive change for both students and yourself. Following the Teacher Success Pathway is not necessarily easy, but it is *easier* than haphazardly problem-solving, squashing obstacles that later just create new obstacles. I ask you to trust the process—and know that others before you have found success with this exact method.

How This Book Will Help You

With the lack of preparation, support, and time educators have to increase their own capacity, this book will provide simple and practical ideas you can begin to implement right away. Regardless of your experience level (novice to experienced), there are strategies and approaches applicable to everyone.

I knew I needed to write this book based on my own lack of preparation, support, and time as an educator. Many undergrad programs spend a majority of their course work on understanding the history of famous educators and their learning theories. A small portion of time is spent on learning how to teach specific subject areas and an even smaller portion spent practicing teaching strategies.

As a result, teachers enter the profession underprepared. Many districts combat this problem by assigning mentors to these new teachers, usually for their first three years. Sadly, these pairings are often unsuccessful due to lack of clarity in the role, limited time to meet regularly, and mismatched areas of expertise. New teachers end up having to teach themselves how to teach better, relying heavily on their colleagues who are also trying to do the same thing, while sitting through monthly professional development sessions way beyond the areas in which they need the most help at the moment.

Quick Note: There are of course amazing mentors successfully guiding new teachers. This is not to shortchange your effort and not acknowledge your hard work. Also, shout out to all the new teachers navigating these challenges and excelling! When you're ready, I hope you reach your hand back and help others learning the ropes. By the way, this book will help you do just that!

Now, new teachers aren't just underprepared—they're under-supported. That continues as they grow into veteran teachers, where it is assumed they have figured it out and can be successful on their own. Pair that with lack of time to effectively plan and collaborate with colleagues, and now we have teachers of all levels scrambling to increase their effectiveness in the classroom.

Although there are many books out there dedicated to teaching strategies to help these teachers grow their craft, there isn't one that provides a pathway.

You might be wondering:

- Where do you start?
- How do you select a singular area of focus?
- Why must you attack your instruction in a particular order sequence?

This book will share not only instructional strategy best practices but also the pathway to follow in order to improve your practice for long-term success in education. This clear road map ensures educators, no matter their experience level, can find their own unique starting point on the path and grow forward in skill and knowledge.

Let's begin by completing a vision cast. Throughout this book you will see sections called "Journal Jots." In efforts to allow you to scribble, note-take, or journal in the way that feels most authentic to you, when you see the circular pencil icon, grab your desired method and pause your reading. It can be tempting to push through to finish reading, but if you truly want to maximize your impact, slowing down to think and reflect is the only way to break through barriers and increase results.

Journal Jots: The Future-You Forecast

Close your eyes and envision *who* you'd like to become after reading this book and applying the principles. Write one to two goals for yourself. This will hold you accountable to not just read the book and apply what you learn but also to grow specifically in the way you desire. Dream big, believe in yourself, and write down your goals. Then post them where you'll see them often. We will visit these goals throughout the book.

I hope you'll also take notes and mark up the text as you read, because that will help you process what you're learning and track your ideas for how to apply this in your classroom.

You might collaborate with a colleague you trust to share your ideas and ask for feedback. You don't have to be a solo learner—invite your friends along!

Successful learning isn't just in the execution phase—where you try these strategies out in your classroom. The process of learning starts right now as you're reading and chewing on what you read. That's when the neurons in your brain start firing and making new connections and pathways. Don't limit how active your brain can become, because that will only limit your growth. Take time to allow your ideas to flow. Slow and steady will prove fruitful in the end, I promise.

> **Quick Note:** As a type-A checklist speed reader, I know just how hard of an ask this is, but I also know after decades in classrooms across the nation that if we don't do this right, we'll be right back where we started—defeated and not an ounce more effective.

When your mind is clear and present, dive in! I'll see you in the next chapter.

CHAPTER 1

THE FORMULA

You cannot stay dry in a flood armed with just a bucket. You have to go to higher ground.

Teachers are armed with tools such as materials and resources. However, they are often not provided adequate training, or even a road map for successfully using the tools they're given. We can't continue to throw tools at teachers and assume they'll be able to use them appropriately and effectively. They're trying to stay dry in a flood armed with a bucket.

More Than a Toolbox

We have to teach the various tool options, how to use them, as well as when. We can do this by making the pathway to solving problems clear. This pathway is how the formula was born. The formula is the key to successfully targeting areas of your performance that will produce the largest results when enhanced. And, the best news is, this formula is not throwing you a bucket during a flood. You'll have appropriate tools to attack your obstacles.

I realized the major problem in increasing teacher effectiveness is that most teachers were haphazardly trying out teaching strategies like magic tricks, hoping one would work. And when it didn't, they'd swap out the tools and try again without success. Not having a clear plan of action not only slows the growth of teachers but also slows the growth of students as well. A bag of unrelated tricks is not the secret to success in the classroom. It is not quantity over quality. We can have fewer tools, and when using them correctly, find tremendous results. In order to fix the problem of haphazard tool selection we need simplified, strong foundational skills (quality) over a bag of fun tricks (quantity). When we prioritize quality over quantity, we target obstacles correctly and efficiently. Then teacher effectiveness will rise.

It's not the fault of teachers that they think in order to get better they need to just gather more tools. It's the fault of those telling teachers that tools equate to success. The implementation of the tool is all the difference. When I hear the "add this to your bag of tricks" sentiment given to teachers, I think of a group of well-intentioned professionals lost in the middle of the woods with a ton of equipment, but not a map to find their way out. Instead, they should consider these types of questions:

- What does each tool do?
- How do they use the tools?
- When do they use it?
- Are some materials more effective?
- Is there an order in which to use them?

Tools without a manual limits the ability of the user to be successful using the tools as intended. The pattern of behavior looks like that shown in Figure 1.1.

Guessing wastes time and energy. No wonder teachers are exhausted! We have to stop the trial and error of teaching tools; the problem isn't the tool, it's how it's being used. And, spoiler alert, the order matters!

My experience told me that I had the ability to draw the map and help these well-intentioned professionals work their way out of the woods, leaving the random bag of tricks (equipment) behind them—at least for now. There will come a time when the bag of tricks can re-enter the game, but for now let's keep it simple.

Let me give you a real example of how a tool without directives can fail teacher performance. A performance rubric can be too vague to be helpful.

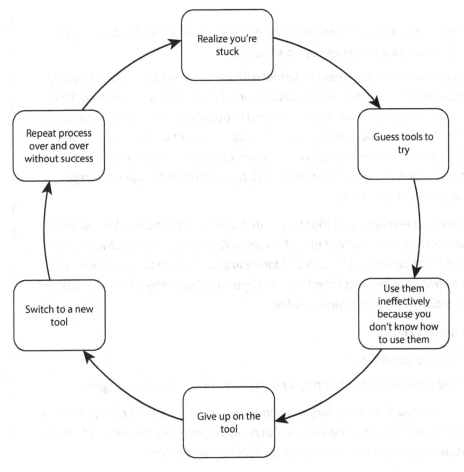

Figure 1.1   Working with tools without a manual.

Lessons from the Trenches: The Order Matters

When I taught elementary school, our district performance rubric was hard to decipher for clear next steps—what does it mean to move between categories labeled "Proficient" to "Accomplished" to "Distinguished" when the identifiers are vague (e.g., most students completed task or redirected misbehaviors some of the time)? Those words are up to interpretation from the observer and lack clarity and direction for how to improve (and by how much).

I remember sitting in an observation debrief with my assistant principal and going over my ratings on the district performance rubric. I asked her over and over, "How close am I to moving up?" and "What do I need to do differently so I can move to the next rating?" Sadly, she too felt the rubric was vague about how to grow through the ratings, so she pulled out a large binder provided by the district given only to adminis-trators for reference. Fortunately, we were able to come up with clear next steps applicable to my performance.

One indicator, for example, was that I presented a lot of professional development (PD) to staff members but only at the school level. We located a few district events I could present at that would show I had a larger impact outside of my school—so I could move from the "Accomplished" to "Distinguished" category in the professional learning portion of the performance rubric.

Teachers need to know:

- *What do I focus on first?*
- *What do I need to do to exemplify an indicator under a specific category?*

In coaching new teachers in my large, urban school district, we used a very effective rubric that clarified what teachers needed to do to progress. But teachers still strug-gled because they needed even more clarity. Teachers wondered:

- *Which category is most important?*
- *What do I focus on and in what order?*
- *How quickly can I move from rating to rating?*

I realized there wasn't a major difference in what made a kindergarten or 12th-grade Honors Chemistry teacher successful. The art of teaching requires the same founda-tional skills that every teacher needs to master. I saw firsthand how lack of thorough planning and practice before execution affected classrooms—with children aged 5 to 18. The new teachers I coached who could master specific skills in a specific order, no matter what subject or grade level they taught, rapidly became more effective.

EXPEDITIONARY
LEARNING

> *This told me order mattered. How to use the tool mattered. And, yes, the tool does matter, too—but we don't need a lot of tools. Success can come from pairing a really strong tool (like the performance rubric I used when coaching versus the one I used when a teacher myself) with clear directives (like a coach helping you prioritize areas of performance on the rubric).*
>
> *I saw firsthand the difference of what happened between teachers using quality tools and receiving guidance in using them. I watched other new teachers in the cohort read teaching strategies, practice them in small groups, and execute them in class. But when it came time to implement teaching strategies live in front of students, it was a disaster. How could that be? These teachers spent a significant amount of time learning and applying their learning in a safe setting before doing it in a real lesson. Why would that method fail?*
>
> *It failed because they were working the system out of order. They worried about behavior before planning a lesson. They focused on student interactions before putting routines in place. Just like we must take care of students' basic needs of food, water, and shelter (Maslow's hierarchy of needs) before we challenge their brain at deep levels (Bloom's taxonomy), we must work the basics of lesson design: before managing a classroom, before engaging students, and before increasing student ownership in the classroom. The order matters. Say it with me . . . the order matters!*

If only teachers knew the pathway to increased proficiency and student outcomes, their time and energy wouldn't have been so wasted. Plus, mentors could provide more targeted support to teachers when they themselves understand that order matters.

The Teacher Success Pathway

I refer to each characteristic of the success pathway as a brick. This metaphor helps learners visualize how to build their own capacity with the sturdiest material for long-term results—brick by brick. Figure 1.2 demonstrates why brick order matters.

Figure 1.2   The bricks of teacher success.
Source: Hakan Kızıltan/Adobe Stock Photos

Figure 1.3   The dangers of progressing too quickly.
Source: benjaminlion / Adobestock

Notice how the visual begins at the bottom and ends at the top. Similar to how a house is built, the first brick is the foundation and must be laid before any other brick (or instructional focus) can be added. And it isn't until the brick is laid that It can become cemented in place through intentional practice. Only then can an educator continue building with the next brick. And if an educator fails to allow the bricks to solidify before moving forward, dangers await them (see Figure 1.3).

When teachers intentionally approach the bricks in the suggested sequence, they experience success faster than they would otherwise. When teachers follow the Teacher Success Pathway, their classrooms run more smoothly, they're able to tackle more content at deeper levels, and their students demonstrate improved learning. When the Teacher Success Pathway is followed consistently over a period of time, notable progress is made—in both teacher proficiency and student achievement.

> **Quick Note:** Some teachers will experience success faster than others depending on whatever extraneous factors they're dealing with. But speed is not the objective. However long it takes to build the foundation, you become more effective and better able to support the learners in your classroom. Trust the program and keep going!

This book will walk you through the Teacher Success Pathway, ensuring you reach your potential without the headaches of figuring it out on your own (ahem, like I did). Each of the four brick chapters will help you grow . . . one brick at a time.

The Teacher Success Pathway is organized into four components:

- Definition of the brick
- Why that brick matters
- How to start in that brick area
- How to master that brick area

Growth requires three processes: learn, reflect, apply!

The layout of the book will help you better understand each concept, assess your implementation of it, and refine your process to become even more successful in the classroom. Plus, there are spots where it would be ideal to journal your thoughts to capture your knowledge growth as you read.

I use this process myself to meet my goals and I put them in this book for you to experience results as well. Learn about each of the bricks at a deep level, reflect on how you are doing in that particular area, and apply your new learning in your setting as soon as possible. The combination of learning, reflecting, and applying ensures that new information is taken into the brain, processed and organized for easy retrieval, and then put to use in a real-life setting. That process is how habits form—and all instructors can benefit from effective habits.

As you grow your craft as a learner, I'd like you to do two things: (1) share this book with others so they too can make the impact they desire and (2) reread this book when components in your career change (e.g., grade level, subject area, job title, etc.) so that you can successfully apply the principles in your new setting.

When you're ready to dive into Brick 1: Lesson Design, turn the page!

PART TWO

BRICK 1: LESSON DESIGN

A lesson plan is more than a standard, objective, and activity. It's about empowerment, accountability, and ownership.

We'll begin our tour of the Teacher Success Pathway working on the first foundational brick, Brick 1: Lesson Design.

Lesson design is the preparation phase of classroom instruction. It is a thorough plan developed by the teacher that includes various components to ensure a successful learning experience for students. The teacher uses the lesson plan during delivery of instruction as a road map for unveiling the learning sequence.

According to the Literacy Information and Communication System (LINCS), effective lesson planning "helps instructors organize content, materials, time, instructional strategies, and assistance in the classroom" (LINCS n.d.).

Organization in a teacher's mind spills over into organization of their instructional materials and space to teach the lesson. Teachers cannot jump into teaching. They first must thoroughly plan.

If a lesson plan is the piece of paper used to outline the learning sequence, lesson design is the thought process of every aspect and component of the learning experience.

Many teachers plan lessons, but few teachers design lessons. Design is the missing piece—and often the answer to obstacles related to the planning and execution of a lesson.

Writing a plan and thinking through a lesson ahead of time sounds easy enough. But it's not. If it were, I wouldn't include this chapter in the book nor would I consider it a foundational brick a teacher must master before moving on to more complex instructional moves. Lesson design solidifies the foundation on which all other instructional bricks rely. When we get this right, every other brick in the Teacher Success Pathway has a greater chance at being successful, too.

CHAPTER 2

OBSTACLES TO LESSON DESIGN

It's very simple: lesson planning matters. If lessons are designed effectively, teachers are prepared to deliver high-quality lessons. However, if the plan is sparse in details, teachers will be spending their brain power filling in the gaps on the fly while teaching live in front of students. This takes away from teachers being able to be present and react to what's happening in the room in the moment. Instead, they are looking for materials, looking up information to answer a student's question, fumbling to fill up time, or confusing their students as they hop around in content in a haphazard way because their lesson was not clearly laid out. This does a disservice to both the teachers and students.

When lessons are planned thoroughly, teachers can use their brain power to react to what is happening in the classroom in the moment. They can pause to clarify confusing content, speed up when students are catching on quickly, access learning materials efficiently, and more. This means students have a greater chance of excelling in the classroom because their teacher is prepared to support and catapult their growth with a thoroughly designed, aligned, and rigorous lesson.

This is why following the Teacher Success Pathway will increase the likelihood that you can efficiently transform your effectiveness in the classroom. Lesson design is foundational and must be mastered before adding on any more layers. It is up to us educators to create environments where students can thrive. Without educators who effectively plan and deliver quality instructional experiences, students cannot be successful.

If you don't believe me, listen to what the Rutherford Learning Group states in their "7 Tools for Developing Teachers and Teaching" training resource: "Many variables affect student achievement. The variable with the largest and most durable effect size is instructional quality, which is largely a product of the teacher's skills, techniques, and approaches to teaching" (Rutherford 2009, 1). This makes it clear why planning is a foundational piece to the development of a teacher's skill, technique, and approach to learning. Proper planning will have the largest positive impact on student learning. This is why lesson design is Brick 1; teachers must truly master this skill before moving on to the other bricks.

Unfortunately, there are a handful of obstacles that get in the way of teachers being able to thoroughly design effective lessons.

Less Time to Plan

Here's a repeat of the Literacy Information and Communication System (LINCS, n.d.) stance regarding organization in the planning phase: effective lesson planning "helps instructors organize content, materials, time, instructional strategies, and assistance in the classroom." Though that statement is accurate, it's also dated—the demands put on teachers today have chipped away at the time necessary to design effective lessons. When the time required to plan dwarfs the time teachers can spend, the resulting lessons are unfinished, slacking in content, management, engagement, or student connection.

Too Much to Plan

Lesson planning is one of the first things future teachers learn to do. Unfortunately, the ideal expectation of what a lesson plan should look like versus the time allowed to create it are at odds with each other, especially because the on-the-job lesson plan templates tend to have numerous boxes to fill out (though fortunately they're not as lengthy as the lesson plans we produced in college). This time-consuming planning process is unrealistic for teachers planning multiple subjects a day.

Although depth of planning is essential to planning an effective lesson, once teachers begin teaching the lesson plan, requirements are focused more on compliance (e.g., *Did you fill out each section of the template?*) than effectiveness (e.g., *Is this a quality lesson?*). Lesson planning becomes an item on a checklist to complete, rather than a habit that teachers practice to ensure their lessons meet the needs of students.

The Lesson Plan Vortex

As if the checklist weren't onerous enough in itself, in efforts to ensure that teachers think through the details from start to finish, schools have been requiring that teachers' completely filled-in lesson plan templates are checked every week by a leadership member. Teachers responded to this additional pressure by completing the required lesson plan templates before spending adequate time actually designing the lesson. Unfortunately, this loss has a doubly negative effect: the students learn less and the teachers "learn" that what they teach is more important than how they teach it.

Teachers in this situation have entered what I call the *lesson plan vortex:* when they're so stuck in the requirements of the lesson plan that they lose their vision to affect student learning. The vortex paralyzes teacher creativity and innovation. It creates an intense focus on details—which can turn into rabbit holes—that don't move the skill needle of students one iota. For example, teachers stuck in the vortex can get hung up on selecting between two texts to model a skill—because students might enjoy the message of both texts. Ideally, teachers would be selecting the text that most clearly showcases the skill that is aligned to the lesson standard and objective. Hemming and hawing over which book students will enjoy more is a distracting rabbit hole; understanding what skill you're teaching, and choosing which text will best support that teaching, keeps you focused on your task. Decision-making becomes easier and faster. Having clarity in the design process saves teachers time in the planning phase by helping them avoid getting stuck in the lesson plan vortex.

The overwhelm of all the details needing to be thought through can leave teachers unmotivated to try something new in their instructional delivery. And so they keep using familiar strategies and techniques to avoid having to think through new pieces to the puzzle. But the familiar can be dull—for everyone in the class. That's why I tell teachers, "Don't be a vanilla [basic and boring] teacher. Be a spicy [innovative and exciting] teacher!" When teachers know how to effectively design a lesson—and effectively avoid the vortex—they can spend their remaining brain power to think creatively and try something new.

Less Time to Collaborate

In my experience the collaboration phase of lesson design is the most important. Ideally, teachers can plan as a group, talking about future lessons and brainstorming ideas. But in order to combat the time shortage problem, some teachers divide to conquer: splitting up the subject areas for each teacher to plan and then sharing their portion with the team. But the planning process is valuable preparation for when standing in front of the class; this means that teachers are underprepared for each portion they didn't plan. Plus, this generic planning approach can't be tailored to the needs of the students in *their* classroom, such as content to review from a previous lesson, higher-order questions for specific students, and small-group pairings. (Note, there is a way to effectively share planning duties among colleagues. I'll explain how in Chapter 6—after discussing the essentials of the first brick.)

* * *

Given all these issues, standard methods for planning lessons are not translating to high achievement in the classroom. Fortunately, all these obstacles can be avoided. But before we get into that, let's consider one important detail of the lesson plan: the day's objective.

Lessons from the Trenches: The Mistake I Won't Forget

I made an embarrassing mistake as a first-year teacher. Our team planned together so I knew what I was teaching and when, but we didn't flesh out a plan—and with the whirlwind overwhelm of my first year, I didn't take the time to write a thorough plan on my own. On the morning of each lesson, I'd write verbiage on the board for the social studies objective, referencing my teacher planner. On one particular day I wrote, "Students will be able to complete an activity on goods and services." My principal happened to be going on walkthroughs that day. She visited my classroom, copied something down on paper and left. We had a scheduled weekly staff meeting later that afternoon.

As I returned to my classroom from afternoon bus duty, I heard my name come over the loudspeaker by the secretary: "Miss Schultek [my maiden name], please report to the library for the staff meeting." It was so odd. I wasn't late. Why were they singling me out? At the staff meeting, the principal talked about her walkthrough and how upset she was with the quality of objective writing in classrooms. She then shared an example. She proceeded to read my objective word-for-word to the entire staff. There was lots of chatter among teachers under their breaths trying to figure out who would write an objective such as that. I turned bright red and felt tremendous shame.

The principal went on to say we cannot write the activities we are doing with students in the objective. We had to focus on what skill they were going to learn through the activity. (It turns out that I'd been summoned to the staff meeting because the principal wanted to make sure I heard what she had to say.)

After the meeting, I talked with my grade-level team. They felt horrible for me. Every single one of them had the same objective in their teacher planner—because we'd collaborated in advance—but when they put it up on the board, they added more to it (skill over activity). That was the difference between my being a novice versus being a veteran.

* * *

Regardless of my poor objective writing, the lesson went well and students learned how to "compare and contrast goods and services around their community." (See the skill-versus-activity difference in what I wrote versus what I should have written?) Lesson learned! I'm glad to report that never again in my career did I receive negative feedback on my objective writing.

Quick Note: I share this story not to embarrass myself all over again but to share another lesson. Teachers of all experience levels struggle with writing strong objectives. We have to intentionally teach this writing and thinking skill in under-grad and graduate school. We have to provide support during on-the-job professional development sessions. And we have to ensure mentors and instructional coaches are building in this practice and feedback. Then maybe teachers' mistakes won't be singled out at a staff meeting, and the teachers won't be humiliated for an area of weakness they need help with. Public shaming does not encourage those who need help to get the help they need; it just creates distance and distrust. Go right to the source and address it privately and professionally.

Grace and guidance over embarrassment and shame.

Fortunately, we can do better than following a student-unfriendly, compliance-based checklist lesson plan. There's a more manageable—yet thorough—habitual process teachers can rely on to ensure the lessons they design are top-notch. Let's get into that now.

CHAPTER 3

LESSON DESIGN PHASE OVERVIEW

Lesson design is an essential component to student success; making time for proper planning and preparation ensures teachers are equipped to deliver high-quality learning experiences to all students.

One way to combat these obstacles of efficiency, collaboration, and quality lesson plans is to get a better idea of what constitutes an effective lesson.

An effective lesson is one in which the teacher has thoroughly designed a learning experience that accomplishes the following:

- Ties the state standard and the curriculum together.
- Aligns all parts within the lesson, and all lessons in the unit are aligned to each other
- Provides scaffolded practice of the skill being taught
- Tailors the instruction to the varying needs of students
- Moves at a reasonable pace, with limited distractions
- Provides students with numerous opportunities to engage with content, the teacher, and each other
- Builds in opportunities to increase student ownership and accountability
- Enables students to successfully demonstrate mastery of the lesson content and/or skill

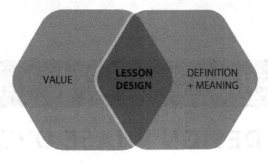

Figure 3.1   Effective lessons require high levels of both value and definition and meaning.

It is easier to design an effective lesson now that it is clear what an effective lesson is. Clear expectations enables teachers to meet the standard of performance.

Effective lessons need be composed of high levels of value and meaning (see Figure 3.1).

When thinking in terms of the big picture about the purpose of your lesson, consider the following two aspects:

Value is the information required for students to reach mastery at their current level, such as standards, objectives, and curriculum topics.

Meaning is the teacher's ability to make that content relevant to students, such as connections to self and world, student interests, and learning styles, and reference previously taught related concepts.

Let's dissect Figure 3.2 to get a clear understanding of the impact that various levels of value and meaning have on student achievement.

If a lesson has

Low value + low meaning: The lesson topic is not relevant to student's grade level content and students do not see the point of the lesson and how it applies to them. This lesson is not likely going to be successful because it lacks both value and meaning.

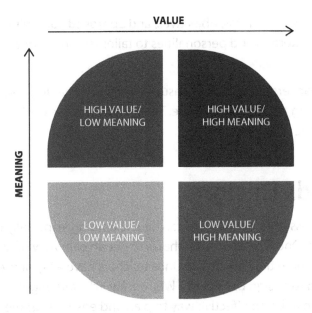

Figure 3.2   The value/meaning matrix.

Low value + high meaning: It might be really engaging for students but have limited impact on their academic trajectory because it is not related to appropriate grade-level content.

High value + low meaning: Students have the opportunity to gain new skills and knowledge based on grade-level expectations but maybe the topic is not of interest; therefore, students can lack motivation and engagement in the learning process. This will hinder their academic growth because they will not put 100% focus into gaining new skills and knowledge.

High value + high meaning: Students are learning appropriate content for their grade and find it extremely interesting. This means they are very invested in learning the lesson presented to them. The likelihood of students mastering content is great.

After reviewing the impact both value and meaning have on student achievement, teachers must attempt to design a lesson with both high value and high meaning as often as possible. To increase the likelihood this will happen, teachers should always reference grade-level standards, objectives, and approved curriculum while also knowing student interests and personalities to tailor lessons to bring high meaning to them.

Two processes teachers can follow to ensure both high meaning and high value are backwards planning and gradual release. These two processes help teachers design lessons that are effective every time.

Backwards Design

Designing every lesson to be effective can be challenging, especially if starting from scratch each time. One way to combat that is to get an overview of where the students are starting and where they are going. Once teachers have a lay of the land, so to speak, they begin to design backwards. *Why backwards*, you might ask? Backwards design has proven to be an effective way to plan and ensure alignment (Bowen 2017)—one of the major pieces to an effective lesson.

The educational company Learning A–Z wrote a blog post entitled "Effective Lesson Plans: The Backwards Design Way" that describes both the established approach and their recommended approach: "Using traditional methods, teachers tend to begin the planning process by reviewing state and national standards and learning objectives, planning instructional activities around them, and implementing assessments that aren't always tied directly to the activities students engaged in or the standards that have been set. Oftentimes, assessments using this method are more of an afterthought and may not be implemented at all" (Learning A–Z n.d.).

In essence, traditional methods of planning are ineffective because the components of the lesson are planned out of order. Some pieces are even thrown together as an afterthought. If teachers' lessons are poorly planned, execution will be challenging at best—and, of course, a poor plan and execution are a recipe for poor student achievement results. However, using the backwards planning method enables the teacher to home in on specific, essential pieces of the lesson—which, all combined, creates a thorough, effective plan.

Following this backwards order, teachers would begin with the topic and skill, followed by how they will assess if that skill was met, followed by determining ideal activities as ways to practice the skill. Again, this backwards approach has proven to be very effective in helping students master content. The order matters. Take a look at Figure 3.3.

Figure 3.3 demonstrates the flow of backwards design: beginning with the standard that leads into the creation of the objective before designing the assessment and ending with planning activities. Placing this simple visual in your lesson planning binder can help remind you to use backwards design consistently in order to align your content to essential and required standards. Now, this is not how many teachers were taught to plan lessons. This is also not how many teachers fill out their required lesson plan template. But trust me: order matters. No matter how long teachers have been teaching, revisiting lesson design principles can eliminate struggles in the classroom. It's essential that teachers go back to Brick 1: Lesson Design.

> How *we plan matters more than* what *we're planning.*

Backwards planning ensures all pieces of the lesson are aligned. If teachers tell students they are going to learn skill X but all the activities during the lesson are unrelated to skill X, then students will not master skill X by the end of the lesson or unit. Alignment is essential so that all pieces of the lesson relate back to the standard and objective.

To make time for quality backwards planning, schools need to implement a quarterly planning day for each grade level or subject area. (A backwards planning template is provided in Appendix 1, as well as on my website; see the next Downloadable Resources box.) This is when teachers gather together for a day of big picture planning for the upcoming quarter. They use backwards design on a different scale than with

Figure 3.3 The flow of backwards design.

EXPEDITIONARY
LEARNING

planning individual lessons. Teachers locate what standards need to be covered for that quarter. Usually, a school district provides a pacing guide that directs teachers in what needs to be taught by when, but if they do not then teachers can decide that collectively. Placing the sequence of topics into a quarterly calendar helps track the trajectory of how lessons build on one another leading up to the end of the quarter. Once standards and topics are plugged in to the appropriate places on the calendar, teachers then design end-of-unit assessments. Knowing what the assessment will measure enables teachers to plan backwards from that point to ensure all lessons are aligned to the skills on the planned assessment. Last, teachers can collaborate on aligned engaging activities, higher-order thinking questions, and so on to place in the individual lessons.

The backwards design method on a quarterly planning scale looks like what you see in Figure 3.4.

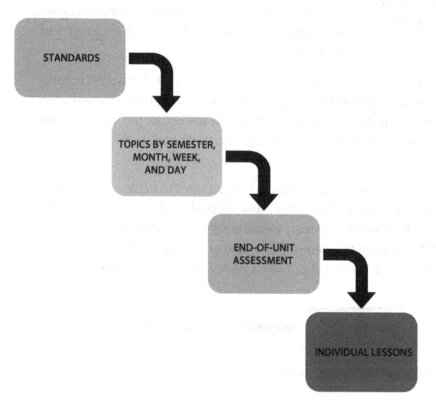

Figure 3.4 The backwards design method in a quarterly plan.

Knowing where you are going with instruction helps ensure everything students learn is aligned and on course for where they need to go for that quarter. Even though individual lessons aren't planned, the road map for how each lesson aligns and builds on each other is created. This sets the foundation for quality lessons to be flushed out in details. All the intense thinking has been completed as a team, leaving teachers to take the skeleton plan and plug in personalized supports for the students in their respective classes.

During a quarterly planning day, it is helpful if other specialized educators come in to meet for a few minutes with the planning team.

- **Content-level coaches** provide support to teachers in dissecting student perfor-mance data and gain a stronger understanding of the curriculum to be taught in the next quarter.

- **Administrators** remind teachers of expectations with designing effective lessons, collaboratively planning, answer questions, and show support of the intense preparation occurring.

- **Other support staff** includes anyone else who works closely with that grade level. They should stop in during their prep period to assist teachers in designing lessons that assist a wide range of learning abilities (especially those protected under laws such as 504 plans and individualized education plans [IEPs].)

When a quarterly planning day is time well spent, the design of the individual daily lessons is easier. All the heavy thinking was completed already and all that remains is tailoring the lesson to meet the needs of students. This can be done a week ahead of time and even the day before, especially if making adjustments to curriculum being covered based on what students were able to master the day previously. A plan is only a plan. It is meant to be changed. If teachers are as responsive to their students' changing needs, as they should be, then adjusting lessons plans should be a part of the design process.

Quick Note: Schools often provide coverage for a grade level for half- to full-day planning time so teachers can spend time mapping out the next quarter, sequencing the lessons (especially if their district does not provide a pacing guide of what to cover, by when, and for how long), and collaborating on how to best serve students. For example, my school hired four subs and they covered our classes all day. Each day for the rest of the week, they covered a different grade level of classes. It was a great way to create phenomenal lessons—and build relationships with colleagues. We repeated this process for quarters 2 through 4 (we did quarter 1 over the summer during our designated PD time).

Downloadable Resources: Backwards Planning Template and Backwards Planning Guide

Visit www.alwaysalesson.com/teacher-essentials to download your free resources!

Gradual Release

The second aspect of effective lesson design is implementing gradual release during the skill practice portion of the lesson. Gradual release is where the teacher presents the new content through direct instruction, then aids the students through guided practice, and ends in independent practice.

As the leader in the classroom, you are in control of starting learning ownership—and then slowly passing it on to students as they demonstrate capability. Start by modeling a skill so students can see your expectations in real time. Then, complete the task again but this time together, aiding students less and less with each repetition. Then let students work on the same task independently, and interfere only when necessary. Your support lessens gradually over time, which is why it's called *gradual release* (see Figure 3.5). This enables students to be successful as they transition from watching to trying with your help to trying by themselves.

Direct instruction is the most efficient way to deliver information to students. Teachers are sharing information directly with students with no interruption. It is informally

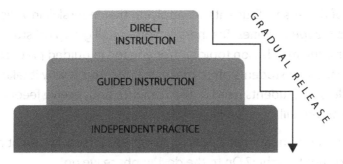

Figure 3.5 The gradual release instruction approach.

referred to as the *I do* portion of a lesson because the teacher models the skill they are teaching. They are doing the skill (I do) while students watch. This often happens during a mini lesson of content delivery and is short in duration, such as 10–20 minutes.

Guided practice follows direct instruction, when students begin to practice the new skill together with the teacher to build competency. Because this is done along with the teacher it is informally called *we do*. This portion of the lesson is longer in duration, such as 20–30 minutes, because students need rounds of practice with assistance to ensure they are successfully executing the skill. Teachers can use their judgment as to when it's appropriate to move on to the next portion of the lesson.

> **Quick Note:** Not all of your students will be successful during the guided practice. However, when the majority of your students are ready, move the lesson forward. You can support the remaining students needing more practice in the next section of the lesson.

Independent practice is the longest portion of the lesson, ideally 30–40 minutes. This is when students practice the skill completely on their own. This shows the teacher what students are able to know and do, which is why it is informally referred to as the *you do* portion of the lesson. Students are applying their new skill in various settings to ensure their knowledge solidifies. Teachers can pull small groups of students to the side to emphasize the mini lesson topic and/or engage in guided practice before sending those particular students off to practice alone. This is why it takes up the majority of the lesson. Students need time to practice and receive feedback to perfect their execution of the skill.

We're learning about foundational pieces in planning a lesson, but what does it look like when it all comes together? On to the design phase we go!

CHAPTER 4

EFFECTIVE DESIGN

We now know a few helpful things before sitting down to design. We know the two foundational pieces for writing an effective lesson plan (backwards design and gradual release) and the importance of high value and meaning for students. We also know we want our lesson design process to be efficient without sacrificing collaboration or quality. These things will be key in how you design. You won't just be filling in boxes on a lesson plan template, you'll be envisioning a learning experience from start to finish, enabling all the details to matter.

A lesson plan is only part of the picture. When you design a learning experience for students, you not only teach content that supports learning styles and needs but also you deliver a clear message that motivates students to take risks and give it their best effort. How they learn because of the environment you create and the lessons you provide is by thoughtful design.

Knowing students is a huge part of designing lessons, which means year after year the lesson will change. It should reflect the students in the room. (Yes, some of the staples found in the lesson, like engagement and management strategies and routines, will be reused in addition to teaching the same topics year after year.)

ASCD author Ellen Ullman, in her online article "How to Plan Effective Lessons," says, "An effective lesson gets students thinking and allows them to interact and ask questions, tap into their background knowledge, and build new skills" (Ullman 2011).

Knowing student interests, personalities, preexisting skill levels and knowledge, and so on help ensure the designed lesson will meet the meaning component of designing a successful lesson. (You can find my Student Learner Survey in Appendix 1, as well as on my website; see the next Downloadable Resource box.) Although there won't be a tidy section on a lesson plan for understanding students, it does weave into the fabric of each portion of the design process.

Downloadable Resource: Student Learner Survey

Visit www.alwaysalesson.com/teacher-essentials to download your free resource!

There are six aspects of design to think through during the lesson-creation phase. As I share these with you, think about how students need to do what Ellen Ullman recommends—communicate with each other and use old skills to build new skills.

Pacing/Time Management

Managing the clock as you design a lesson ensures you can teach your *entire* lesson without rushing through content and/or running out of time—thereby leaving ample time to respond to student questions in the moment. A great way to do this is to include time stamps in your lesson to remind you to keep to the clock. For example:

> *Five minutes for students to enter the classroom, unpack their backpacks, and begin the activity listed on the front board.*

You can then put those same time stamps at the bottom of each presentation slide, use sticky notes to signal moving into the next section of the lesson, or even set timers for each section of the lesson.

As you deliver lessons and better get to know your students, you'll become more accurate with your guestimates for how long each section of the lesson will take.

As you further gain mastery, you can allow students to dictate your pacing by using the level of their comprehension to signal movement to the next portion of the lesson. For example, if students are moving quickly and easily through the warm-up, you can begin the teaching point sooner. Or, if students are struggling with the guided practice, you can do an additional example together before moving into independent practice. Of course, these additional examples themselves are also planned—but just to be used as a necessity.

Checks for Understanding (CFUs)

Stopping periodically and throughout a lesson to check in on student understanding will ensure you catch misconceptions quickly and deepen understanding through clarification. On June 23, 2017, I shared a quote on Instagram about the importance of CFUs. It said "If you aren't checking for understanding through your lesson, you are missing opportunities to throw your students a life vest." A pause to ensure the majority of students are comprehending the lesson content gives you an opportunity to clear things up before moving on. This increases the likelihood students don't spend an entire lesson in confusion and then perform poorly on an assignment or assessment. CFUs are life vests—added support in the learning process.

Designing quality CFUs takes thought and time. Vary the level of thinking about the concept by asking low-level questions (e.g., Who discovered the theory?) to high-level questions (e.g., What would happen if one step of the scientific method was missing?) Scripting out specific CFUs holds you accountable for asking quality questions that are aligned to the lesson content and that push students' thinking to high levels. Designing quality questions takes time. Feel free to plan together as a team of colleagues for the questions you want students to be able to successfully answer. You might even meet with a mentor or coach to devise questions until you get the hang of it on your own. Planning ahead for the most important questions for students to answer helps guide their learning, ensuring they will be successful in demonstrating their level of understanding by the end of the lesson. You can even write specific student names next to these questions to remind you of whom you want to check in on during the lesson.

Stack your questions so that they increase in complexity and take note of where most students drop off in understanding. You'll have to unpack that section on a deeper level before proceeding. For example:

> [*John*] *What are the three types of communities?*

> [*Desiree*] *How are each important to the community?*

> [*Andy*] *What would happen if we did not have a variety of community types in our cities and towns?*

There are three types of checks for understanding:

- Ask clarifying questions to uncover specific areas of misunderstanding.
- Have students rephrase important teaching points, especially to each other.
- Restate directions or outcomes prior to a transition.

Be sure all students have a chance to answer. Even if you call on only a handful of students (ranging in performance levels), have students jot down their answer or create a lengthier pause for think time so all students have a chance to formulate an answer. Pairing students up for a quick discussion enables all students to be actively involved, increasing their understanding and building relationships with peers. We want to avoid having a small percentage of kids understanding and moving the lesson forward when the rest of the students have a shaky understanding at best. Every student deserves the opportunity to learn and be held accountable to learning at high levels.

A helpful tip for knowing how to come up with authentic, challenging, helpful CFUs comes from author Stiliana Milkova. She wrote a piece for the Center for Research on Learning and Teaching called "Strategies for Effective Lesson Planning." As part of the fourth step in preparing a lesson plan, she recommends: "An important strategy that will also help you with time management is to anticipate students' questions. When planning your lesson, decide what kinds of questions will be productive for discussion and what questions might sidetrack the class. Think about and decide on the balance between covering content (accomplishing your learning objectives) and ensuring that students understand" (Milkova n.d., 3).

You might plan questions that are too low or high based on how students are performing during the lesson. As you get to know students, you'll hear their questions in your head as you're designing your lesson. Use those to guide how you support students, phrase activity directions, and so on.

The goal is to cover content and ensure students achieve mastery of the stated objective, but rushing to finish a lesson on time doesn't help students. You can't get too behind by rarely finishing the lesson you designed, but you also need to be mindful of appropriately pacing a lesson to meet students' needs and levels of understanding. This is why you revisit the next day's lesson prior to teaching it to make pacing adjustments based on prior days' lesson content coverage. As Stiliana says, balance is key in effective lesson design.

Transition Routes

Thinking through how students will move about the classroom (or access learning materials) during the lesson ahead of time will diminish distractions during learning. Decide the most efficient ways for students to move from one location to the next and then walk it yourself to make sure you've thought through all obstacles that could arise. Then, teach students the expectation of how to transition (route, noise level, and time limit). It's essential to hold students accountable for moving quickly and quietly to their learning areas so that they do not lose out on learning time. As you're planning transition routes, pay attention to your lesson pacing and be realistic with the transition route. For example:

Students will transition from their desks to the reading carpet in three minutes by pushing in their chair, walking to the end of their row, finding their spot on the carpet, and sitting down silently.

Students will require a lot of repetition for practice to meet the expectation of a transition routine. Don't expect to teach it once and students to be successfully doing it. For example, these transitions can take practice to do in an organized fashion:

- Going from their desk to the reading center
- Moving from one classroom to the next
- Putting materials away from one subject and beginning learning in a new subject

Citing the work of Professor Douglas Brooks (1985), Harry K. Wong and Rosemary T. Wong shared the following in their book *The First Days of School*: "Effective teachers spent time organizing and structuring their classrooms so the students knew what to do to succeed" (Wong and Wong 2009, 3). The planning phase is just as essential as explicitly teaching expectations to students before having them repeatedly practice with feedback.

Teacher/Student Actions

Identifying specific actions both the teacher and student should do from the start of the lesson to its completion ensures clarity and productivity. For students, knowing what you want them to do during each aspect of the lesson ensures there is no down-time for misbehaviors to occur. Assigning a student action throughout your lesson enables you to notice areas where students are idle and prevent "nothing to do" moments. Assigning yourself actions forces you to be intentional with each minute that you're with students, whether its circulating with a purpose, pulling a small group, or distributing materials. You too won't be left with idle time and nothing to do. When you and students are together, the time spent will be purposeful. For example,

Teacher passes out activity paper while students read directions on the board silently.

Material Organization and Distribution

There will be multiple times throughout a lesson when students will need to access materials. Some materials are applicable for numerous subjects or lessons, so they might remain in students' desks or in a community bin, for example, sticky notes, tape, erasers, pencil sharpener, and so on. Other materials might be specific to the lesson and need to be distributed to students efficiently, for example, mini clocks, hundreds chart, manipulatives, and so on. Deciding how to get these materials to students quickly is essential to using time wisely, leaving time to teach the lesson versus losing time distributing materials.

Students pick up their lesson packet at the table near the door on their way into the classroom in the morning.

The goal is to save time with logistics of running a classroom so you can save as many minutes as possible for instruction. Students benefit from more time asking questions, collaborating with peers, and engaging in rounds of practice. Tightening up a menial task such as organizing and distributing materials prioritizes student learning.

Eventually, you can have students in charge of passing out these materials to each other while you work 1:1 with students or in small groups. This is a long-term goal, and we will discuss this in a later chapter.

Differentiation

Edu-leaders in my EduLeadership Facebook group (https://www.facebook.com/groups/609598144007188) mention the wide range of learning abilities among students to be a factor in why teachers cannot deliver their lesson as they planned it. Regardless of whether students have different home lives, varied experiences with preschool, or inconsistent teaching during the pandemic, students will always perform at varying rates because of the way individual people process information. In order to close the gap over time, group students together by the skill needing reinforcement, build in time to review previously taught skills, and provide options to practice at home. You will never have all of your students performing at the same level at the same time because every child is uniquely different. All you can try to do is help each child grow to meet (or exceed) the expected level of performance by their grade level. Designing lessons to meet student needs is also a skill needing practice. You must get to know your students' learning styles and struggles in order to differentiate to meet them right where they are and provide a bridge of support to get them to where they are expected to perform. Simply, collaborate with peers, seek out a mentor, ask students what they need, communicate with students' parents, and keep trying new ways to reach students. Differentiating is an ever-changing puzzle, but pays off tenfold when students reach their potential because of how you supported their growth through the learning process.

* * *

Teaching is 10% being on stage and 90% planning.

These six design aspects in your planning habits will increase the likelihood your lessons are effective and productive.

Many of us get into teaching because of a desire to lead someone in a learning experience, but that's such a small piece of what educators do. Just like performers, the real magic is in what happens before the performance that makes the actual, live performance so great. Without thorough preparation, the performance would be lackluster. The 90% off stage might not be as fun as the 10% on stage, but without the 90% there'd never be the 10%. Meaning, if we don't plan for excellent instruction, it won't magically happen. When you put in the time and effort where it matters (planning phase), you will reap the rewards of experiencing the greatest joy and outcome of the 10% that follows. Students deserve teachers who plan high-value, high-meaning lessons that meet their needs.

CHAPTER 5

GETTING STARTED WITH LESSON DESIGN

Our objective is to design a thorough, effective lesson:

- A lesson plan is the thought process for how to deliver the content of the lesson.
- The lesson plan template is the organizational structure to which educators fill in their lesson plan content.

There are two parts to getting started. The first is determining what your lesson plan *needs* to include. Your school or district might require you to use a specific format, so check there first. It's also possible that they would approve your using a different format as long as it meets their requirements.

If you're free to use your own format, the important part is having a place to think through the details and being able to play around with the visual layout of the lesson plan until you find one that makes the most sense for how you think and how you teach.

Lesson Plan Components

Regardless of the format, the basic components of a lesson plan should include, as discussed, a standard, objective, assessment, direct instruction, guided practice, and independent practice. (Note that a Lesson Plan Checklist is included in Appendix 1, as well as an example Lesson Plan Template in the format that works best for me; you can also download them on my website; see the next Downloadable Resources box.) Let's review each of these components in turn.

Standards

What do students at this specific grade level in this specific state need to know by the end of the school year?

Locate your state's standards for the subject(s) you teach and mentally process the contents. Read through any supporting documents that break down the standard into knowledge strands so that you are clear on all skill/topic components covered within the standard. Note, it often takes days, weeks, and/or months to cover an entire standard, so don't rush this step.

Here's an example of a standard:

CCSS.ELA-LITERACY.RL.3.2(*): Recount stories, including fables, folktales, and myths from diverse cultures; determine the central message, lesson, or moral, and explain how it is conveyed through key details in the text.

*The code is as follows: CCSS = Common Core State Standard; ELA = English Language Arts; Literacy, RL = Reading Standards for Literacy; 3.2 = third grade, second standard. (Core Standards n.d.)

Note that following the standard is not sufficient for designing a lesson. What's called for is understanding what the standard means and being able to break it up into bite-sized skills that move the students along a learning trajectory—and this is a process that must be practiced often. Collaborate with colleagues to practice locating a grade-level standard, bulleting out a list of skills related to that standard, and sequencing the learning of those skills into potential lesson topics. A quarterly planning day is perfect for doing this type of task. Knowing what a standard means and all it encompasses is a planning action that separates good teachers from great ones, and great ones from excellent ones. Practice will get you there.

Objective

What do students need to be able to know or do by the end of the lesson (as stated by the state)?

Objectives are small portions of the standard that can be taught in a single lesson. Printing out a calendar to use as a pacing guide can help you plan how many days, weeks, or months will be needed to cover the entire standard. Once you've mapped that out, you can write out individual objectives for each day: often one-sentence statements that describe what students will be able to know or do by the end of the lesson.

As for the phrasing of the objectives themselves, check with your administrator to see if there are specific guidelines to follow when writing objectives and where/if they should be posted in the classroom and/or shared with students throughout the lesson.

Educator Madeline Baird states, "Write the objective on the board and read it before starting the lesson. I know some districts require this. Sometimes as 'I can' statements. Reading it together before the lesson sets the tone and gets everyone on the same page. After the lesson, it's helpful to read it again and to talk about how the objective was met. [For example] 'What did we learn today?'" (Google doc comment to the author, November 21, 2022).

Quick Note: Here is an example of an objective:

Students will be able to state the moral of the story "Grandmother Spider Brings the Sun" by citing three events to support their claim.

Many objectives start with "Students will be able to . . .," followed by the skill they will master by the end of the lesson. As noted, the objective can also be rewritten as an "I can" statement in the voice of the student. For example, "I can state the moral of the story 'Grandmother Spider Brings the Sun' by citing three events to support my claim."

EXPEDITIONARY
LEARNING

Note: It takes practice to (1) learn what amount of content can be taught in a single lesson, (2) understand your students' background knowledge and learning speed, and (3) build in support for both the students who need more practice and those who are ready to move on. Do not expect that you can quickly master objective writing; this too requires collaboration and practice. Keep tinkering with individual objectives until you find what works for you and your students.

Assessment

> *How will students demonstrate mastery of the skill mentioned in the objective covered in the state standard?*

In order to determine if students mastered the skill specified in the objective, we need to create a means of assessing that skill. An assessment can be long or short. It can be formal (like a silent, independent written or digital test) or informal (like a work sample or an answer on a sticky note as an exit slip). Whatever method you choose, it must determine if students mastered the skill outlined in the objective and standard. If you decide to do a short informal quiz at the end of class, be sure you ask only the most essential questions to determine the level of understanding. One-word answers or multiple choice will not suffice. We need a clue into students' thinking. For example, if you ask students to solve a math word problem, you can review their strategy and their answer to determine if they've mastered this skill.

Assessments should inform instruction. They're not just grades in a grade book; they're information to guide your next sequence of lessons, perhaps by adjusting student groupings for intensive instruction, tweaking differentiation options, or scripting specific examples to include in tomorrow's lesson as a review. Use this valuable intel to your advantage.

Veteran educator Chelsea Henley shares:

> Assessment can take place during a lesson as well as at the end. I think it is impor- tant to work in little assessment tools throughout lessons in order to better

understand your students and how to best help them. I liked to use a quick assessment during math that would allow me to see who was understanding the concept and who needed additional support and practice. Students would sit on the carpet, and at the end of the mini lesson, they would complete a problem on their whiteboards, and hold it on top of their heads (facing up, so only I could see). If it was correct, they got their problem set to take to their seat for independent practice; if they were still on the carpet, we would work through examples from their problem set together (that way they weren't behind, but still got support). This was a quick way for me to see where students were, and also adjust my instruction. (Google Docs comment to author, December 31, 2022)

A few notes to keep in mind:

- Because grading can take up a lot of time, be intentional about what and how you grade.

- You don't have to grade everything. You might just glance at answers to locate trends among student responses and identify any major misunderstandings.

- You might plan a quiz where just one essential question assesses student mastery (e.g., you'd focus on the answers to number 3 on everyone's paper).

- It's important to give feedback to students as soon as possible. If students make repeated mistakes or lack understanding for a lengthy period of time, they can become frustrated; they also lose precious time that could be spent mastering other skills. But when students learn of their mistakes and misunderstandings and can remedy them quickly, they progress much more quickly.

Quick Note: Here is an example of a simple assessment task to gather information on how well students understand the concept taught in a lesson:

State the moral of the story "Grandmother Spider Brings the Sun" and highlight three events in the story that support your moral. Then write three to four sentences explaining how these events teach the reader a lesson (moral).

Direct Instruction

Teaching point: how will you teach the skill to students as outlined in the objective and measured in the assessment?

Whether you use a 10- to 15-minute mini lesson or a longer direct instruction method, plan out your content delivery, paying close attention to academic vocabulary and key concepts that students must grasp before moving on in the curriculum. Keep it bite-sized and focused on essentials.

Reference the gradual release process for how to roll out content effectively for students. The teaching point is the modeling or direct instruction portion of the lesson.

Note: It can be helpful to practice your teaching point while you're getting stuff done outside the classroom; once you solidify the content in your memory, it's easier to deliver concise, confident instruction in the classroom. It also enables you to be more present to what students are doing in front of you, instead of needing to focus on what you're saying or doing. We are all learners, but teachers should be first to master the content. (Remember: order matters!)

Quick Note: This is an example of what a teacher could say during the direct instruction mini lesson: *"Today, we're going to learn about stories that have a moral. A moral is a lesson the author teaches us through the events in a story.* [Point to anchor chart of definition so students know they can reference this throughout the lesson.] *I'm going to read you a story called 'Sulwe' written by Lupita Nyong'o* [2019]. *Watch as I find clues throughout the story for what the lesson, or moral, might be.* [Read story and jot down clues on sticky notes.] *Now that I've collected my evidence of clues on these sticky notes, it's time to decide the moral of this story.* [Read all clues out loud and think out loud about the commonalities.] *I think the moral of the story is that we all look different and, because of that difference, we are all beautiful. We can be proud of who we are and how we are different. Sulwe's journey shows us that being 'the color midnight' is what makes her powerfully unique and beautiful. This moral encourages me to be thankful for what makes me different (like being an artist and the youngest in my family). My differences make me unique and I can be proud of them."*

In purposefully designing lessons, the intent is to guide learners from not having a skill or knowledge to successfully demonstrating the new skill or knowledge. In the book *Instructional Design: Principles and Applications,* Leslie J. Briggs and coauthors discuss the procedures of lesson design: "The purpose of providing learning guidance is to model or show learners what appropriate actions constitute correct performance. If learners can observe performance before they have to do it, they are in a better position to perform themselves. A teacher may provide learning guidance by showing all the steps to completing a problem. In other cases, the guidance may be a suggestion about how to go about carrying out a task" (Briggs et al. 1991, 201).

This means it's essential that teachers are clear in the direct instruction phase of their lesson so that students can imitate execution of the skill being taught. Once a strong model is demonstrated—perhaps a few times—students continue to receive guidance as they move through the lesson with gradual release. Just like a swim teacher might help a child learn to swim by first holding them aloft in the water while they practice kicking—and then gradually lessening their hold until the child can swim on their own—classroom teachers are guides, offering support as students learn to demonstrate skills on their own.

Guided and Independent Practice

How will students practice this skill outlined in the lesson objective?

After you've modeled the skill during your mini lesson or direct instruction of the teaching point, it's time to guide students in practicing together—guided practice.

Once students demonstrate progress with guided practice, they can move on to practicing the skill on their own—independent practice. This should be a similar, but different, activity focused on the same skill.

Differentiate to ensure that all levels of learners successfully practice and master the skill. Students learn at different rates, and retain a different percentage of information as the days progress, so teachers need to ensure there are additional supports in place. For example, you can modify an activity down to the essentials to support certain students in moving at a slower pace (a "remedial" option)—and you can devise a different level of activity for the students who could benefit from a deeper dive into the topic (the "acceleration" option). One ideal acceleration approach is to assign an open-ended task that could be used daily for a specific unit of study; the added benefit is that this increases efficiency, because you won't have to offer fresh directions every day.)

Downloadable Resources: Lesson Plan Checklist and Lesson Plan Template

Visit www.alwaysalesson.com/teacher-essentials to download your free resource!

Sample Practice Script

Let's see what the end of the read-aloud portion of the mini lesson might look like in action.

> *Now that you watched me read a story, tracking evidence for a possible moral, I want you to try it with me. We're going to read* Our Class Is a Family *by Shannon Olsen. Use your notebook to jot down clues for a possible moral. We'll review these at the end of the story to find common ideas that help us determine our final moral of the story.*

[Read entire story out loud, jotting down clues on sticky notes while students jot down clues in their notebooks.]

> *Now, talk with your partner, sharing your evidence to come up with a possible moral.*

[After two minutes:]

> *Now, let's come back together and share what we think the possible moral might be.*

[After that:]

> *You all nailed it! The moral of this story is that family can be those you surround your-selves with, like teachers and classmates. School is a home, too, a place where you are*

safe and loved for exactly who you are. Nice work, students! Now it's time for you to try this on your own. You're going to read mini stories at your stations. You'll highlight your evidence on the mini story, and then write a two- to three-sentence moral for each.

[After 10 minutes:]

Let's all come back together for a discussion.

[Prompt students with questions about the moral of a story, highlighting a few mini stories students read during independent practice.]

One last point: the primary goal of teaching students is for them to master a skill or gain new knowledge. Although, of course, it's great to have fun along the way, that takes a backseat to the rigor of the learning. That's why it's smarter to choose activities as the last phase of the planning process—so you can focus your planning time on your primary goal. Once you've aligned the activity to the standard and objective, you can have fun bringing learning to life.

Journal Jots: Sample Practice Script

What stands out to you about this lesson example?

CHAPTER 6

MASTERING LESSON DESIGN, PART 1

I started off Brick 1 with a quote: "A lesson plan is more than a standard, objective, and activity. It's about empowerment, accountability, and ownership." It's time to go to the next level by focusing on how you can build student empowerment, accountability, and ownership into your lessons.

We are no longer filling in a lesson plan template; we are designing a lesson from start to finish. Just like when putting on a play, all the details from curtain open to curtain close matter. And, the order in which we plan those parts matters. Thorough and intentional planning is key!

Luckily, as you build the habit of designing a lesson instead of planning one, you'll be able to reuse a lot of your structures. We'll call these your *core moves*. They will become staples in your lessons, no matter the subject. Simply rinse and repeat (maybe adding a bit of flair here and there, especially as you plan with your colleagues and incorporate their unique approaches). And because this approach avoids the pitfalls of inefficient planning processes, your brain is free to focus on delivering quality instruction and responding in the moment to student needs.

For example, one effective core move is to use sentence stems to aid students in leading discussions in small groups. (This is a great core move for building empowerment and ownership, which we'll cover in Brick 4: Student Choice and Ownership.) Sentence stems are the beginnings of sentences, such as "I think . . ." or "I agree with [student name] because . . ." Sentence stems provide students with a verbal template

Effective Task Sharing

Sharing the planning duties among colleagues saves time and reduces workload. Logistically it makes sense, which is why it is such a common practice in schools. But as I described in the "Less Time to Collaborate" section in Chapter 2, this approach can lead to educators being unprepared to teach the portions they didn't plan. So if teachers are going to continue to divide subject area planning duties, then I highly suggest the following:

1. Discuss each subject as a team so everyone is aware of the standard being addressed and content being covered for that week.

2. For the material each teacher is responsible for, write subject-specific plans that are bare bones: just standard, objective, assessment, and activity.

3. Meet again as a team to review the bare-bones plans, ask questions, and personalize each plan to students' particular needs (e.g., differentiating the activity, drafting small-group topics and pairings, scripting questions or additional materials, etc.).

Following this approach, teachers can each deliver a similar lesson that is both aligned to district curriculum and differentiated to meet the unique needs of their students.

Note: Although this three-step process enables teachers to cut down on planning time, it does add preparation time, because you'll need to (1) review the plans together to discuss specifics and (2) flesh out the bare-bones plans to best serve your students.

Whether you plan lessons yourself or together with colleagues, it's important to take the time to understand the design of the lesson flow, the content delivery, and the level of mastery for assessment. Pay most attention to supplementing instruction for the students who need to remediate or accelerate. Lesson design is the foundation for everything that happens in the classroom; taking shortcuts here will sabotage efforts in the other brick areas.

to say as they gather their thoughts to share with peers. It moves peer discussion from one-word responses to back-and-forth dialogue. You won't need to use this every day, but if you use it often students will know what's expected of them and can readily launch from this familiar task into learning a new topic.

In his book *Atomic Habits,* James Clear states, "There is no longer a need to analyze every angle of a situation. Your brain skips the process of trial and error and creates a mental rule: if this, then that. These cognitive scripts can be followed automatically whenever the situation is appropriate" (2018, 45). So, as teachers internalize lessons and create repetitious procedures, they're able to be more present to effectively react to what is happening in front of them, and their instruction flows naturally and efficiently.

Clear goes on to say, "Your brain is always working to preserve your conscious attention for whatever task is most essential. Whenever possible, the conscious mind likes to pawn off tasks to the nonconscious mind to do automatically. This is precisely what happens when a habit is formed. Habits reduce cognitive load and free up mental capacity, so you can allocate your attention to other tasks. . . . It's only by making the fundamentals easier that you can create the mental space needed for free thinking and creativity" (46). This means that when teachers or students operate in routine, their brains have space and energy to think more creatively, which enables them to produce enhanced learning experiences of deeper understanding leading to greater academic gains. What a win-win! Make designing lessons a habit.

In *Atomic* fashion, as you gain proficiency in your lesson design process (and only when you *and* your students are ready), feel free to get creative and mix up the format of your lesson from time to time. For example, instead of a warm-up, kick off the lesson with a hands-on discovery activity. This new energy can spark student engagement while providing context for the day's lesson. Just be sure to never sacrifice quality for the sake of creativity. To help students achieve at high levels, it's essential to infuse instructional rigor in every lesson.

The Glossary of Education Reform (2014) discusses *rigor:* "While dictionaries define the term as rigid, inflexible, or unyielding, educators frequently apply rigor or rigorous to assignments that encourage students to think critically, creatively, and more flexibly."

It's our responsibility to provide quality learning experiences that meet the needs of our students, and rigor is part of that responsibility. In her book *Powerful Lesson Planning Models: The Art of 1,000 Decisions*, Janice Skowron discusses Charlotte Danielson's "Framework of Professional Practice," in which planning and preparation is one of four domains of teaching responsibility (Danielson 1996, 3–4). Skowron affirms:

> The difference is the details. . . . It is not difficult to recognise classrooms that are alive with purposeful activity and exude a feeling that "there's important work going on here." Students are engaged in their work. They understand the direction and importance of their activity. The teacher is a facilitator—coaching, questioning, and providing resources for students at opportune times. There is an atmosphere of authenticity that resembles real life. Independence is balanced with interdependence as a means to learning. Some of the time, students learn with others in small groups, some of the time they work independently, and other times they are part of whole class activity. Such a classroom does not just happen. It is the result of careful and precise planning by the teacher. (Skowron 2006, 1)

Let's look at what a thoroughly designed lesson could look like in comparison to a lesson plan template to be filled in. Following is an example using the same standard, objective, and assessment examples from Chapter 5 in the section, "Lesson Plan Components."

Standard, Objective, and Assessment Example

Standard: CCSS.ELA-LITERACY.RL.3.2: Recount stories, including fables, folktales, and myths from diverse cultures; determine the central message, lesson, or moral and explain how it is conveyed through key details in the text.

Objective: Students will be able to state the moral of the story "Grandmother Spider Brings the Sun" by citing three events to support their claim.

Assessment: State the moral of the story "Grandmother Spider Brings the Sun" and highlight three events in the story that support your moral. Then write three to four sentences explaining how these events teach the reader a lesson (moral).

Notes About This Example

- The objective doesn't just list the activity the students will complete during that lesson; it focuses on the skill (stating the moral) and explains how students will demonstrate this (citing events).

- Practice writing objectives from a standard. Multiple objectives can be made from a single standard, so, just like students need rounds of practice, you'll be able to have rounds of practice, too.

Direct Instruction Example

1. Introduce *moral* and provide an anchor chart.

    - A moral is a lesson the author teaches us through the events in a story.

2. Model by reading aloud *Sulwe* by Lupita Nyong'o, jotting down evidence for the moral.

    - Prayer to God (p. 8): "I want to be beautiful, not just to pretend."

    - Mama's advice (p. 13): Sulwe means star (brightness) and Sulwe wants God to turn her skin lighter, but Mama says, "Brightness is not in your skin . . . brightness is just who you are . . . you are beautiful to me . . . real beauty comes from your mind and your heart. It begins with how YOU see yourself, not how others see you."

    - Journey on a star (pp. 16–35): Night and Day sisters with each having a very specific job to do for the land and people. When night left due to poor treatment, everyone missed her and what she provided ("deepest rest . . . grow and dream"). And "When you are darkest is when you are most beautiful. It's when you are the most YOU."

    - Authors note (p. 43): "What is on the outside is only one part of being beautiful . . . working on being beautiful inside. . . . Know you are beautiful because you chose to be."

---

3. Review moral evidence and conclude: *"The moral of the story is we all look different—and because of that difference, we are all beautiful. Let's be proud of who we are and how we are different. Sulwe's journey shows us that being 'the color midnight' is what makes her powerfully unique and beautiful. This moral encourages me to be thankful for what makes me different. My differences make me unique and I am proud of them."*

4. Ask students, *"Did you see how I read the story, and jotted down big events that might help me figure out the moral? I then looked at all the evidence I collected to see if there was a lesson repeated over and over. That helped me know the moral of the story."*

Notes About This Direct Instruction

The fact that this lesson includes specific details (direct quotes and page numbers) from the read aloud that are evidence of the moral enables you to draw students' attention to these specific pages, to model a think-aloud while jotting down this as potential evidence, and to prompt students with questions about story events that taught a lesson—all while being present and responsive to whatever happens in the classroom.

*   Designing a lesson means you know where you're going and how you'll get there. This intentionality brings clarity to the direction of the lesson, all leading to an aligned end point.

Guided Practice Example

Let's read one more and try to decide on the moral together.

1. Read *Our Class Is a Family* by Shannon Olsen. Ask students to track evidence in their journal while you track as well. Evidence:

    *   Cover page and title page: "Our class is a family"
    *   Pages 5–6: "But family doesn't have to be who you're related to. It can be another special group who love and care for you."

- Page 8: "where all your time is spent . . . school."
- Page 10: "make it like a home"
- Page 11: "where we can be ourselves and make memories with one another."
- Page 14: "our classroom is a special haven"
- Page 18: "In this classroom of four walls, we will stick together"
- Page 21: "We're a classroom family"

2. Students turn/talk to swap morals and evidence.

- Hudson and Lily
- Avery and Elijah
- Peyton and Grayson
- Etta and Rhett
- Jason and Juan
- Tessa and Keegan, and so on

3. (At teacher's discretion) Students come back for a quick share out.

4. Teacher summarizes moral: family can be those you surround yourselves with like teachers and classmates. School is a home, too, a place where you are safe and loved for exactly who you are.

Notes About This Guided Practice

The fact that the pairings of students are already listed and/or visibly posted makes the turn/talk process efficient because it identifies whom students must speak to.

- Basing these pairs on seating assignments also aids efficiency.
- It's wise to keep pairings the same for a few days to build routine and collaboration before switching them up.
- Thinking through the details saves time during the lesson for learning. Also, because the teacher doesn't have to figure out who should pair together and

> what they should talk about, they're available to offer feedback on transitioning or partner talk.
>
> • The stories selected here were recommended by Sharon Brandwein (2021).

Independent Practice Example

Thinking ahead enables you to be more effective in the moment.

1. Have students move to centers to read mini stories and decipher moral (Singer 2021). (30 min)

   • *Strega Nona* by Tomie dePaola = keeping promises

   • *The Rainbow Fish* by Marcus Pfister = giving to others brings happiness

   • *The Little Witch* by Anna Elizabeth Bennett = the power of friendship

2. Pull a small group with Amory, Jason, Lily, and Juan to review point of view from yesterday's lesson. (15 min)

3. Do 1:1 check-ins with Shonda and Barrett for reading comprehension and reteach moral if necessary.

4. Post on board: Early Finishers grab their independent reading book and complete a journal entry on the moral of that story. (Illustrate if time allows.)

5. Call everyone back together for a class discussion. Ask questions below:

   • *"Remind me, what is the moral of a story?"*

      • Story events teach a lesson

   • *"Where did you look for the moral?"*

      • Cover of the book, in illustrations, in words on the page

   • *"What did you do while reading to help you think of the story's moral?"*

      • Track story events in notebook.

   • *"How did you decide what the moral of the story might be?"*

      • Review tracking in notebook and look for repetition.

- *"What was similar about all the characters in the stories?"*
    - They all had to learn a lesson to overcome their problem.

6. Pass out copy of *Grandmother Spider Brings the Sun: A Cherokee Story* by Geri Keams (1997).

7. Have students complete exit ticket:
    - *"What does the term* moral *mean?"* (1 pt.)
        - The lesson of the story
    - *"What are three ways to find out the moral of a story?"* (3 pts.)
        - Look at the pictures, read the word, track the evidence.
    - *"After reading 'Grandmother Spider Brings the Sun,' what do you think the moral of the story is? How do you know?"* (2 pts. each)
        - Don't underestimate the capability of other people based on how they look, what they know, or what they do. You might just be surprised.

8. Grade and adjust teaching point for tomorrow's lesson; create a small-group reteach lesson for any students who scored 0%–60%.

Notes About This Independent Practice

- It's helpful to list out specific materials for the lesson because thinking through the details of all items needed creates a seamless learning experience for students. Then, collect these items and place them in an accessible location to help prepare for the lesson.

- When you script out specific questions to ask students in advance, you're able to design higher-order thinking questions related to the standard and objective. (Thinking of quality questions on the fly is challenging.)

- To have also scripted the (hoped-for) correct answers reminds you to not accept answers that are just approximate. Prompt and prod to get students to formulate a thorough answer.

- These answers might also appear on an assessment, so bringing up the question-and-answer in class enables students to grapple with the connection and solidify that learning in their brains before the assessment.

Preparation takes time in the moment but saves time in the long run.

- It's also ideal to determine beforehand how to score the assessment. The more details that are addressed in advance, the more freedom you have to be in the moment with your students.

CHAPTER 7

MASTERING LESSON DESIGN, PART 2

You've seen two clear examples of how teachers could plan for lessons. Before we dive into the last portion of an effective lesson (assessment and data collection), let's pause to consider the benefits and costs of the two lesson plan examples from Chapter 6.

Journal Jots: Lesson Design Reflection

Now that you've seen two versions of a lesson plan, I'm hoping you noticed some differences in how the second one was designed. What stands out to you about this second lesson example?

As you can see, there is quite a difference between the two lesson plans. The first lesson plan is sparse in detail but has all the lesson components most schools require teachers to plan, including which materials they need and in what order to accomplish tasks. The second lesson plan is designed to account for the flow of the lesson, from partner pairings to specific questions to be asked. When you *design* a lesson, you're called on to focus on all the details necessary to make the lesson successful.

The level of detail plotted out in the second lesson plan is much more effective preparation—down to taking the time to ensure the picture books chosen meet the standard and learning objective, which was to "recount stories . . . from diverse cultures." Selecting texts that are diverse enough in types of characters showcased and the story line events cannot be done effectively at the last minute. Excellent teachers prepare weeks in advance, tweaking as the days grow closer to the actual lesson. This is why a quarterly planning day is helpful, because a team of colleagues can spend time in the school library locating texts for specific standards.

If you're like many teachers, the level of detail in this second lesson plan might have made you a tad worried. So let's talk some of your possible fears.

- Yes, this takes longer to do.

- Yes, you can reuse a lot of systems or core moves (e.g., turn-and-talks, transitions, etc.), so planning can become less think heavy.

- Yes, it does get quicker in time.

- No shortcuts will create the same results as doing it thoroughly.

- Yes, you can plan multiple lessons a day at this level. Why? Because when you start noticing all the details that helped make your lesson successful, and saw the reward in student mastery by the end of the lesson, you'll find a way to prioritize designing a lesson over planning one.

All that said, we all know that lessons can fall flat. Students might not comprehend as quickly as you thought they would, some students might be absent for their small group, technology might go haywire, or a fire drill might eat up your entire class time. Consider how you'd respond if you'd cut corners with the first lesson plan. If you're unfamiliar with your lesson and the lesson starts to fall flat, it will be challenging to get things back on track. You'll be emotionally and mentally frazzled. But if you've thoroughly planned, it's easy to make adjustments in the moment because you know your lesson well. This is why I highly suggest practicing your lesson—or at least specific components of your lesson—so that when it's time to stand in front of students you're confident and clear in your delivery.

Journal Jots: Planning Versus Designing

If you were to explain the difference between lesson planning and lesson designing to a friend, what would you tell them?

EXPEDITIONARY
LEARNING

Creating In-Class Data Collection Procedures

We've touched on assessment and even grading it a bit, but I want to make sure we discuss the importance assessment plays in the long-term academic gain trajectory. Although there is some sort of assessment planned for each lesson, ideally teachers informally assess all throughout the lesson—taking note of details such as who is acquiring skills and knowledge and at what pace, what portion of the lesson seems to be tricky for most students, and what areas do specific students need additional practice at a later date and time. All of that information is helpful in designing future lessons, adjusting course during a lesson, providing additional supports to students in the moment, and even sharing specific examples with parents during conferences or on report cards.

The data you make note of during a lesson are just as important as the data points in the assessment portion of the lesson. Ideally teachers are 24/7 data collectors, using all clues found along the way to direct the path forward. This is why knowing a lesson inside out is advantageous, because you can then make sound judgments in the moment based on the data you're collecting.

If collecting data seamlessly throughout a lesson seems daunting, then—just as you design specific questions to ask students, or develop time stamps for activities— decide at what specific points in the lesson (usually while students are working quietly) it makes the most sense to collect data. Simply walk around the classroom with a roster on a clipboard and jot down observational notes to reference for future lessons, conferences with parents or students, and/or evidence for IEP/504 students. This informal data will help you adjust tomorrow's lesson plan to ensure it meets students right where they are—what is difficult from today we want to touch on again, what can we skip tomorrow that students are mastering right now, and so on.

Table 7.1 provides an example of what a classroom roster with informal data might look like during a lesson. You can then refer back to this when you're preparing to deliver the next day's lesson.

Table 7.1 Data Collection Example

Student Name	Date	Subject Area	Notes	Follow Up
Joshua W.	12/7/22	Math	Transposing numbers → incorrect answers	1:1 check-in
Layna M.	12/7/22	Math	Rushing to solve vs using problem-solving process	Reminders before indep practice
Leah S.	12/8/22	Reading	Mastering sight words but relies on pictures for comprehension	Small group
Thomas B.	12/8/22	Reading	Speed reading, but enjoying Magic Tree House series	1:1 check-in
Juno A.	12/9/22	Science	Limited info in scientific method chart, but understands process	Spiral review as entry activity

Notice how this sample includes time stamps with dates that mark moments in time. This is helpful when reviewing a student's learning trajectory over a period of time. Some teachers use a separate sheet of paper per subject area; others record all stamps for a student on one page. If you (1) develop the habit of noticing students in the learning process, (2) jot down what you see, and (3) create a follow-up plan, you can ensure that your lesson design procedures remain strong all year long.

As you build your new habit of transitioning yourself from planning lessons to designing them, use the Lesson Design Guiding Questions (in Appendix 1, as well as on my website; see the next Downloadable Resource box) to support you (just like teachers support students as they gain new skills).

Downloadable Resource: Lesson Design Guiding Questions

Visit www.alwaysalesson.com/teacher-essentials to download your free resource!

Developing Your Own Systems and Habits

If you find yourself spending too much time designing lessons, remember that any new habit takes hours of practice to form into muscle memory. In the blog post "How Long Does it Actually Take to Form a New Habit?" on James Clear's behavior psychology website, he shares,

> On average, it takes more than 2 months before a new behavior becomes automatic—66 days to be exact. And how long it takes a new habit to form can vary widely depending on the behavior, the person, and the circumstances. In Lally's study, it took anywhere from 18 days to 254 days for people to form a new habit. In other words, if you want to set your expectations appropriately, the truth is that it will probably take you anywhere from two months to eight months to build a new behavior into your life—not 21 days. Interestingly, the researchers also found that "missing one opportunity to perform the behavior did not materially affect the habit formation process." In other words, it doesn't matter if you mess up every now and then. Building better habits is not an all-or-nothing process. (Clear n.d.)

The more you do it, the easier it will be and less time it will take. Plus, many aspects of your lesson design can be replicated day after day, so you do not have to reinvent the wheel for each lesson.

There are ways you can help yourself and your colleagues succeed with lesson design:

- Print and enlarge the Lesson Design Guiding Questions (see Appendix 1).
- Place them in your lesson planning room.

- Make copies and share with colleagues on your team or in your school building.

- Save a copy to your computer for easy access as you type up your plans.

- Leave a copy near your lesson materials as a reminder as you teach.

- Use technology to project questions from lesson plan onto a board to prompt students throughout the lesson, limiting the likelihood these planned questions would be skipped or forgotten by you, the teacher.

Going Beyond the Curriculum

Sometimes the curriculum provided by the district is not thorough enough to effectively teach a topic. In this instance, teachers have to go beyond the curriculum to supplement with additional information found elsewhere. It's important to only use trusted websites or other materials so that the information gleaned is accurate and appropriate for the grade being taught.

Going beyond the curriculum is one way teachers can master the lesson design process. Instead of relying only on the information provided, teachers dig through additional resources to pull together a lesson that is thorough. This way teachers are able to study the topic at a deeper level, ensuring they have a strong understanding before presenting it to students. Plus, this deep dive into additional materials enables teachers to more effectively answer student questions that come during the lesson. Having additional background knowledge and understanding how previous and future topics connect to the lesson ensures students can move beyond surface-level understanding. Mastering the depth of the content of a lesson is a major piece to mastering the design of the lesson. Teachers can script stronger questions, develop more in-depth activities, and present relevant facts and details to enhance the lesson. A great time to engage in this type of activity is during a quarterly planning day with colleagues. Each colleague can grab a resource to gather additional information on the same topic and share what was found. Then add these teaching points into the lesson as background information, guiding questions, or used with extension activities for students ready for more challenging practice on the topic.

By moving beyond the curriculum, teachers grow their knowledge and skill set while simultaneously enabling students to do the same. When a teacher teaches only surface-level content, or relies only on the limited materials provided, students are at a disadvantage, missing the opportunity to understand content at deep levels. When a strong teacher teaches, students are able to achieve at higher levels. This benefits the achievement results of the current lesson but future lessons as well.

Ways to move beyond the curriculum include using a planning protocol that incorporates norms, goals, and expectations, such as the following:

- Topic dives into resources outside the provided curriculum in order to gather additional information to build into a lesson

- Discussion about what is and isn't working in content delivery and lesson design so that future lessons can be productive and successful in student outcomes

- Personalizing lessons based on student needs where teachers can use their own discretion to adjust a lesson

- Asking for support from instructional coaches, mentors, and other teacher leaders in content planning and delivery

If you're wondering what this might look like, an example of a 45-minute planning agenda is shared in Table 7.2.

As you can see, the bulk of the time is spent in research and discussion mode. The actually fleshing out of a lesson happens on a teacher's own time—so they can digest their own learning and present the material in a way that meets the specific needs of the students in their classroom. The purpose of a planning protocol keeps teachers on task to learn the content at a deep level and collaborate together to design a learning experience that is thorough, engaging, and personalized to students. If the discussion is fruitful, fleshing out the lesson into a template should not take much time because all of the thinking has been done, and now writing it down will go quickly. A planning protocol holds colleagues accountable for doing the behind-the-scenes work of understanding the material they are presenting to students in a thorough way while also using the ideas and talents of colleagues to enhance the design of the lesson. Students benefit when

Table 7.2   Planning Protocol

Time Stamp	Task	Notes
5 min	Greetings Announcements Celebrations	
5 min	Intention setting/goal for the planning session Reflections: what's working and not working?	
15 min	Topic dive into supplementary materials Share out	
20 min	Design lesson outline Discuss delivery options Share related learning activities	
ON OWN	Personalize lesson Ask for additional lesson design support (if needed)	

teachers spend the necessary time preparing for a learning experience—researching, writing, and collaborating.

Overall, finding a system that works for you is how you can overcome the common obstacle of lesson design taking too long—and resulting in low-quality instruction. More important, though, is collaboration. When you come together with a team of colleagues, the goal is not to fill in a lesson plan template. The goal is to discuss the upcoming lesson and brainstorm unique ways to deliver the content as well as ways to meet the unique needs of students. The time together should be spent in dialogue as you think, share, research, model, brainstorm, and so on. Then when it comes time to design the lesson on paper, the heavy lifting (thinking) of the process in which you will deliver the lesson is already done! You and your colleagues have fleshed out a quality lesson and now you just have to track it on paper and personalize it for your students. This, too, will become more efficient over time.

Virtual Instruction Side Note

Planning lessons virtually can save time. Instead of using a lesson planning calendar, use a shared platform where your colleagues and yourself can plan together as well as administration and other teacher leaders can leave you feedback. When content is planned online and others have access, it is more efficient to review plans and leave specific feedback about sections of your lesson. For example, in Google Docs you can highlight words within the text and leave a comment. This helps to know what exact part of the lesson needs some tweaking and pushes the thinking of the teacher to make the future lesson even more effective for students.

Internalizing Your Lesson Plans

Internalizing your lesson plans will help you spend more time in the moment responding to student needs. Internalizing means you are familiar with the materials enough that you don't have to reference it often during delivery. By no means do you need to memorize a lesson. The more in advance you plan, the more time you have to adjust and internalize plans. This results in a closer execution to what you actually planned. You won't lose time looking for materials, referencing your lesson plan for page numbers, discussion questions, or flow of teaching. It will be in your long-term memory as you deliver a high-quality lesson with ease.

A member of my EduLeadership Facebook group (https://www.facebook.com/groups/609598144007188) uses an internalization technique with her teachers. Adina

EXPEDITIONARY
LEARNING

Cintron-Medina is a middle school principal at Hoboken Dual Language Charter School in New Jersey. She says, "I have been working with teachers on internalizing their lesson plans as well. So although they plan out a lot of really great teacher moves, they either forget the meaty questions they scripted or miss a chunk of the 'good stuff.' I did that myself when I was in the classroom! I have helped teachers avoid this by helping them use slideshows for support and a chance to practice with me whenever possible."

Adina is referencing a technique I, too, used when I was a classroom teacher. I created PowerPoint slides for each section of my lesson plan and would include any important information on these slides such as timers, vocabulary terms, discussion questions, activity directions, and so on. This was helpful for students to reference, but it was originally designed to keep me on track and took the pressure off me having to remember everything I had planned. It was my safety net to ensure that the high-level instruction I planned I actually delivered.

Quick Note: The biggest way to prevent misbehaviors is to master the first brick of lesson design. As Marcia Tate shared with instructional coaches at the Teaching Learning Coaching [TLC] Conference in San Antonio, Texas, "a teacher's best defense against classroom management concerns is an engaging lesson." It's essential to master Brick 1 before moving on to Brick 2 because you can put preventative measures in place well before you're live in front of students.

As you design your lessons, think about how students will react throughout the lesson. When you assign teacher and student actions in your lesson, you're already preventing misbehaviors from occurring because you're thinking through transitions, material distribution processes, student partners, and so on. These habits create structure that decrease the likelihood students are left with time on their hands to act out. Passing ownership to students by assigning specific actions to them throughout the lesson builds responsibility and investment in learning. This is an example of how interwoven these bricks become as you become a more masterful teacher.

EXPEDITIONARY
LEARNING

Speaking of internalizing information, let's see how well you're internalizing the information shared with you in this chapter.

Lesson Design Scenario Practice

Take a look at a common lesson design scenario and then answer the follow-up question. Marcos is in his third year of teaching. He wrote lengthy lesson plans during his student teaching placement and his first year teaching second grade. His second year of teaching, he began to follow suit with what other teachers were doing and wrote down the bare minimum in a lesson plan notebook. He was often flustered during his lesson and couldn't seem to find all of his materials. Most lessons ended early and Marcos let the kids talk to pass the time. Now during his third year, his principal, Mrs. Delgado, called him into the office. She told Marcos his teaching performance has decreased year after year. She wanted to know why he seemed ill-prepared and lacked understanding of content even though he's been teaching the same curriculum for three years now. Marcos shared his lesson plan book that looked more like a monthly calendar with a few items written in each day than an actual plan. Mrs. Delgado realized Marcos is not planning effectively and set him up with a mentor in the building whose lesson planning process is effective and efficient.

Journal Jots: Lesson Design Mentoring

If you were Marcos's mentor—the lesson design whiz—how would you help him develop stronger lesson planning habits? Script out what you would say.

Don't peek if you haven't yet completed your scenario practice! Do not read further until you've spent time reflecting and writing your response to the scenario. This will ensure you process your new learning before receiving feedback to solidify your application. Consider the following:

Key Points

- Many mentorship programs require new teachers in their first three years to receive additional support. Marcos is in his third year of teaching.

- Changes in Marcos's planning process over the years (thorough to minimum) are affecting his preparedness in delivering high-quality instruction to students.

- Oftentimes, Marcos does not use the entire class period to teach or for students to practice their new learning.

- After three years, Marcos's performance is decreasing rather than increasing.

- His principal is concerned and partnering him with a veteran teacher with strong lesson planning habits.

Overall, Marcos's situation is common in education as teacher planning time becomes more and more limited, but their task list continues to lengthen. Finding a planning process that Marcos can follow for every lesson will help save time due to using a familiar structure. Marcos has demonstrated in the past that he can design thorough lessons (as seen in his student teaching placement and first year on the job). This means with a gentle reminder of the importance of lesson design, plus a walk down memory lane for using a thorough (not always lengthy) planning process, Marcos will build more effective instructional habits. Next year, Marcos will most likely exit mentorship support so it's essential to help him solidify this foundational teacher essential now. As a mentor, you should share what works for you and maybe what other colleagues use so that Marcos can see many examples and try out a few until he finds one that helps him perform strongest in the classroom. The goal is not to write an amazing lesson plan, but to deliver a strong learning experience day after day. A lesson design habit and/or protocol will ensure that happens.

* * *

Before you move on to the next brick, let's assess where you are right now with the first brick for classroom and career success by taking the Lesson Design Self-Survey (in Appendix 1, as well as on my website; see the next Downloadable Resource box). Honesty will help you clearly see the specific areas of lesson design to focus on in order to improve your planning skills.

Just like grades inform instruction, lesson plans can inform your future teaching of the same content. After a lesson, take time to write down what went well and what you would change if doing it again. This will help you during content review at the end of the quarter, semester, or year and in future years teaching the same content.

Downloadable Resource: Lesson Design Self-Survey

Visit www.alwaysalesson.com/teacher-essentials to download your free resource!

I am lucky to learn from the only other educator in my family, Richard Jacobs. My Uncle Rich is a retired professor of educational leadership and public administration at Villanova University. He also chimed in on my EduLeadership Facebook group, sharing, "IMO [in my opinion]: The best lesson plan is the one written after the material has been taught. An outline should precede a plan. That way, the plan can be improved upon from year to year." Instead of moving on to the next lesson, take a few moments to reflect on the plan or outline you used to teach the lesson and make note while things are still fresh in your mind as to what to add, change, or keep. This is worth your time and better serves your future students.

The goal for this book is to help you grow your craft one brick at a time. After reading this chapter, your instructional foundation as a teacher is now one brick thick! And, most important, you have the most important brick in your arsenal—the brick that which all other bricks rest and rely on. Without the lesson design brick, no other teacher essential can be successful or effective. Following the sequence of the Teacher Success Pathway will ensure you build the strongest instructional practices possible.

Where you like to take notes or journal, track your thinking. It can be messy and disorganized. It's a way to enable your brain to process the information you learned in this chapter, organize it in your brain, and prepare it for output. Your reflection will enable these new ideas to solidify into new learning while also forming into actions you can implement immediately. Don't be shy in approach or short in words—let your reflection flow.

Revisit the goals you set when first cracking open the book:

- Who do you want to become after implementing the principles in this book?
- Are you on the right track to make that a reality?
- What steps can you take right now to move closer to becoming the person you dreamed of becoming?

When you're finished, move on to the next chapter so we can keep building strong teacher essentials for classroom and career success.

PART THREE

BRICK 2: CLASSROOM MANAGEMENT

One of the major reasons why teachers struggle with classroom management has little to do with their content knowledge or their passion to teach. It all comes down to clarity.

Let's continue along the Teacher Success Pathway! Our goal is to grow our craft one brick at a time, and you've mastered the foundational brick of lesson design. It's time to move on to Brick 2: Classroom Management.

CHAPTER 8

UNDERSTANDING CLASSROOM MANAGEMENT

Classroom management is not found in a single tool or strategy. It is a combination of environment, support, and prevention.

Classroom management focuses on creating the environmental circumstances for students to be the most successful as often as possible. It is easily confused with behavior management, a technique that focuses solely on how the behavior of others meets the expected behavior requirement (e.g., sitting with hands folded at the desk).

The Three Rs of Classroom Management

The truth of the matter is, we cannot control anyone. These attempts at managing behavior (like the stop light system) have short-term results. When motivation runs out, behaviors return to their original state (as seen with students frequently landing on red, often referred to as *repeat offenders*). Furthermore, depending on the age and energy level of students, sometimes the impulse control is not yet developed. Interestingly enough, many students that exhibited the most distracting behaviors we were trying to control were boys.

Turns out, there is a reason for that. Occupational therapist and cofounder of The Kids Coach, Roisin Sullivan (n.d.), says, "Teachers commonly tell me that it's the boys in their class that are the 'troublemakers'—the ones [who] act out, won't sit still during lessons,

---

Lessons from the Trenches: Focusing on What Matters Most

As a classroom teacher, I always had strong control over classroom operation, but I never tried to make students behave. We had a stoplight behavior management system in which all students had a clothespin with their number written on it. All pins would start the day on a green circle. If students did not adhere to classroom rules, they would move their pin down the stoplight to a yellow circle and if misbehaviors continued, they would end up on a red circle. At the end of the day, students would record their behavior color in their agenda, followed by my signature. This would be taken home for their parents to sign daily. This ensured two-way communication about student behavior in the classroom. The idea behind this system is that if students are behaving, they will have more time for learning. And if they were busy misbehaving, then they miss instruction and perform more poorly than if they did behave. Having parent support in the open dialogue format about student behavior did help most students achieve green throughout the year.

I never thought anything of this system. It was required and every classroom throughout the school used it. Parents were familiar with it because every grade level used it. Students seemed to be motivated to stay on green. However, there were a few instances when students made it to red in the first few minutes of the day. I attempted to keep them motivated by allowing them to move back up the stoplight color system if they made good decisions throughout the day.

But for some students, this stoplight system failed them. They spent more time on red, spent the majority of the day distracting themselves and others, and got so discouraged that they no longer tried to earn a green. Students like this ended up with an individualized behavior plan on the corner of their desk that was designed together by the special education teacher and me. These behavior plans were often short and sweet, giving students a goal to master a handful of behavior expectations ("raise hand to speak"). These behavior plans would constantly change as students mastered certain behaviors and began working on a new handful of expectations.

> *Although this was more successful overall because it targeted specific classroom rules and learning behaviors, it still aimed to control behavior.*
>
> *As an instructional coach of new teachers across the district, we used specific techniques to manage behavior. One specific method focused on how students sat at their seats, and teachers were asked to constantly redirect students if they were not sitting as instructed.*
>
> *Lessons became a distracting hand signal performance redirecting students. Secondhand off-task behaviors occurred as a result of constantly reminding students to sit properly (feet on the floor, straight back, hands folded on the desk, facing forward, etc.).*
>
> *When I started my consulting work, I helped teachers and their coaches move away from this obsessive focus on details that didn't affect learning. For example, if a student needs to stand because they've sat all day and are able to maintain concentration and work output, then the desired results of learning is achieved, regardless if they sat in a specific position or stood. This forced teachers and leaders to rethink their policies on behavior management, wondering what was actually helping or hindering learning. We were getting caught up on things that didn't matter.*

and don't behave as well as their girl peers." Roisin shared that brain development in boys and girls is different. Boys are processing in the cerebellum, which is related to movement and doing. This explains why boys are active and might fidget more, act out, or misbehave more than girls. We know though that children cannot sit for long periods of time. Roisin is a huge proponent of movement in the classroom as well as active recess times.

Just as we learned in the lesson design chapter, we must know our kids. Not just as boys and girls, but as individuals. And most of these individuals need to move to process information, take a break from learning, or to get out anxious energy.

Roisin probably is very against our stoplight behavior system, and the more that I learn so am I. The only way to truly help students successfully learn in a classroom is to control the environment instead of the people.

Classroom management is not behavior management. It focuses on creating the environment so that it is primed for learning to occur. This enables students to express their unique personality, learn in a manner that works best with their style of processing, and provides structure to what can often be a chaotic environment.

Children respond best in a safe environment where they feel loved and cared for. If you try to correct children's behavior from head to toe all throughout the day, they will not feel loved or cared for. They will feel inferior and attacked. They will withdraw and disconnect from any potential engagement opportunity with whatever stimulus is making them feel bad. Being under a microscope for extended periods of time increases their anxiety and frustration, making many students rebel—the exact misbehavior you're trying to avoid.

The best way to disappoint yourself is to try to control other people. It's impossibly unhealthy. It is true that children need routine and guidance, but they do not need a dictator. Instead, as educators, it is our job to help children learn and grow skill sets that will help them out in the workplace and in future academic environments.

It is helpful to have high expectations and hold students accountable for following structures to maintain order in a classroom full of children. However, providing a structured learning environment is not the same as forcing compliance. Students have free will to follow requirements and expectations, with knowledge that consequences follow if not meeting expectations. Students also have freedom to learn and grow in their own style. Therefore, educators shouldn't hold strict one-size-fits-all behavior requirements.

As mentioned, behavior management is not the same as classroom management. We need to shift from focusing on behaviors to focusing on how we structure and operate a classroom. Teachers can control the classroom, but they cannot control a student's behavior. They can influence a child's behavior, but they cannot control it. Influencing behavior happens through managing a classroom—the systems, routines, procedures, norms, and protocols that you use. Create the conditions you desire to influence student behavior. Clarity in how you run your classroom will have the greatest influence on the behaviors you desire.

If you don't set the expectation, no one can meet the expectation.

Systems and routines are created out of purpose. If you cannot figure out why it's important to have a particular system or routine, you don't need it. Think about safety, respect, and efficiency as the reason for having systems. A routine should enable students to learn in a safe way while respecting the classroom environment and the people within it. Most important, though, is efficiency. Systems enable common behaviors to occur in the fastest, safest way possible so that there is more time left for learning. When these systems are used over and over again, the classroom operates on autopilot, whereby if the teacher is out of the room for whatever reason, everything can still occur as it should. Students know and follow the expectation.

Systems set the tone for learning to take place. Having a system sends the message to students that learning is the most important thing we do in this classroom, and because we value learning, we adhere to expectations and routines to ensure we spend the majority of our time learning. This enables teachers to influence behavior. Teachers are planning how they want students to behave, teaching students how to meet the expectation, and holding students accountable for doing that every day. The specificity and clarity in having routines and consistently using them enables teachers to create the classroom climate they desire and one that prioritizes learning.

As teachers are developing their routines and classroom management strategies, there are three characteristics to keep in mind, as authors Jason E. Harlacher and Sara A. Whitcomb state in their book *Bolstering Student Resilience*: "Consistency, connection, and compassion are the cornerstones to helping students choose and practice successful behaviors and coping skills" (Harlacher and Whitcomb 2022). I agree. These three Cs set the tone for learning, ensure all students can be successful, and teach students to rely on these principles in life as well.

- Consistency ensures students know what is expected of them daily, no matter what. Everyone is held accountable to the same level of meeting the requirements.
- Classroom management systems flop when relationships with students aren't the foundational piece established. Students need to know you care about them as people and you'll do your best to ensure everyone is safe and successful.

- Compassion is how you show grace to misbehaviors and less-than-desired choices. Understanding the role of a teacher is to facilitate the growth and maturity of another individual and means one has to be compassionate on the imperfect path of learning.

In considering all that we've just talked about in terms of routines, resilience, and influencing student behavior, the next few chapters will discuss three elements that will ensure the classroom management system you design for your classroom can stand the test of time. The three Rs are relationships, routines, and roping students in with engaging content (see Figure 8.1). This three-pronged approach will ensure you're focused on managing a classroom and not just student behavior. This will maximize your impact and instructional time.

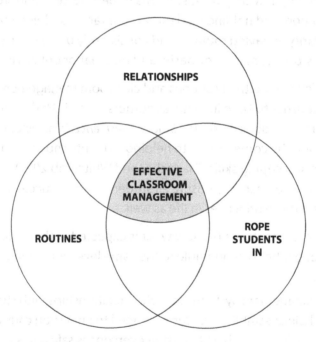

Figure 8.1   The three Rs of classroom management.

The Impact of Classroom Management

When a teacher structures a classroom for safety and efficiency, students have the opportunity for more time on task. This means students gain additional instructional time because the routines and procedures that run the classroom are efficient. When students can transition around the classroom and gather materials effortlessly, they dig into learning quicker than in a classroom that is disorganized and not methodically structured.

When students have more time on task, they have additional opportunities to solidify their learning, either through more repetitions of skills, more time to ask questions, or varied ways to collaborate with peers to deepen their understanding.

Classroom management affords students a richer learning experience. They can learn more content and at deeper levels because of structure and routine. This translates to higher student achievement in the classroom.

When I reached out to edu-leaders in my EduLeadership Facebook group (https://www.facebook.com/groups/609598144007188) about what is the major factor affecting teachers from delivering the lessons they planned, they mentioned student misbehaviors. Even if you master Brick 1: Lesson Design, you can still have a challenge ahead of you in Brick 2: Classroom Management. Regardless of how well planned you are, you'll struggle to execute this plan if students aren't physically or mentally ready for the experience.

Ensuring your environment readies the minds and bodies of students so that they can learn is of upmost priority when its time to implement that 10% of teaching (delivery of instruction). This includes having a welcoming environment, clear directives on entering the classroom, consistent routines daily, acknowledgment as a contributing member of the classroom family, encouragement to make good choices, celebration of progress and met milestones, and so on.

Students misbehave because they lack clarity in what they are to be doing, and oftentimes there's no repercussions for deviating from the expectation. If you can be consistently clear and follow through with consequences, misbehaviors will be a rarity in your classroom. That leaves more room for learning to occur, increasing the likelihood academic gains will be made by students.

Lessons from the Trenches: Set the Expectation

I got a lot of comments about my classroom for various reasons. However, the most popular feedback related to the vibe of my classroom. The fluorescent light bulbs in the classroom were harsh and gave students headaches—especially when it reflected on bright white paper on their desks. Each year I taught, I started to stock up on lamps from the Back-to-School sale at Walmart as students headed back to college. These multicolored lights were in each learning area around the classroom and provided ample light for students to work.

The school provided a CD/cassette player (don't joke about how old I am!). I purchased a CD with calming jazz on it and had that playing every morning as students came in to work, during all independent work activities, and during packing up at the end of the day. Students knew they could not speak louder than the music, which was strategically placed at a low volume.

On the front board was a welcome message. Students knew to read this every morning as they entered. They were to complete, but the sequence of items stayed similar. For example:

1. *Unpack.*
2. *Turn in your homework at the back table.*
3. *Begin morning work at your desk.*
4. *When finished, read silently in your secret spot. (Students with good behavior and academic performance could earn having a secret spot: a spot of their choosing in the room where they could work independently.)*

I stood at the doorway and said "Good Morning" to each student by name. It was my way of appreciating each student for arriving on time, pouring into them with a personalized greeting so they felt special, and a chance to start the school day off on a positive note. Many students experienced hardships prior to coming to school, so a fresh start beginning at my doorway was a way I could control how the rest of their day went.

EXPEDITIONARY
LEARNING

> *These are the ways I helped ready student minds and bodies so that they were ready to learn as soon as they entered. Other classrooms had students throwing backpacks at each other, talking in loud voices, numerous questions to the teacher for what to do, and instructional time lost when the bell rang because of having to get things in order. In comparison, my classroom was calm and focused because every decision I made was intentional for the outcome I wanted—students unpacked, ready to learn when the bell sounded.*

If we want to affect student learning, we must get a hold of how we run our classroom, down to the details. (Sound familiar? How we design lessons directly affects how we are able to execute our plan.) These expectations should be explicitly taught often throughout the year. This means teachers plan what the expectation will be, post the sequence in the classroom for easy reference, teach the system to students, and allow them to practice and receive feedback. But we can't stop there. Just because we taught it one time doesn't mean students will meet the expectation on a repeated basis, especially after a long break away from school. Revisit expectations as often as necessary—maybe even build in practice time, too. This reminder builds muscle memory for meeting expectations so students can achieve mastery.

Without effective classroom management practices, teachers are unable to maximize time spent learning. In her article "Effective Classroom-Management & Positive Teaching," Katharina Sieberer-Nagler (2015, 164) cites research that correlates effectively managed classrooms with student learning:

- "The National Union of Teachers reported in a [1988] survey . . . that more than a third of teachers experience disrupted lessons as a result of misbehavior and that half of them believe that school discipline is a greater problem today than it was years before" (citing Merrett and Wheldall 1990).

- Another study "reported that some teachers spend as much as 30 to 80 percent of their time addressing discipline problems. . . . Teachers must be able to establish appropriate student behavior in their classrooms to maximize time for learning" (citing Levin and Nolan 2007).

This is why it's essential that teachers set up strong classroom management systems so they can offer students a high-quality learning environment where they spend the majority of their time gaining knowledge and practicing skills. It is our duty to ensure all students learn and grow in our care. Classroom management is one way to do that. It is unacceptable to lose 30% to 80% (or up to four hours) of instructional time. How can we expect students to be ready to move to the next grade level if the majority of their academic time is spent on things other than academics? As teachers, we can control our own classroom and ensure the percentage of off-task behaviors are minimal. Sharing classroom management strategies with colleagues during planning is one way to influence other teachers to maximize the learning time in the classroom as well.

In addition to lost instructional time, dealing with misbehaviors constantly does not build relationships with students. If you are constantly having to redirect a student, they feel attacked, singled out, and that you don't like them. This can make them act out more, or worse, disengage entirely. It is very difficult to get a student reengaged after they feel defeated and disliked.

Elementary educator Chelsea Henley agrees: "Optimized learning time is clearly the number one goal with classroom management, but I also think it is important for emotional wellness and overall satisfaction of both teachers and students. If things flow well and are productive, everyone feels better!" (Google Docs comment to author, January 11, 2023).

Classroom culture is something every teacher can control, in any classroom. As the Children's Literacy Initiative defines, "Classroom culture is created through the language we use, the responsibilities we encourage, and the procedures we teach. A purposeful classroom culture teaches children the social-emotional skills they need to succeed in the world—in and out of school" (CLI n.d.)

Our responsibility as teachers is to not just teach content, but to teach children. That means we help them develop skills and habits to operate in future classrooms and out in the world itself.

CHAPTER 9

GETTING STARTED WITH CLASSROOM MANAGEMENT

Classroom management doesn't have to be super complicated, but it needs to be consistent and appropriate.

Three principles will help you get started with classroom management: relationships, routines, and roping students in (see Figure 9.1). We will discuss each of these principles at length to ensure you are able to successfully get started with classroom management.

R1: Relationships

Education is a people business. The human-to-human connection is most important. If we create a laundry list of rules and force students to comply, they'll never blossom as individuals. Before diving straight into learning and enforcing routines, put relationships first. Get to know each other as people, and then as teacher and student. If students aren't personally connected, they will not abide by the structure you put in place nor will they rise to the academic excellence they are capable of. Show respect and interest in your students by getting to know their names as quickly as possible, have a pleasant attitude, learn about their interests, and maybe even attend their extracurricular activities.

Edutopia shared a quote on Instagram (June 19, 2023) by Ashleigh Warner, a psychologist: "Beneath every behavior is a feeling. And beneath every feeling is a need. And when we meet the need rather than focus on the behavior, we begin to deal with the

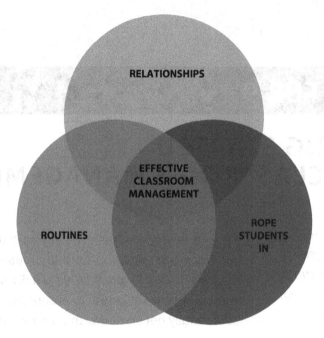

Figure 9.1 Relationships and routines help rope students into the lesson.

cause not the symptom." The only way to get to the root of a problem is to understand the person first. Relationships are the conduit through which those feelings, needs, and behaviors become crystal clear. Then you can begin to problem-solve.

Lessons from the Trenches: The Whole Student

As a teacher, I liked to get to know my students with a survey. During Back-to-School/ Meet the Teacher night, I got to meet my future students. They got to walk around the classroom and find their cubby, their desk, and meet their friends. On their desk was a small gift—a welcome certificate, brand-new "Welcome to ___ grade" pencil, and this survey. They could fill out the survey that evening with the help of their parents or take it home and return it the first day of school. It provided so much insight into how students viewed themselves as students. Many were surprised I was asking their preferences and parents were thankful I was willing to tailor my teaching and interaction to their child's needs. At the end of the year, parents filled out another survey to provide feedback on their perspective of their child's learning journey (see the End-of-Year Student Reflection/End-of-Year Parent Reflection sheets in Appendix 1, as well as on my website; see the next Downloadable Resources box). Their replies help me make adjustments for the next year, but the real value in this exercise is that they sit down together and think through the year. That conversation paves the way for future conversations about how the student experienced their grade level (strengths, weaknesses, needs, etc.) and what support they need from their parents to be successful. Many parents commented that they appreciated the opportunity to contemplate the year together and that they never thought to talk about it with their child before. I hope parents and students continue to have these conversations together.

Note: I communicate with parents throughout the year, so this is not the first time I request feedback. But because the ups and downs of the year have usually been neutralized by the end of it, the feedback tends to be logical and unbiased.

Downloadable Resources: End-of-Year Student Reflection Sheet and End-of-Year Parent Reflection Sheet

Visit www.alwaysalesson.com/teacher-essentials to download your free resource!

When teachers know their students well, they can design more interesting, relevant lessons for them. Connecting with students throughout the year is important for classroom culture to thrive.

The effect that positive classroom climate can have on student learning is immense. As famous educator, author, speaker, and leader, Dr. Brad Johnson reminded his Instagram audience: "Effective teachers don't focus so much on rules, but more on relationships, routines, and expectations. If you focus mainly on rules, you will spend

---

most of the year enforcing them. But if you focus on relationships, routines, and expectations, you rarely have to defer back to rules" (August 7, 2022).

Let this be your reminder to build the culture and the environment for success and you'll rarely have to focus on the rules. Refreshing students on expectations will increase the likelihood they can meet the expectations on a daily basis. Revisit these expectations after long breaks from school (e.g., summer and winter break) or after having a substitute teacher. A classroom is a place to learn, and in order for learning to take place, we put structure in place to manage the process. We are not controlling people—we are controlling the environment so that people can succeed.

R2: Routines

Routines provide structure to a classroom that can easily get out of hand with 20+ children in it. Routines provide a road map for how to operate in the space, hold students accountable for their compliance and interaction, and prevent the potential for misbehaviors to distract from learning.

When teachers get stuck in poor planning mode, they end up being reactionary in managing their classroom. Preparation is the key to a smooth-running classroom, both in the written lesson plan and execution phase.

Quick Note: Remember, Brick 1: Lesson Design must be solid before moving into Brick 2: Classroom Management. If you find you are having a lot of misbehaviors and are unable to decrease or eliminate them, then revisit Brick 1 to see if something in the planning phase can sort out the issue. Being proactive has stronger long-term results than being reactive.

This means teachers spend a significant amount of time thinking and developing their systems, rolling them out to students, holding students accountable, revising systems that aren't working, and celebrating the success of student learning habits.

In building strong routines in the classroom, there are three steps to work through in order to build a successful classroom management system. These three steps will focus on routines in relation to where, what, and how routines are executed in the classroom.

Classroom Management Planning

1. **Formulate your philosophy based on classroom management.** This will set the tone for what students will accomplish in your care. It should be supportive and encouraging. Grab your favorite note-taking item to brainstorm answers to the following questions. Feel free to revisit these questions yearly and see how your responses change and shape your experience as a leader in the classroom.

    *   What are your beliefs and attitudes toward managing a classroom of students?
    *   What is it you hope to provide for children?
    *   What management strategies feel most aligned to your values and beliefs?

    Getting clear on what you believe before creating systems ensures you will stick with what you plan because you believe in your methods.

2. **Plan and prepare your classroom management systems.** Setting up structure for classroom management is to think through how to operate a successful lesson within the desired parameters. Aspects of instruction such as volume, pace, location, format, and direction prevent misbehaviors and increase time on task.

    Managing behaviors is *reactionary*. You have to wait for behaviors to arise before you can apply consequences to discourage future behaviors. When you manage a classroom, you set up structures and routines to *prevent* misbehaviors from happening. No longer are you waiting for the fire to ignite so you can stomp it out. You are setting up your learning experiences so that fires cannot exist in the first place.

    Plan the following for each section (subject area/class period) of your teaching day:

    *   Expectations: What do you want/need to happen?
    *   Responsibilities: Who does what? Why?

- Routines: What do we do every _____? Why?
- Procedures: How do we do X?
- Transitions: How do we change course?

When you design your system, don't just think through the logistics of how it will operate start to finish. Think about how you will hold students accountable for meeting these expectations. It's essential that when you teach the system you share your rationale. Use your favorite note-taking item to brainstorm how you frame your systems for your students.

Why does this matter to and for students? How does this affect them when they follow or don't follow the system?

This builds interest and motivation in meeting expectations. The responsibility of being a student is multifaceted, and students need to know what they signed up for, how to be successful, and what happens when they fall off the learning expectation wagon. When they see the big picture and feel how it is connected to them, they now have a reason to adhere to the system.

3. **Set up your learning environment.** You want the environment to be inviting. Natural light and bright colors can welcome students and get them excited for learning. Arranging desks in pods or a circular shape encourages collaboration and a sense of community. Decide the level to which you desire students to collaborate before choosing your seating arrangement. There will be various learning areas in your classroom and each area will have its own structures for learning and material management. Physically setting up your space on paper first will enable you to think through hot spots in your classroom that need to be put out (e.g., tight squeeze entering and exiting the area, too many materials in one place creates a mess, etc.). Once you have maximized the learning space on paper, set up the physical space. Place expectation reminders in the learning area to hold students accountable for following the protocol. Be flexible enough to make additional changes once students begin to operate

Having a strong classroom management plan ensures learning can remain front and center in your classroom.

in the space. It might be a sound thought or even look good on paper, but until you see it in action you are not going to be certain it's the best option.

When you introduce your structures, systems, and processes to students be sure to begin by explaining their purpose. You want students to be invested in their learning and be willing to meet expectations to do so. This holds them accountable and motivates them to be successful. By providing the rationale behind requirements, students better understand the teacher's approach and how their choices affect the success of their peers and themselves.

When designing routines, there are five common aspects of instruction to manage:

- **Volume:** How loud should students be conversing with each other at each section of the lesson? What signal will you give to alert students they have breached that boundary (e.g., cannot speak louder than the quiet music playing)?

- **Pace:** How quickly should students be completing tasks or transitioning? Time tracking each section of your lesson will keep you on pace to finishing the lesson as planned within the allotted time frame (unless purposely lengthening an instructional section due to misunderstandings, gaps in preknowledge, etc.). Instead of thinking about the length of a subject area or period (e.g., language arts 10:00–11:15), we need to break up each section of the language arts lesson to make sure we stay on track with what we planned. This can be shared with students and even posted on the board if helpful (e.g., use a timer to track efficient transitions without being rushed chaos).

- **Location:** Where are students to be working and retrieving learning materials? What are the expectations within each location (e.g., classroom library process versus math manipulatives center)? Label the learning areas with an expectations poster so students can be responsible learners and have the visual reminder of how to operate in the space.

- **Format:** How are students to respond or complete assignments? Is there a common format to follow (e.g., heading a paper, problem-solving process, preplanning, writing a graphic organizer, etc.)?

- **Direction:** What is the process to move about the room to and from these locations? Are there specific movement directives to keep transitions orderly and efficient (e.g., rotate to the right, walk around desk formations instead of through, etc.)?

Decide what routines and procedures will be used often in the classroom, for example, pencil sharpening, gathering materials, transitioning to centers, partner discussions, and so on.

Think through that procedure from start to finish, detailing how students should complete it for safety and efficiency. Once you have designed your procedure, focus on "hot spots" where students might get distracted (e.g., everyone turning in homework at one place at the same time will encourage dialogue, misbehaviors, and chaos).

Once you have thoroughly planned your routines and procedures, it's time to teach it to students before holding them accountable for meeting expectations. (It is expected that you will need to tweak the routine as necessary as students implement it.)

Quick Note: Be careful to not over-teach your management systems. Teach your most important system first with multiple opportunities for students to practice. You want students to process the information and build muscle memory, so it becomes an automatic habit. Then slowly add in additional systems as students get the hang of the previous system. This can take the first few weeks of school (and refreshers after long breaks from school) for every routine to be taught and practiced. Slow and steady ensures students retain expectations and have had time practicing meeting them.

Avoid the major misstep of making new routines and procedures for every single activity in every single lesson. This is confusing and students will never master a routine. You'll spend more time teaching the new routine than doing the new routine, not saving any time for actual learning. The secret is in developing routines and procedures than can be used time and time again no matter the subject area or lesson topic (e.g., passing in/out papers).

Decide what student responsibilities will be and what your expectations of those responsibilities will be. It is a student's personal responsibility to get an education, and your professional responsibility to provide it. Students should know their role as learners requires daily effort and work output to help them achieve their goals. Teachers can lay out the road map for students to do just that and experience a successful school year. Plus, if students are in charge of routines as a classroom job, they are more likely to meet behavior expectations because of the added responsibility of leading a routine. Educator Madeline Baird says, "I had enough jobs for every student and I had students apply for jobs. I would then hire each student for a job and train them. At each quarter they would apply for new jobs. Students who did the job the previous quarter would train the next student on their job and if the student ever had a question about the job they would go to their 'supervisor' for questions. It was a fun way to get routines done and for students to show ownership. They loved it" (Madeline Baird, Google Docs comment to author, November 18, 2022). The classroom is not only your space but also the learning home of students. They should be involved in operating their learning home and, in turn, take pride in the efficiency and productivity occurring in the space.

Having a repeatable system creates automaticity, freeing up mental space in the brain to focus on processing new learning instead of reacting to the learning environment. For example, if you pass out papers the same way in all subject areas every day of the week, students no longer think about receiving the paper, they are focused on you for direction on how to complete the task. This is an efficient use of class time getting students to work right away, and they are capable to begin because their muscle memory is working on autopilot to receive the assignment. By saving time with structure, that time can be reallocated throughout the day for additional lessons, working with small groups of students, or repeated practice of new skills.

Your word choice has a huge impact on the result of your classroom behaviors.

Your directions are an opportunity to bring clarity to expectations for students. There is a difference between asking students to be "quiet" instead of "silent." Decide ahead of time what you want and then communicate to students. Being concise in your word choice ensures only the main points stick with students so they can meet expectations and the lesson can move on efficiently. Short, purposeful directions have urgency, leaving room for repeated practice to strengthen skills. It's also a good idea to have students get in the habit of pausing a task and standing still during directions. Their full attention will eliminate confusion later in the lesson. Posting directions for students to reference throughout an activity cuts down on question asking and confusion, leaving more time for on-task learning. Placing time stamps near the directions help students manage their time as they move through sections of a task.

Quick Note: For example,

- 2 min: Read word problem and underline key words.
- 5 min: Solve word problem and double check with a second strategy.
- At 15 min bell: Go back to confusing problems and try again.

There is less likelihood for misbehaviors to occur when teachers are clear in words and expectations. In his short publication *Classroom Management*, Walter Doyle (1980, 6) notes how much instructional time is wasted by misbehaviors: "Students learn more when more time is spent in productive work rather than in confusion and misbehavior." Misbehaviors are distracting to other learners. It interrupts their productive work. Therefore, teachers who are effective classroom managers prevent misbehaviors before they happen so that students do not get distracted at all, increasing their productive work time.

When we get so focused on catching misbehaviors or redirecting unwanted behavior, we route all our energy into reacting instead of being proactive. If we put routines in place for structure it leaves little room for misbehavior to crop up. Why? Because with structure comes clear expectations. There's no gray area to exploit. And when we consistently use the same systems and processes to run our classrooms, students experience success when meeting those expectations. Structure stamps out gray area. Consistency builds muscle memory. And a feeling of success builds motivation to continue meeting expectations.

The key to effective classroom management is prevention. Teachers lose significant instructional time putting out fires, meaning addressing misbehaviors of students. To maximize instructional time, teachers should create a classroom environment that is structured to avoid common time suckers like talking out of turn, finding partners, side conversations, and so forth.

If you remember in Brick 1: Lesson Design, we discussed planning for student misbehaviors in a way that will actually prevent them. Scanning the room helps you catch misbehaviors quickly. When you're working with students, always face the majority of the remaining students and look out and up to scan the room.

Moving about in the school building is another popular time misbehaviors occur. Instead of standing in the front of your class of students to walk them to the next location or in the back of the line, stand in the middle. This enables you to scan your lane and address the front and the back with ease and effectiveness. Have students stop every so often at predetermined landmarks to ensure the class is keeping pace together as a unit and are meeting hallway behavior expectations. For example, students might walk to the end of a hall and stop before receiving the go-ahead signal to turn down a new hall and stop at the next landmark.

CHAPTER 10

ADDRESSING MISBEHAVIORS

Misbehaviors are an outward manifestation of something occurring on the inside.

Misbehaviors alert us that something is disconnected. Sometimes students are disconnected from us as leaders in the classroom, or from each other as peers, or even from the applicability of the content. Either way, it is a signal that we cannot ignore.

It might take time and extra hands but getting to the root of the misbehavior will serve the student best in the long run. You put the time in up front, and you see all the reward in the end.

When we use an unrelated solution to a problem, the connection to better behavior choices never reaches its destination.

Let's turn to the basics when it comes to misbehaviors that arise despite your systems and procedures you put in place (especially the structures to prevent misbehaviors to occur in the first place).

The following steps will help you address misbehaviors without distracting from the lesson.

1. **Redirect:** When dealing with misbehaviors, the first choice is to redirect the unwanted behavior to the desired behavior. For example, if students are standing at their seats and shouting across the room you would say, "Sit down and work silently by yourself on your assignment." They now know what they should do and are easily able to get back on task. Instructional time didn't suffer dealing with misbehaviors, and it provided as a reminder to all students the expectation for learning for that moment in time.

Redirecting behavior will happen but it doesn't have to eat up loads of instructional time. It can be quick and effective, just like in the example.

- Decide what "off-task" behavior is (e.g., fiddling with a pencil, chatting with peers, playing on technology).

- Redirect behavior by reminding students what they should be doing (e.g., face forward versus stop turning around in their seat).

- If the misbehavior continues multiple times, apply a consequence related to the infraction (e.g., playing on technology = lose device privileges for remainder of lesson).

Note: A nonverbal redirection, like tapping on a student's desk as you walk by, would be ineffective if you had not already explained to students what the tap on the desk meant. Some students will still respond with "Huh? What? Why are you doing X?" This is their desire to save face in front of students or continue receiving attention, albeit negative attention. Tapping on the student's desk is the least intervening action to redirect, but it might lack clarity without other interventions occurring before it. For example, maybe you had already paused midsentence to get their attention and waited for them to abide by expectations before saying "thank you" or quickly spoke their name before getting back into the lesson. Those interventions lead up to the tap, which is the least intervening action to get their attention.

2. **Address 1:1:** When redirections are not working, it's time to address a student for a misbehavior. You want to avoid the whole class watching the conversation, so get students working first. Have a back pocket activity you can implement on the spot if you need to step away to take care of a misbehavior or unexpected circumstance. This activity should be something they are very familiar with so they do not need lengthy directions or clarifying questions before getting to work. This allows for a seamless transition from managing the environment back to instruction. For example, students could read silently from a text and pull out key words

that summarize the concept or read the next two paragraphs in pairs. The second example is helpful because the noise generated by the out-loud reading conceals the noise coming from your private conversation with the student.

Addressing the misbehavior is best by walking over to the offending student, whisper the expectation, encourage them to rise to meet it, and get back to the lesson. This quick redirection is personalized, intimate, and avoids creating a scene because students are already working on the back pocket activity and you addressed it quickly.

- Ensure students know that when a misbehavior occurs, it's in the moment, and after it's redirected, the student can start over fresh. A fresh start policy allows students to make mistakes without feeling like there's no way to turn things around. A sense of safety in a classroom encourages students to continue trying their best, even when they have a lapse in judgment. Forgiveness and forgetfulness go a long way to build a strong classroom culture where students can be themselves and grow. Elementary educator Chelsea Henley states, "Each child deserves a fresh start; people change, and sometimes you can be the person to make a difference for that child" (Google Docs comment to author, January 21, 2023).

- Assume positive intent. Some days there are more misbehaviors than normal, but students are imperfect people learning how to operate in their environment. They may push the limits to explore what they can get away with, but most of the time, the average child does not come to school to purposely misbehave. Assume that when a misbehavior occurs it was a misjudgment or accident. It's not an attack on you or your instruction, rather a child experimenting in a social environment. Most students aren't thinking through ramifications before they act. The more redirection they receive, they will begin to make the connection and meet expectation. In the meantime, assume students want to learn, want to behave, and want to be in your classroom. Give grace. Redirect to the expected behavior. Start over fresh.

3. **Self-reflection:** Get students back on track and encourage to meet expectations once again by incorporating a self-reflection aspect. This increases ownership that students have a choice in how they respond in their learning environment.

It also reminds them of the expectations and brings clarity for how their behavior is unacceptable. This self-reflection can be used later to talk 1:1 with the students in depth to find out additional information if the misbehaviors continue to occur or it could be used during parent-teacher conferences to show the growth in meeting expectations. Either way, the self-reflection is not only about the current misbehavior but also about bringing awareness to the decisions that lead up to the problem. A reflection is a preventative measure for future misbehaviors.

4. **Consistency:** Be sure to consistently address students not meeting expectations. This sends a message that expectations apply to everyone, that you have high expectations of all learners, and that your classroom is a fair and honorable place to be. This increases student responsibility, ownership, and empowerment.

5. **Recognize and reward:** There will be students who consistently meet expectations. Avoid bribery but acknowledge those putting in the effort to be responsible learners, for themselves and those around them. This could be verbal or written praise in private or in front of others. Simple, yet effective. This is important in order to motivate students to adhere to protocol and consistently meet expectations. We are all human and experience days where we might not want to put in the extra effort to adhere to requirements. However, when students know their teacher sees their effort, on their best and worst days, and acknowledge their choice to meet expectations, they will be more willing to comply. Students will work hard when they know there is a benefit, and a teacher giving positive attention to good choices encourages the hard work to continue.

There will be a time, when your classroom management strategy and skill level is top notch, but you're still experiencing consistent disruptive misbehavior from a student or students. At this point, know it is not your management system that needs to be reworked, it's your approach to that particular student. Diving deep into your relationship with that student will help you pinpoint the root of the problem. Maybe that student desires more attention and is unsure how to get it and acts out for you to notice them. A quick hand on their shoulder or thumbs up during instruction might be all they need to know you recognize their hard work and appreciate them. Or maybe the student is very physically active and struggles to sit for long periods of time. Knowing your students' learning habits and preferences will help you problem-solve quickly, enabling that student to bounce on a ball while learning or squeeze a stress ball to relieve anxious energy. If you are still unable to pinpoint why the misbehaviors occur, meet with the student and their parent(s). An open discussion will increase self-awareness for the student and build a team partnership with the parents as you all try to problem-solve together. Students may have unique learning needs, but they shouldn't get in the way of others learning. Addressing the problem head on will save you time and frustration in the long run. Plus, you've helped a student learn tools and strategies they can take with them as they progress through the grades so they can be a successful learner no matter the classroom environment.

Lessons from the Trenches: Addressing Misbehaviors

Over the years, I've been challenged with various student misbehaviors. Most were the common ones, such as talking out of turn, running around the classroom, taking other students' materials, copying each other's work, and telling on each other. I was able to address most of these with the structures I created in the classroom, but there were some extreme behaviors and challenging obstacles that I didn't know how to solve on my own—which is when I turned to others for help: colleagues, our special education team, the administration, even the internet. Fortunately, we had a team on staff that specialized in brainstorming solutions to classroom challenges— collaboratively discussing options to better support the students, from environment changes to alternative assignments. I share several examples here (with names changed for anonymity).

A few points before we get started: (1) When going this route, documentation is always recommended to track the interventions you're trying and their outcomes. (2) Don't wait to ask for help. The quicker students receive support, the better off they'll be. (3) Know that sometimes we have to get creative and think outside of the box to meet our students where they are and enable them to be successful in our structured learning environment.

EXPEDITIONARY
LEARNING

Norman

Norman was in my third-grade class in my first year of teaching. He was high energy and full of life. He made me laugh and the entire class rallied around his shenanigans. His favorite trick was doing cartwheels into the American flag that hung high on the wall. At the age of eight, he was taller than I was and had more energy than the entire class of students combined. He performed average academically, mainly because he could concentrate only for so long before breaking out in song, drum solo, or an athletic pole-vaulting event. But because I was just a first-year teacher, his behavior always threw me off. I would deal with him while the whole class watched. Minutes of instruction time ticked away and we'd have to finish the day's lesson another day.

We had a behavior management facilitator on staff who often stopped by to check on Norman. He told Norman he'd reward him with 1:1 time, guy-to-guy, if—that's if—he made it through the entire day without incident. Because Norman's father wasn't in the picture, Norman thrived off male attention, but even that strong incentive wasn't enough; his antics would kick in soon after the start of class.

We tried all sorts of solutions—get out energy in the bouncy corner, visit a buddy classroom to complete work in a different environment, win a prize for meeting expectations. . . . He still ruled the roost.

Except when his mother showed up, which was often. Right in the middle of instruction, she'd fly into the room and holler Norman's name at top volume. To this he'd sit down with his tail between his legs and complete his work silently for the rest of the day. (Despite her intrusive manner, I knew she was trying to support my efforts to maintain an orderly environment.)

It was so clear that he wanted to do well, but he just couldn't control his impulses.

We got him evaluated and he qualified for medical intervention in relation to ADHD. It helped him remain focused for longer periods of time. He was able to control his outbursts without losing his zeal for life. (It helped that he now sat in the front row, so there were fewer distractions in front of him.) We were able to implement a behavior plan with three simple goals: raise hand to speak, walk when indoors, and complete all assignments before socializing with peers. It took all of us working together to help Norman succeed.

Jay

Jay was in my fifth-grade class in my fifth year of teaching. He was handsome and had a heart of gold. He so badly wanted to be liked but didn't know how to socialize well. He aggressively entered conversations, pushed and shoved as a way to build connection, and told on his classmates for things they didn't do just to get attention. He also struggled academically and because of that engaged in distractive behavior to avoid assignments. This was the year we departmentalized across the grade level, so I shared him with a colleague across the hall. We often chatted after school about ways to help him, compare behaviors in class, and think of new ways to structure our lessons so he could experience success.

We overheard him reminiscing about fishing with his grandpa, but had since broken his fishing pole and lost his grandpa. So we bought him a fishing pole and presented it to him one day as the classes dismissed for recess, telling him how proud we were of how hard he was working. He immediately broke out in tears and ran to us for a group hug. He was just a little boy in a big boy body, in need of love, acceptance, and guidance. For the first time, I understood how badly he wanted to belong.

After that, Jay showed up to class on time having completed his assignments—not exactly correctly, but completed all the same. He paid attention as best he could and participated when he could. He still needed learning supports such as shorter assignments, multiple breaks, and talking chips, but we focused on learning and not his physical behavior when learning (e.g., standing, tapping, or humming).

His permanent desk spot was in the back near the door, so he could easily step out if needing to jump to refocus or stand up and pace when processing information. It only took a warning glance from me for him to know he had crossed the line of distracting others, and he learned how to calm himself and return his focus to the lesson. In time his learning habits improved and he was able to move into a cooperative group during a lesson. He learned how to calmly approach his friends, listen to their jokes, and chime in when he could. Over time, his academic performance showed gains, and his confidence in who he was and the value he contributed to the classroom skyrocketed. The smile on his face to feel included—and knowing he'd earned it all by himself—was worth all the stress of trial and error to get to that moment. All because of a fishing pole.

Jay taught me to look beyond the surface, that a simple act of kindness can make such a huge impact. When we listen to our students for who they are as people, and dig deeper to understand their needs, we can provide solutions that affect them for years to come. The way we show up to support students as people first and students second can shape the trajectory of their academic career—and beyond.

Monica

Monica was in my second-grade class in my fifth year of teaching. She'd immigrated from Mexico and was staying with her aunt and uncle until her parents could join her. When I first met her she walked right up to me with the biggest smile and gave me a huge hug. She loved people and school, and fortunately my loving classroom environment encouraged students to immediately welcome her. She sat in the front of the class and answered every question—although often off-topic and always in broken English.

I had no experience teaching in a foreign language, so I dusted off whatever Spanish I could remember from high school and tried my best to communicate. But I also learned how much we can communicate in other ways, without a common language.

Because our school was very diverse, Monica was able to speak Spanish during recess and lunch. She also attended ESL classes multiple times a day with various grade levels, which improved her English in class. Her accent was adorable and she was so proud of herself when she would ask, "Can I sharpen my pencil?" or "Can I go to the bathroom?"

Sometimes, what we teach kids has more to do with the person we help them become and less to do with the grade on their paper. Monica grew in confidence that year. She needed boundaries and rounds of practice with routines, but she thrived in a foreign environment.

Her big smile and long brown pigtails remain in my heart and mind. Her lack of language skills pushed me to advocate for additional services for her, dig into my bag of tricks to meet her where she was academically, and lead with love.

Katy

Katy was in my third-grade class in my eighth year of teaching. She arrived with an extensive IEP, which outlined in detail the triggers of her aggressive behavior tendencies—which she could not control—as well as her academic and behavioral goals (such as waiting her turn to speak, refraining from profanity, sitting in a chair properly, and working on second-grade-level learning standards). Fortunately, Katy had a 1:1 aide who stayed with her throughout the school day to provide additional support, which included keeping her safe.

Katy regularly erupted without notice. Thankfully, her aide would escort her out of the room so as not to disrupt the instructional flow. During these times, I would direct student attention toward me, jumping into an intriguing story related to the content until the distraction was gone and we could return to our work. It happened so often that sometimes I'd gather the students out of harm's way for an impromptu mini lesson.

One day Katy was so uncontrollable the aide couldn't get her out. She was kicking the aide and nearby students, cussing vehemently, spitting on herself and others, and throwing items from my desk. I rushed into action: "Students, stand up. Line up at the door quickly and quietly. Go into the hallway and sit against the wall." Recognizing my tone of voice, the students knew the situation was unsafe, and (mercifully) followed my instructions. I followed them out into the hall and completed the rest of the lesson without materials while Katy came down from her frenzy. (She later apologized to me and her classmates.)

So, what to do? I understood that Katy deserved to have a quality education and be exposed to grade-level content and peers. I believe in inclusivity. I was taught that no child should be left behind. But that didn't take away from the fact that the rest of the class deserved a quality education, too—which called for a safe learning environment that didn't erupt into chaos without warning on almost a daily basis. So I had to speak up. In the scariest meeting of my life, I met with the IEP committee and said Katy needed to be in a 1:1 learning situation with a full-time aide—that the harm she caused in class was unacceptable for everyone else. I felt she should be exposed to same-aged peers only at lunch, recess, and potentially specials (art, music, PE, etc.), but she was too disruptive to the classroom environment.

The committee had a hard time deciding how to ensure special education services were honored while also honoring what was best for the students. In part because Katy's parents didn't participate in the discussion, the district ruled in my favor. Katy was assigned a one-on-one aide to help her manage her emotions and meet academic requirements in a more intimate setting.

I firmly believe everyone deserves a quality education, so all the Katys out there deserve the extra attention they need. And, the rest of the kids also deserve a quality education—one that is safe and predictable, that sets them up to learn and grow—so, we must be able to draw a line in the sand if the situation becomes untenable. I value that this experience helped me find my voice in advocating for all the students in my class. I am thankful for how Katy taught me to be flexible, to think on my feet, to put emergency plans in place while keeping instruction going—and to protect all of my kids at all costs.

Sometimes, classroom management techniques aren't enough, and we must allow professionals to intervene with our neediest learners. When I put strong systems in place and Katy didn't succeed, I paired up with the special ed department. When those systems in place didn't help her succeed, we involved the school and district. Don't stop until you find the answer to help a child to learn and grow.

Laura

Laura was in my third-grade class in my eighth year of teaching. She was quiet and withdrawn. She arrived with a 504 plan that allowed some academic support as we went through the IEP process to get her additional services. At the time, her goals were to write her name and achieve kindergarten learning standards, which meant I had to expose her to third-grade content—but have her complete kindergarten-level assignments on that content. Quite a challenge!

During this time, the Bouncyband manufacturer offered a complimentary Bouncyband in exchange for a blog post review. What's a Bouncyband? I learned it's a thick rubber "bar" that fits onto desk legs to provide a bouncy footrest. According to the Yerkes-Dodson law (and Bouncyband.com), "physical stimulation can improve and help achieve optimum mental performance when one is neither overstimulated nor understimulated"—that movement can "stimulate the brain and boost mental performance."

I decided to try out the Bouncyband with Laura. She'd sit in her chair and complete her work while kicking her feet against the bouncy band. The resistance from the band allowed her to get out anxious energy and maintain focus. It worked tremendously for her. The Bouncyband decreases distracting, off-task behaviors and increases learning outcomes by providing additional structure. It definitely increased Laura's performance.

Classroom management isn't always routines and procedures; it can also be tools designed for specific student needs. Laura taught me that collaborations in the community can bring benefits far beyond your wildest imaginations. I continue to advocate for staff members and students out loud because you never know who is listening and able to help. We are truly better together.

Bruce

Bruce was in my third-grade class in my seventh year of teaching, and he arrived well into the school year. He had the same legal first name, last initial, and nickname as another student in the class. Because a child already in the class was referred to by said nickname, to avoid confusion I used Bruce's legal name instead of his nickname. This created a lot of friction—he wanted to be called his nickname, and I resisted.

His anger intensified at random throughout the year until his mother finally came in for a parent-teacher conference. She too was angry about why I refused to call her

EXPEDITIONARY
LEARNING

son by his nickname. I was able to decipher that his legal name was given by his father, who was not in the picture. I assumed using his legal name brought up bad memories, so I suggested they could legally change that name.

When I reflect back, I realize I could have easily had two Bruce Bs and just dealt with any confusion over which one. And today, given students' preferences over their names as well as their pronouns, I would have honored each student's choice. My point in sharing this story is that it taught me there is always more to the picture. Oftentimes student misbehavior has more to do with what is happening outside the classroom than what is occurring in it. I am thankful for that conversation with Bruce and his mom. May we extend grace before jumping to conclusions. Managing a classroom comes back to prioritizing your learners, because many of the best interventions occur at the personal level. If you allow individual students' needs to drive the solution, you can create an environment where all students can succeed.

I share these stories to demonstrate how there are just some things that only first-hand experience will teach you. Experiences like these helped me develop my classroom management, and I know I learned more from my students than they learned from me. Everyone makes mistakes, but you can also grow tremendously from each student and each experience. Don't focus on doing things perfectly; instead, focus on learning something every time. Then your stories will make you smile in remembering how much those students grew along with you.

Most misbehaviors will be minor. The examples I share with you are to demonstrate the creativity and intention required to meet every student's needs. Luckily, you will be able to solve common misbehaviors through prevention, attack unique misbehaviors in the moment without missing a beat, and even troubleshoot the more difficult misbehaviors with the support of your colleagues and school leaders.

Set the scene and tone for how the classroom will operate and students rise to the challenge. You spend your time, energy, and brain power where it matters most—instruction—instead of trying to control behavior. That's the power of influence.

Journal Jots: Visualization

Let's do a quick exercise. Answer the following prompt by writing anything that comes to mind—don't censure your thoughts.

Visualize a guest walking into your classroom while you're teaching.

- What is the energy in the room?

- How does it make the guest feel?

- What is the noise volume?

- Where are students and you (the teacher) located?

- How are the students relating to one another? How are the students relating to you as the teacher?

- Are misbehaviors present? If so, how are they handled?

Now that you had a chance to imagine what you truly desire, you're better able to open up your problem-solving muscles to work through whatever challenges you're currently facing. So let's see how we can get the current version of your classroom to transform into the visualization you wrote about in the Journal Jots.

In Appendix 1, as well as on my website; see the next Downloadable Resource box, you'll find my Classroom Management Guiding Questions. Take time to read each question and ponder the honest truth. This will help you get clear on what you desire and bring to light obstacles that are keeping you from making your philosophy a reality. (If you haven't begun teaching, skip the questions related to previous experience.)

Downloadable Resource: Classroom Management Guiding Questions

Visit www.alwaysalesson.com/teacher-essentials to download your free resource!

CHAPTER 11

MASTERING CLASSROOM MANAGEMENT

Students need to love learning, but more importantly they need to be able to love learning.

You've likely gained some momentum with your classroom management strategy by putting relationships first and routines in place. I'm guessing your intentionality has made a difference in how smoothly your classroom operations and learning experiences have gone. Once you feel your students are successful and productive in the learning environment you've created, it's time to step it up a notch and really get your classroom operating at high levels of learning.

Some students come to school already loving the idea of learning. Others, however, need positive experiences in order to fall in love with the process. For those students, the environment has to set them up for success so that they have access to engaging learning opportunities. Consistency and availability make all the difference for students to build learning momentum, stretching their knowledge and skill sets in new ways. This is how you hook and keep lifelong learners before you even teach them anything.

Consider these two questions as you reflect on the effectiveness of your classroom management strategy:

- **Consistency:** Are expectations the same each day so there is a flow to the day?
- **Availability:** Are engaging learning experiences available to all students each day?

EXPEDITIONARY
LEARNING

Even if you have the most thorough plan and best intentions, if you are inconsistent in how you operate your classroom, the mixed signal will encourage misbehaviors to crop up. When you master lesson design, you know you have made engaging learning opportunities available for every student every day. Now it is time to ensure your structures and routines are consistently applied during those lessons for every student every day.

If you find yourself off track with consistency, ask yourself why. What is getting in the way of you being able to consistently enact your management plan? Once you know the origin for inconsistency, you can begin to troubleshoot that area to allow for consistency to begin to develop. Make the adjustment as soon as possible so that you can get back to the thorough management plan you designed.

Quick Note: Remember, you'll find success in your classroom performance and effectiveness when you pay close attention to this sequence: perfect lesson design before classroom management. You may have to go back into the design phase to tweak what is not working before progressing forward again into classroom management.

Most important, when things go awry, the whole day doesn't have to be wasted because you didn't execute as consistently as intended. Extend grace to yourself, too!

When you allow an obstacle to throw you off, students pick up on that and very quickly your classroom can spin out of control. Keep composed, take a deep breath, decide your next step, and execute. Slowly you'll find your flow again. Your strength as a teacher is measured by how well you manage the hiccups, not how perfect your day runs.

In addition to consistency, there's one more way to master classroom management. Let's turn to our third and final R principle in implementing strong classroom management systems.

R3: Rope Students into Your Lesson

Roping your students into your lesson means you create such appealing learning experiences that students cannot help but engage. The act of roping in means to bring forth. Your instructional choices are a way in which you can bring students forth toward the learning opportunity. When you consistently teach in appealing ways that meet your students' interest levels and learning styles, you'll hook them on learning in your classroom. They will want to show up and learn from and by you.

There are a few ways to rope students into your lesson so that misbehaviors become extinguished:

1. **Quick, just-right pacing:** Reference your lesson plan to keep your delivery of your lesson in pace with what you planned. This goes back to internalizing your lesson and reusing structures and routines so it's automatic and efficient. The goal is to move fast enough to keep student attention—not too fast students will experience frustration trying to keep up and not too slow students will experience boredom from the slow pace.

   Once you know your ideal pace and you manage the lesson and environment to allow for that pace to flow, you'll need to be on the lookout for speed bumps and fast lanes:

   • Speed bumps mean you are flexible enough to adjust time if students need to slow down to better achieve, but you don't want to get too far behind that you can't get through what you've planned. However, in the case that the lesson needs to be extended a day, not only adjust your current lesson pacing but also adjust your weekly/monthly topic calendar so you can still hit all required content while taking time to meet student needs.

   • Fast lanes mean you are ready to accelerate the speed and direction of the lesson if students are grasping material quicker than expected. Teachers are masters at adjusting the pace of the lesson to meet the needs of the learner. Classroom management is the secret weapon to accurate and successful pace adjustment.

2. **Student discourse and interaction:** There is a major misconception about the sound level in a teacher's classroom equating to strong classroom management skills. Many believe a silent classroom means learning is happening at high levels due to compliant behaviors. Whereas others believe the opposite—loud classrooms mean high levels of learning and compliant behaviors because the learning process requires communication (and communication can increase the volume in the classroom). It turns out voice level is not an indicator on its own as to the quality of learning taking place in a classroom. As long as the noise volume is accompanied by on-task discussion, then the noise level is productive and should be allowed.

> **Quick Note:** Here's another example of how I use music in my classroom as a noise-level boundary. I set music at a certain volume, and then tell the students they can't talk any louder than the music—meaning, if they can't hear the music, they are too loud. This is just one way to help students self-regulate their volume during productive discourse.

In her book *Effective Classroom Management: The Essentials,* Tracey Garrett confirms the notion of noise volume and active learning: "Teachers often believe that a well-managed classroom is equivalent to an orderly and quiet environment, but the reality is that a productive learning environment can often be noisy because learning is not a passive activity. Learning requires talking, sharing, discovering, experimenting, and questioning, all of which can create noise" (Garrett 2014, 1).

Children have an innate desire to talk to themselves, others, and the environment around them. They desire connection and like to practice their language skills they are acquiring. Talking is a major part of learning. It enables the mind to process material by speaking it out loud, writing it down, and asking questions to peers.

This means teachers need to encourage their students to talk. And by doing so, students will learn what is and isn't appropriate (sound volume, topic, behavior, etc.). Instead of fearing your classroom will quickly get out of hand, decide ahead of time what protocol you will put in place to allow the freedom of discourse. Knowing it meets a student's need for a sense of community, their desire to talk to their peers, and natural part of the learning process, build that into the lesson. When you give them what they want and desire, but you also put parameters around that, they are going to be much more successful in the activity or assignment. They feel that their need is fulfilled but they also are willing to adhere to the boundaries because of the excitement in doing it in a way they desire. They would rather talk with boundaries than not talk at all. Honor that.

There are many student discussion activities to try, but I will give you three examples that increase in student flexibility and ownership. The first enables you to start small with parameters and work your way up to more robust discourse opportunities as your management strategy and student response are capable of handling.

Quick Note: Some classes of students are never able to engage in discourse at high levels, depending on their age, maturity level, or even energy level. It might take all year to work your way up, or some classes are ready much earlier in the year. Put the parameters in place and allow students to show you when they are ready.

- **Turn-and-talk:** Students will turn to their elbow partner to discuss a prompt. This provides them voice in the learning to share their ideas, while also practicing the protocol for a managed learning environment. This will teach students how to communicate (e.g., sentence stems, staying on topic, noise volume, back/forth dialogue, etc.). Here is an example:
  - Teacher: "Turn and talk to your partner about why suburban, rural, and urban communities need each other."
  - Student A: "I think they need the rural ones because they have cows and can give milk or chickens can give eggs."
  - Student B: "Yeah! The city doesn't have that. I think they need the urban ones because they have stuff to do like a museum or a show."

EXPEDITIONARY
LEARNING

- Student A: "I agree. Rural is boring so they need something to do. Oh! And people need houses so the suburban one is important, too."
- Student B: "Yup. They each give something to the other one."
- Teacher: "Students, turn back to me. Hands up to share one reason you and your partner talked about."

- **Gallery walk:** A gallery walk is where students collaborate in mini groups at a poster hung around the room and rotate to stations to discuss various prompts. Students use their background knowledge of the simple turn-and-talk activity and apply it in a new setting with the knowledge that if they are unable to learn within the set structure, they will revert back to simpler activities. This allows for a larger discussion group with a lengthier discussion topic so students can stretch the boundaries of discourse and interaction with peers. Here is an example:

  - Teacher: "Students, you are going to travel in your table group of four to each poster around the room. You will spend one minute reading the prompt on the poster, two minutes talking to your group about the prompt, and one minute to write your answer on the poster. Then we will rotate to the next poster and repeat the steps. When we have visited all posters, we will share out a summary of each topic poster."

- **Socratic seminar:** Your end goal would be to have open discussion with the whole class, following the protocol and respecting the boundaries. In his article about an instructional technique called the Socratic method, Jack Maden (2021) shares, "The Socratic method is harnessed by teachers to 'draw out' knowledge from students. The teacher does not directly impart knowledge, but asks probing, thought-provoking questions to kickstart a dialogue between teacher and student, allowing students to formulate and justify answers for themselves." This requires the highest level of management of a classroom to keep the discussion on track, all students involved in the dialogue, fresh ideas coming to the table, misbehaviors at bay, and so on. This is rewarding to students because they are experiencing freedom in their learning all while you are strengthening your ability to manage a classroom with a lot of moving pieces.

  - Teacher: "Students, bring your chairs in the center of room and make a circle. We are going to have an open discussion on the topic of whether or not all children should go to college. The rules are (1) one person talks at a time; (2) before sharing your own comment or question, you must first respond to the person who spoke before you; and (3) agree or disagree respectfully and with reasoning.

3. **Offer choice and voice:** You rarely have to manage student behavior when they are motivated to engage. One way to encourage motivation to engage is to offer choice in learning activities and build in opportunities for students to voice their opinions and takeaways about the topic of the lesson. These are components all teachers should strive to implement into their classroom structure. Building in choice and voice increases student motivation and investment in the learning process because they feel valued as individuals and have freedom to be unique while still adhering to structures and expectations. (We will discuss this in more detail in Brick 4: Student Choice and Ownership.)

4. **Differentiation via small-group instruction:** There are times in a lesson when students will need to receive additional support to affirm their learning. This can be done in small groups for students needing remediation (review and additional practice) or acceleration (extension with challenging, related activities). Small-group instruction can become quite tricky due to all the moving pieces.

In order for differentiation to be effective, students not receiving additional instruction should be working on an assignment that spirals past skills. If not, they will have questions and interrupt your small-group instruction. You want the independent task to be in a format they are familiar with for completing assignments in and of content they have previously learned. If they have simple clarifying questions, you can have a protocol in place for them to quietly and quickly check with a peer.

During small-group instruction, sit so you are facing students and can catch misbehaviors early before it distracts too many students. Hand signals or a snap work well to get their attention and provide redirection. When small-group instruction is used often, students will get used to the routine.

Students who are in small groups should alternate so they do not feel targeted to always have their name called to meet with you. However, if a particular student needs to receive instruction multiple times a week, try to skip a day in between if possible. If you are truly using data to formulate your groups, they should change based on the current skill being taught. It should be rare to have the same small group of students for every skill all year long. If this happens, it's time to look at a more intensive intervention.

There will come a time in each lesson when you need to differentiate instruction, providing small-group instruction to students needing additional time to master specific skills. This requires intentional classroom management structures designed in the planning phase of your lesson:

- Post a list of student names, locations to report to, and materials needed.

- Explain expectations for noise volume while working solo, in small groups, and during transition.

- Thoroughly plan transition routes with rounds of practice with feedback for students.

Table 11.1 shows how a teacher could display clear directives for small-group instruction so that all students can be successful with the transition.

Normalizing small-group instruction for all students is essential so that everyone receives what they need without feeling isolated. This might come in the form of small-group instruction or 1:1 meeting. We want differentiation of using various learning supports for all students, not just ones who are struggling academically. Fairness and equity are essential for student well-being.

Table 11.1 Small-Group Directions

When	Who	Where	What	Volume
10:00–10:15	Jessy, Lauren, Robert, Shanika, Damien	Back table w/ Ms. S	Red writing folder and notebook	0–2: silent, solo working with occasional soft whispers for questions
	Layna, Maurice, Jack	Library w/ Mr. J	Rough draft of personal narrative	

When differentiating instruction, you'll have to ensure students not needing assistance are able to continue to learn on their own while you meet with other students. Think of a clown spinning multiple plates in a circus show. Your eyes and ears are on the student(s) in front of you needing more assistance, while your eyes and ears are also scanning the environment to ensure all students are on task and do not need your assistance. A simple signal such as a bell to call a small group together (labeled on the front board) is an easy cue and system to implement in all subject areas.

We want all students to have access to the learning supports they need without distracting others during the learning process. For example, maybe students need additional learning materials to aid in completing an academic task and they'll need to quietly retrieve these items without disturbing other students (e.g., dictionary, calculator, word wall, math manipulatives, etc.).

Differentiation requires a lot of organization because students are working on different skills that require different materials. Keeping materials accessible and organized while also facilitating multiple learning activities at one time requires skill and intention on part of the teacher.

- **Missed instruction:** Students will be absent at some point and need to access prior day lesson materials. Decide how students should locate those items and catch up to the current day's lesson content. Teach students your procedures and follow up to ensure items are completed and students have a thorough understanding when they miss a lesson. This might mean they join in on small-group instruction for review with other students needing remediation.

- **Finished early:** Don't forget to have additional tasks for students who finish assignments early. If students are left with nothing to do, they will entertain themselves, distracting others and preventing a productive work environment. Students should know where to go to receive instructions on early-finisher work and complete the assignment that reviews or builds on past skills requiring no intervention from the teacher. Thoroughness is key!

Elementary educator Chelsea Henley shares a strategy she used in her classroom to remain organized while allowing students access to ongoing assignments: "I used 'ketchup, mustard, and pickle' folders in my classroom for independent work during small-group time. Any work that they couldn't finish during the day went in the ketchup folder, and they could use this time to 'catch up' on assignments. The mustard folder had current assignments that they 'must' complete and turn in. The pickle folder had a variety of activities they could 'pick' from. This helped keep students on task, but also gave them a little bit of freedom in what they were working on while I was meeting with small groups" (Google Docs comment to author, January 11, 2023).

Virtual Instruction Side Note

In a virtual classroom, management might look different. It requires a different set of skills and strategies that do not work in an in-person setting. If teaching a live class virtually, pacing is just as important. Students can sit and stare at a screen only for so long. You do not have the luxury of creating activities incorporating movement, although you can suggest students at home try to change position. Because you do not know everyone's home environment, having enough room to move around while learning (especially with a stationary computer) is challenging. Allowing additional brain breaks or time away from the computer (with countdown) enables the pacing of a lesson to feel manageable for students.

The operations in a virtual classroom are different. Student jobs are different (e.g., paper passer might be replaced with choosing music for a dance break). Students accessing materials can eat up instructional time if files aren't opening or students have to log in to access or cannot print or cannot save, and so on. Plan for a way for instruction to continue moving forward for students who are ready while you remedy tech challenges.

Virtual instruction can feel impersonal at times because you are not physically together in the same room. Personalizing the lesson helps students feel seen while learning at home. Using their interests, referring to their recent experiences, and requiring students to use each other's names can make the lesson come alive even from afar.

Journal Jots: Scenario Practice

Let's take a look at a common classroom management scenario:

Juanna is a fifth-grade teacher in her sixth year of teaching. She has transitioned to a new school serving a new population of students. They're rowdy preteens focused more on being popular than scholarly students. Arriving late, turning in incomplete assignments, and putting forth limited effort are a daily occurrence. Juanna struggles to keep their attention and meet their academic needs. Student grades are dropping below the school's pass rate.

If you were Juanna's mentor (and classroom management guru), how would you help her develop a stronger environment that supports learning? Script out what you would say.

Don't peek if you haven't yet completed your scenario practice! Do not read further until you've spent time reflecting and writing your response to the scenario. This will ensure you process your new learning before receiving feedback to solidify your application. Consider the following:

Key Points

- Juanna is most likely teaching students at the top of the totem pole, because fifth grade is the last grade in elementary school. Being "top dog" might play into student misbehavior.

- Juanna has been teaching for six years. This is a significant amount of time for her to perfect her instructional methods and teaching style. She is considered a veteran teacher.

- Transitioning to a new school can make any teacher, even a veteran, feel brand new all over again. How the school operates (protocols, expectations, rules, etc.) can take time to learn and adjust to.

- Students at the new school are of a different demographic than Juanna is used to teaching. This means they have different needs and backgrounds than she is familiar with. This requires time to gain experience in navigating the nuances.

- Students are in control of their own behavior and choices, such as attendance, work completion, and effort.

- Juanna is in control of her own behavior and choices, such as delivering instruction that resonates with students while also meeting their unique academic needs.

- Student performance is decreasing until the current instructional model changes.

Overall, although Juanna has experience teaching, she does not have experience teaching this demographic of students, and therefore, going back to the basics like a novice teacher will be helpful. She will need to learn new classroom management strategies that work well with these particular students. Prioritizing her struggles and attacking one at a time will ensure she gets back on track being the effective veteran teacher she is. For example, as a mentor you might suggest the following sequence: building relationships with students, incorporating student interests into lesson content, design differentiated lesson plans, as well as data collection and analysis of student academic levels. Over time, Juanna will experience fewer obstacles relating to management because she went back in sequence to strengthen instruction in the lesson design phase while implementing misbehavior prevention in her execution. (Brick sequence makes all the difference!)

Before you move on to the next brick, let's assess where you are right now with this brick for classroom and career success. Check out my Classroom Management Self-Survey, which you can find in Appendix 1, as well as on my website; see the next Downloadable Resource box.

Downloadable Resource: Classroom Management Self-Survey

Visit www.alwaysalesson.com/teacher-essentials to download your free resource!

Remember, the goal for this book is to help you grow your craft one brick at a time. After reading this chapter, your instructional foundation as a teacher is now two bricks thick! Following the sequence of the Teacher Success Pathway (lesson design before classroom management) will ensure you build the strongest instructional practices possible.

 Journal Jots: Tracking Your New Learning

- What connections can you make?
- How are you feeling about your classroom performance?
- What new ideas came to light?

Write it all down. No need for it to be perfectly written or thought out. Let your brain guide your pencil and get it all down on paper.

Don't forget to revisit the goals you set out to read this book:

- Who do you want to become after implementing the principles in this book?
- Are you on the right track to make that a reality?
- What steps can you take right now to move closer to becoming the person you dreamed of becoming?

When you're ready, move on to Chapter 12 so we can keep building strong teacher essentials for classroom and career success.

PART FOUR

BRICK 3: STUDENT ENGAGEMENT

We have to intentionally create engagement opportunities, layering them in such a way that it supports students from the obvious to the inference.

Let's continue along the Teacher Success Pathway! We are meeting our goal of growing our craft one brick at a time and you have mastered two bricks: lesson design and classroom management. Let's work towards Brick 3: Student Engagement.

CHAPTER 12

UNDERSTANDING STUDENT ENGAGEMENT

Student engagement relates to the way in which students interact with the content being taught, each other as collaborators, and the teacher delivering the information. Those three essential components ensure students process their learning at high levels.

Classrooms of strong instruction leverage student engagement as a way to bring the learning to life. These classrooms are not sit and get, when students sit for lengthy periods of time consuming knowledge. These classrooms are vibrantly loud, full of students leading the learning—where learning is seen in action.

> **Quick Note:** Brick 2: Classroom Management shared how students need to talk while learning. Having strong protocols in place for discourse to happen makes it easier to focus on making those discussions as meaningful as possible.

What Student Engagement Does

As discussed, we cannot control people. We cannot force students to want to learn or engage at high levels. However, we can create the conditions in which students would be interested in learning and motivated to engage. In their book *Strategies That Promote Student Engagement: Unleashing the Desire to Learn*, Ernestine G. Riggs and Cheryl R. Gholar share, "Teachers cannot give students the desire, drive, or will. No teacher, parent or any other stakeholder has the power to make students learn. Drive, will, and effort must emanate from the learner. However, teachers can awaken and cultivate these elements through authentic and creative teaching" (Riggs and Gholar 2009, 6). This type of teaching refers to the engagement strategies educators use to encourage and entice students to participate deeply in the learning experience. We cannot force students to learn, but we can create the conditions in which they want to learn and therefore make the active choice to engage in our lessons.

As I shared in the quote at the beginning of the chapter, its essential educators are intentional with how they provide engagement opportunities to students. They must plan and execute experiences that range in difficulty from easy to engage (low-level knowledge recall) to challenging to engage (high-level critical thinking and analysis). This is what I meant by supporting students starting from obvious straight facts to making inferences about their new learning, all through engage- ment strategies. By layering engagement of varying difficulty levels, students can deepen their learning without maxing out their brain muscle. If we ask students to low-level engage often and throughout a lesson, they remain in the passive state of learning. It's too easy and they check out. Similarly, if we ask students to high-level engage often and throughout the lesson, they will become cognitively exhausted from overworking their brain with new learning. This is frustrating and discourages future engagement. To best help students take in, process, and put out new learning, we layer engagement opportunities (think, write, speak, and produce) at their independent learning level.

To do this, students need to grapple with new learning in a variety of ways so that the knowledge moves from the ears to the brain and then stored into their long-term memory. This is done through listening, talking, writing, and producing (see Figure 12.1).

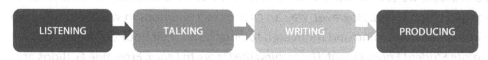

Figure 12.1   The continuum from listening to producing.

- Students first listen to the teacher share the new information, connecting it to prior learning, and modeling the new skill.

- Students now can ask and answer questions or share thoughts with a peer.

- Writing down the new information continues to move the information from short-term memory to long-term memory, increasing the likelihood students will retain the information learned and use it at a later date.

- The last phase of learning is to produce something based on the new skill learned. When students have to create their own version of this new information, understanding deepens.

Through this process of interacting with new learning by connecting with peers, the content itself, and the teacher, the information moves along the continuum from being heard, spoken, written, and re-created.

As you can see, how information is taught to students matters. Engagement is a major piece to teaching. Although the teacher is the facilitator of learning, they are not the lead learner—the student is. Teachers provide the opportunities for students to grapple with new learning, but they are not doing the work for them. Remember, the one doing the work is the one solidifying the knowledge. Without engagement, a lesson sounds like Charlie Brown's teacher, halting student achievement growth in its tracks.

Lessons from the Trenches: Who Rode the Bike Today?

A mastermind is a community of colleagues who put their minds together to problem-solve and goal set so that collectively they create one master mind. Teacher leaders include those in positions such as instructional coach, specialist, professional development (PD) facilitator, curriculum coordinator, or administrator. In a recent meeting with 10 instructional coaches in my teacher leader mastermind, we discussed where our teachers were performing on a scale of 1–10 in student engagement in their classrooms (1 = low-level interaction, 10 = students learning at high levels with limited direction from the teacher). Most of the coaches scored their teachers at a level 5 or 6 when it comes to student engagement, meaning they are attempting to have students engage in deeper ways but are inconsistently successful lesson to lesson and throughout the lesson itself.

This scoring activity and discussion helped coaches know what instructional skill to focus their support on for teachers. I shared the following connection I thought might help teachers better understand the importance behind increasing the level of student engagement in teacher lessons and highly suggested coaches share it with their staff members.

We have all heard analogies of the importance of learning to ride a bike by riding a bike. We can't sit through a lecture on riding a bike and go out and do it. We have to be physically involved with multiple trials and feedback in order to solidify the new skill into our muscle memory.

Similarly, students need to have more ownership in their learning for the new knowl-edge to stick. If at the end of a lesson a teacher feels like they themselves rode the bike the entire lesson, then engagement wasn't rigorous enough because students didn't do enough of the learning themselves. However, if the teacher feels that students rode the bike during the lesson, they are growing in effectiveness as leaders of learning.

I even told coaches to print off pictures of bikes and post them around the school. This would serve as a visual reminder to teachers to engage, engage, engage so students are actively involved in the learning process. I'll ask you to do the same. Put a reminder on your desk or in your planning space so that it will be top of mind to push engagement to higher levels.

When teachers search the web looking for engagement ideas, they tend to be organized into three categories: behavioral, emotional, and cognitive. This tends to help teachers get very clear on what they want students to do and how—such as participating by following all classroom rules for on-task behavior, demonstrating positive emotional responses and attitudes, and thinking and discussing the content at deep levels.

Source: mark1987/Adobe Stock Photos.

Therefore, teachers must ensure they are creating engagement opportunities that connect to all three aspects of the learning experience—behavior, emotions, and understanding. It's not enough to incorporate one aspect in a classroom lesson. When all three aspects of the learner are addressed, student learning solidifies at a faster rate and student motivation to continue learning increases as well.

Why Student Engagement Matters

When students sit idly at their seats, listening to a teacher deliver content, they are passively involved, which limits their comprehension of the material. Arizona State University's online blog written by Gabby Unangst (2021) discussed the drawback of being a passive learner, stating "they cannot use the skills of what is learned in a real-world situation." Whoever does the work, gets better at doing the work. Therefore, if the teacher is doing all the cognitive lifting, then the teacher strengthens their knowledge. But the teacher is not the one who has to pass the grade level or subject area; the students are the ones needing the practice. Therefore, students need to be doing the heavy cognitive lifting.

> **Quick Note:** To revisit the bike analogy: those who practice riding the bike, get better—and can eventually ride the bike on their own.

It's important to mention equity when we discuss engagement in the classroom. Educators must create the conditions whereby all students have access to the learning experience and are invited to engage at multiple times throughout the lesson. In an educational science journal article, author Kimberly D. Tanner (2017) discusses "Structure Matters: Twenty-One Teaching Strategies to Promote Student Engagement and Cultivate Classroom Equity." She notes that

> there are a host of simple teaching strategies rooted in research on teaching and learning that can support [subject area] instructors in paying attention to whom they are trying to help learn. These teaching strategies are sometimes referred to as "equitable teaching strategies," whereby striving for "classroom equity" is about teaching all the students in your classroom, not just those who are already engaged, already participating, and perhaps already know the [content] being taught. Equity, then, is about striving to structure [subject area] classroom environments that maximize fairness, wherein all students have opportunities to verbally participate, all students can see their personal connections to [the content], all students have the time to think, all students can pose ideas and construct their knowledge of [the content], and all students are explicitly welcomed into the intellectual discussion.

Tanner goes on to share the 21 strategies educators should consider to increase equitable engagement in their classroom, organizing them in these categories:

- Giving students opportunities to think
- Encouraging, demanding, and actively managing the participation of all students
- Building an inclusive and fair classroom community for all students
- Monitoring your own and students' behavior to cultivate divergent thinking
- Teaching all of the students in your classroom

As you are designing engagement opportunities, refer to these categories and ask yourself if you are meeting each of them on a consistent basis in your lessons. How you

EXPEDITIONARY
LEARNING

create equitable conditions will model to students how to engage in equitable ways with their peers. Taking ownership in how the classroom is run, the expectations for learning, and how students rally around each other to create a safe community will increase the likelihood that all students are successful.

The goal in education is to reach and effectively teach all students. We as educators must make the consistent effort to engage all of our students throughout our lessons because everyone has a right to an equal education opportunity as a citizen of the United States. This means educators have to ensure the engagement strategies and/or activities are accessible for all students. For example, a physical activity might inhibit someone with a physical disability to engage at high levels like the rest of the able-bodied students. Or students whose first language is not English might struggle with a reading engagement activity if they are not provided a dictionary, word wall, or translation. Teachers must ensure their engagement opportunities are equitable for all students to perform at a high level, and if they cannot, they must provide the accommodation so learning can solidify and the student can participate fully. Students should not be at either an advantage or disadvantage during an engagement opportunity; everyone should be able to be successful without obstacle. This means as teachers we'd be wise to have accommodations ready for every lesson in case we encounter a new learning barrier.

Thorough planning will enable you to think through equitable engagement opportunities ahead of time. It gives you time to reflect on your ideas, collaborate with peers for new ideas, and gain perspective on the learning experience through the eyes of each of your students.

A study on student engagement conducted at Saint Xavier University in Chicago, Illinois, tested ways to help fourth-grade and seventh-grade students feel more engaged with reading, and thus do it more (Carey, Cameron, and Leftwich 2013). Those ways were: teacher conferencing (the teacher interacting with students individually), teacher modeling ("independently reading alongside students as a means of modeling reading behavior"), and student choice (of what they read). In addition, "students engag[ed] in book talks with their peers."

The findings included that "when reading becomes more of a social practice, and students are taught ways . . . to further engage in their reading, pleasure in reading increases." Numerically stated: before the study, 47% of students self-reported that "they loved to read independently"; at the end of the study, that percentage had increased to 59% (87). The researchers noted that two of the three "interventions" they tested were very effective. First, they "saw drastic improvements in students being engaged when [teachers] read alongside them and participated with them in the reading process" (87).

As for the second helpful variable, not surprisingly, "the opportunity for students to choose their books directly correlated with their increased motivation levels to read independently" (74). Less surprisingly, they also found that "although students may have had a solid understanding of their reading interests, we observed [they] still needed further assistance and strategies in choosing reading material at their appropriate level. . . . [W]hen a student chooses text at their proper level, they are able to better engage in the text" (88). (We'll return to the subject of reading choice in Brick 4.)

This reminds us educators to not shy away from peer collaboration among our students in efforts to maintain a quiet, orderly learning environment. Productive dialogue aids in student learning and meets their needs to connect with one another. We can use their desire to talk with peers to our advantage if we build in academic talking activities, even during reading—an often quiet, solo activity. Reading and comprehension are related but not guaranteed, meaning we don't always understand what we read. But if we build in time for collaboration to enhance understanding before, during, and after reading, students will improve their reading and comprehension skills.

Best of all, the researchers found that high engagement decreases misbehaviors in the classroom, leading to increased time on tasks and better overall student performance (see Figure 12.2).

Therefore, if teachers can figure out how to engage students effectively, they will not have to manage or redirect behaviors as often, leading students to be on task during lessons. On-task behaviors lead to increased learning and greater academic outcomes for students.

Reverting back to our four bricks of the Teacher Success Pathway (lesson design, classroom management, student engagement, and student choice and ownership), if

Figure 12.2   One of the many benefits of high student engagement.

teachers can plan for students to be specifically and highly involved during the lesson and set up the classroom environment so that it manages operations effectively, students will engage at high levels throughout the lesson. The sequence of how teachers attack misbehaviors and lack of engagement is crucial. The order matters.

Table 12.1 outlines what engagement is and isn't. This should serve as a reminder at a quick glance while also enabling you to reflect on the current engagement students are experiencing at this moment in your classroom.

EXPEDITIONARY
LEARNING

Table 12.1 What Student Engagement Is—and Isn't

Category	Engaging	Not Engaging
Interaction	High interaction • Interaction with content • Interaction with peers • Interaction with the teacher	Low interaction • Head nods • Thumbs up/down • Yes/no answers
Environment	• Noisy and on topic • All students have access to the learning opportunity	• Quiet and orderly • Specific students singled out to participate
Choice	• Ownership of learning with students in the driver's seat making decisions	• Compliance driven without choice or voice (one size fits all)
Emotion	• Positive feelings toward learning • Being eager to learn	• Apathetic and disconnected
Options are . . .	• Varied in difficulty and type • Simple and replicated across topics • Modeled with live feedback	• Only academic or cognitive • Available only to specific grade levels or content areas • Confusing, complicated, or distracting • Only explained on the front end

CHAPTER 13

GETTING STARTED WITH STUDENT ENGAGEMENT

You don't need flair and fireworks to make a lesson engaging. You need a deep understanding of content + passion + real-life connections.

Social media can often distort a teacher's mind as to what is normal and what is expected for classroom setup, material acquisition, classroom management, and student engagement. The pressure to put on a show for students just for them to learn is sacrificing the art of teaching. Rich, rigorous, engaging lessons can occur without a theatrical production. No set props. No costumes. No lyrical battles. Great instruction can happen in a tiny classroom without technology gadgets or other flair and fireworks. It's up to the teacher to plan for engagement and then execute it at high levels. Trying to do too much too fast will limit the power of engagement and a lesson can quickly get off track. (Then you'll quickly find yourself sliding back to Brick 2: Classroom Management.) The key is to start small, do it well, and then expand your strategy tool belt.

Approaching Engagement from Three Directions

As mentioned in Chapter 8, engagement is a three-pronged approach (see Figure 13.1). Engagement with the teacher, their peers, and the content help move the information

Figure 13.1   Engagement is a three-pronged approach.

into long-term memory due to the variety of ways in which students are asked to recall or reuse the information.

In order for students to take in their new learning, make sense of it, and store it in long-term memory, they have to engage in a variety of ways until the material is no longer novel and easily retrieved. But be careful: even memorizing math facts or spelling words for a short period of time does not result in true understanding. Students can easily remove that information and replace it with new information once it's no longer needed. (In addition to the fact that memorization does not determine a true understanding of spelling patterns or math foundations.)

Engagement helps this information stay accessible to students, even if they have moved on to another topic or subject area. That's because engagement involves more than just the brain. When students process information, they can write, speak, or even move. Involving other parts of the body helps cement this new information. Understanding your students' learning styles ensures they receive instruction in their preferred method of learning at some point during the instruction of a specific topic. This means learning styles do not need to be met every portion of the lesson every day; however, it should be incorporated during the teaching of a topic, and engagement is an easy way to build in learning styles (e.g., visual, auditory, kinesthetic, creation).

Some simple ways to implement the three-pronged approach are as follows:

- **Teacher:** Ask questions, answer questions, participate in a model, and so on.

- **Peers:** Retell information, reteach a concept, share connections, and so on.

- **Content:** Read information from a text, fill in main points on a graphic organizer, highlight main idea and details in a passage, and so on.

Be cautious with students remaining at a low level of interaction as a form of engagement. Low level does not aid in information processing. Examples of interaction are giving a thumbs up, hands raised, or nodding their head to a question. These are surface-level engagements but do not help process learning; they're simply student actions with no effect on solidifying knowledge. Plus, it provides the teacher with limited information about the depth to which students understand. Being able to listen to or read student response provides clues into how well students understand a topic.

Also, beware of excessive talkers. Do not confuse word count for active engagement. Edutopia shared a quote image from an educator named Amy P. on Instagram stating, "Years ago, a conversation with a quieter student convinced me to change 'class participation' to 'class engagement.'" (Amy P. 2022). It should not be a contest to see who speaks the most. Assess involvement in learning no matter how it looks in each student. Getting students to engage is essential to deepen their learning. However, knowing each student has different needs and personalities, how they engage will differ. Educators should know and understand their students well enough to create a variety of engagement opportunities personalized to the students learning in their classroom. Quality over quantity; the goal is deep, rich engagement that results in a stronger understanding of the content.

Remember, engagement begins in the lesson design phase when educators plan ways to engage students with specific questions or activities with ideal responses in mind. Author Greg Wilson agrees with planning for engagement. He wrote a journal article called "Ten Quick Tips for Creating an Effective Lesson" in which he talks about writing formative assessments for pacing, design, preparation, and reinforcement. Student engagement is a form of assessment, albeit informal. His point is valid and affirming of moving away from interactive questions that lead to unhelpful data points and replacing them with intentional engaging questions (whether written or verbal) to gather informative data points. He says, "Asking 'Does everyone understand?' almost always produces false positives. In contrast, if any substantial fraction of your learners cannot do a formative assessment correctly, you know right then and there that you need to re-explain the most recent material. When you start doing this, you will feel like you're going more slowly, but that's because you will now be teaching at the speed at which your audience can learn rather than the speed at which you can talk" (Wilson 2019).

Please note, these interactions might help you decide if you want to move on in your lesson or pause to model another example or round of practice. But a better way to gather that information is to provide a deeper engagement opportunity where student answers will demonstrate the level of understanding versus if they're ready to move on or not.

For example, let's say you just modeled for students how to subtract across three digits. You've completed two more similar problems together as a class and you're curious if students are ready to move into independent practice, solving 10 more similar problems on their own. Fight the urge to say, "thumbs up if you're ready to move on to your worksheet." Instead, say something like "On your whiteboard, solve this next problem. Turn it over when you are done. When I say 'Show,' you'll hold up your boards facing me. I want to not only see your answer but also how you went about solving it." Instead of the interaction request, the information gathered from this engagement opportunity is helpful in guiding your instruction forwards or backwards depending on what you find. You'll scan student whiteboards and look for patterns of errors. If the majority of students are making similar mistakes, model a problem bringing attention to this commonality. If the majority of students demonstrate proficiency (not perfection), move on to independent practice and pull an impromptu small group or stop by to work 1:1 with students needing additional help.

Stopping to do a check for understanding (CFU) (from Chapter 4) provides useful knowledge to you as to where your students are currently performing. Don't be afraid to use longer wait times after delivering new information. Students need to process your question, access the answer to your question in their brain, formulate their answer, raise their hand, and deliver their response. This process takes time, and we should honor the process by waiting silently for the majority of students to respond. This also encourages all students to think of the answer to your question instead of waiting for a peer to raise their hand and get them off the hook for having to do the thinking. It's helpful to have everyone come up with their answer and then pick someone to share out. Now more students are doing the heavy cognitive lifting, rather than a handful.

Oftentimes when we plan high-level questions to build authentic engagement into a lesson, we expect students to rapidly respond. However, these types of questions require students to think at a deeper level and educators should make adjustments to their lesson pacing to accommodate this. Educator Chelsea Henley shared how she allowed for wait time in her early elementary classroom, "When I would ask a question that was a quick answer with only one option, I would have the students respond as a whole. To provide thinking time for everyone, they would have to put their answer in a bubble (hold it in their mouth with their cheeks puffed out). Once I saw everyone was ready, I would say 'release' and everyone would share out the answer, hopefully in unison. This would give everyone a chance to think before sharing, and not compete to yell out an answer the fastest" (Chelsea Henley, Google Docs comment to author, 2021).

It's essential that educators know and understand that engagement is a dance between how a teacher plans and executes opportunities and how students respond. Student response is also something teachers can plan for:

- Ideal responses
- Ways to build on student answers
- What to do when incorrect answers arise

Jack Kuninsky, a teacher at Gwinnett School of Mathematics, Science and Technology in Georgia, shared in the EduLeadership Facebook group (https://www.facebook.com/groups/609598144007188), "Plans often focus on what teachers will do, less on what students will do. There is often an assumption that students will participate, ask questions, answer questions, and make the lesson flow. But there aren't specific plans in place for how the students will be engaged and required to participate in the lesson (student-centered activities, cold calls, turn and talks, formative assessments, etc.). If student participation is left to hope and chance, and they don't come through, the lesson will not run as the teacher envisioned" (Kuninsky 2022). This is why teachers are intentional with how they plan their lessons, manage their classrooms, and engage their students. Great teaching is more than happenstance. It's thoroughly planned and executed.

Building Engagement into Your Lesson

Before implementing engagement opportunities centered on new content, have students engage in the strategies with nonacademic material. Educator Madeline Baird shared about a training she attended on Kagan Structures (2023) for student engagement. "They instruct teachers to practice engagement moments/opportunities with nonacademic content first. That way students are only having to process and practice the routine of engagement versus the routine and the content at the same time. Once the routine is mastered, then students will be able to use the engagement opportunity more effectively with content—resulting in less behaviors and blank stares" (Madeline Baird, Google Doc comment to author, November 22, 2022).

Follow these simple steps to start building engagement techniques into your classroom lessons:

1. Separate your lesson into three parts: direct instruction, guided practice, and independent practice.

2. Insert a short, simple engagement opportunity at each of those three sections of the lesson:

   - **Partner talk:** Student partners are assigned ahead of time and projected onto the front board for reference. They turn to this partner sitting next to them and answer the prompt that is also projected onto the front board. Once both students have responded to the prompt and each other's responses, they turn toward the teacher. A timer will keep students on track. For example, 30

seconds to read prompt and reflect on own answer, partner 1 shares for
1 minute, partner 2 responds for 30 seconds, partner 2 shares for 1 minute,
partner 1 responds for 30 seconds. The prompt might even come with a
discussion sentence starter to help hesitant students begin the dialogue
with ease.

- **Stop-and-jot:** Students read the prompt on the front of the board or that the
  teacher speaks aloud and writes down their response on a piece of paper in
  front of them. This helps students process the information without the pressure of having to share out. A timer is suggested to use here as well. Teachers
  can even use both strategies mentioned back-to-back, allowing students time
  to reflect independently first before chatting with each other. This is effective
  when the prompt is more complicated or open ended.

  This can be really helpful after a whole-class discussion to help students
  digest the information they gathered from peers. A reflection journaling
  sheet could be used often for all subjects and be a quick informal data point
  to collect while also giving students a chance to sort out their learning.

- **Website forum chat:** Students can log into their protected class website for
  classroom discussion. Teachers provide a prompt for students to write a three-
  to four-sentence paragraph responding to the prompt. They then have to
  refresh the discussion to see their peer's responses and must leave a one- to
  two-sentence reply on two or three peer's comments.

3. Reflect on engagement techniques and reuse in subsequent lessons if it went
    well. The more students use a technique in a variety of settings or subject areas,
    the easier it will be to employ.

4. Adjust to do fewer engagement moments if student misbehaviors increase
    dramatically or do more if students are adhering to expectations. The more they
    engage in purposeful activities to process knowledge, the stronger their under-
    standing will be.

Engagement comes about by intentionality, not happenstance. But the engagement
opportunities you create don't need to be complicated or lengthy. Use them purposefully at moments in your lesson where students need to pause a minute to absorb

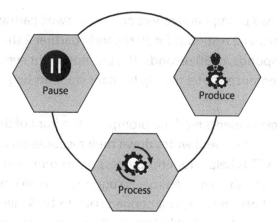

Figure 13.2   We engage students to pause, process, and produce.

knowledge or get additional practice with a new skill. It's like a learning marathon with engagement water stations sprinkled throughout the route, so students can pause (think), process (organize and store information), and produce (create something based on that new skill/knowledge) (see Figure 13.2).

It's important to mention student pairings are essential for the engagement opportunity to be successful. Consider achievement levels, energy levels, social personalities, modeling explicit expectations paired with student practice, and so on. It would be frustrating for a high-performing peer to be with a low-performing peer if the discourse was heavily skewed toward one student contributing more to the conversation. The same would be true with a talkative student paired with a shy student resulting in one child contributing more than the other during the conversation. Be thoughtful in your pairings. Peers performing closer in level would make for a better-balanced conversation. Student personalities too similar might create limited or excessive discussion, so avoid putting both ends of the spectrum together or two identical personalities together. This takes some time to figure out the best pairings for the class, so feel free to keep their "engagement buddy" for a few weeks before changing up the pairings. By that point, achievement levels and personalities might shift, giving you more options than when you started the process. Subject areas might shift pairings, too, because oftentimes students do not perform at the same level in every subject area. Use your discretion for how long to keep partners. You might switch only a handful of people at a time due to behavior struggles or you might choose to change everyone at a designated time (e.g., weekly, monthly, quarterly). There is not one right answer because people change and grow so your system for partnering students will adjust in real time to be as responsive as possible to your students' current academic and social needs. Get started by using the Student Pairing Sheet (see Appendix 1, as well as on my website; see the next Downloadable Resource box.)

Downloadable Resource: Student Pairing Sheet

Visit www.alwaysalesson.com/teacher-essentials to download your free resource!

During a professional development session as a teacher, I learned about a seating chart strategy for the classroom. I drew six large squares on a piece of paper and divided each square into four quadrants. The upper left was for a high-achieving student, the upper right was a high-medium-achieving student, the bottom left was a medium-low-achieving student and the bottom right was a low-achieving student. This meant that whether the students turned to the partner to their side or across from them, they would be able discuss content while contributing similarly in the conversation. Avoiding pairing up the diagonal partners meant students wouldn't be paired with someone polar opposite in terms of cognitive ability or academic performance. Placing students next to other students that are complementary ensures it's a productive experience, and not a frustrating one. (Note, the same strategy can be followed with personality, interests, or behavior.) (See Figure 13.3.)

Figure 13.3 shows four student cards. In the top-left corner the teacher would write a code for personality or behavior traits (shy, talkative, aggressive, loud, etc.). In the top-right corner the teacher would code for academic performance (high, medium-high, medium-average, medium-low, low). Being conscious of the codes while pairing students will ensure the student pairs are as productive as possible.

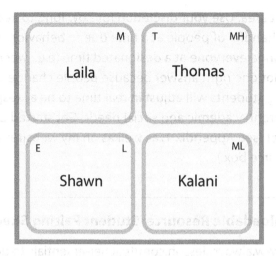

Figure 13.3 Student pairing example.

- Laila is coded with M in the top-right corner for medium or average academic performance. She does not have any other codes, which means she is easy to pair up with most students.

- Thomas is coded with T for talkative in the top-left corner so he should not be paired with another talkative student or a shy student—because either pairing would likely be a frustrating experience with minimal academic gains. Thomas is also coded with MH for medium-high in academic performance. He pairs well with Laila because their academic levels are close enough that they would equally contribute to the conversation.

- Shawn is coded with E for energetic in the top-left corner because he's been diagnosed with ADHD. He is also coded with L for low academic performance. It's important that any student paired with Shawn be close in ability level and a calmer demeanor (assertive but not shy) to help keep the pair on task. It wouldn't be helpful to pair a low student with a low student because the discussion might stall due to lack of understanding of the content. Pairing Shawn with a student who performs better but not too far apart helps Shawn process new information, because it's conveyed in terms students understand.

- Kalani is coded with ML for medium-low in terms of her academic performance. She is not shy, talkative, or energetic, so she would make a great complement to a student with any of those descriptors.

Crafting Student Pairs

1. Decide what categories and codes you want to use to identify students' demeanor and academic performance (e.g., letters like in the previous description, numbers from 1 to 5, with 1 for the struggling students and 5 for the accelerated students, etc.).

2. List out your choices for later reference as needed. (The same strategy can be followed with personality, interests, or behavior—whatever suits.)

3. Write each student's name on an index card.

4. Add codes to note their demeanor and performance.

5. Try out pairing the students so they'll have optimal chances for a productive conversation. This means don't have pairs that are too similar or too different.

6. Once you have your students paired up, create a pairs list for future reference. (See Appendix 1 for my Student Pairing Sheet, as well as on my website; see the previous Downloadable Resource box.)

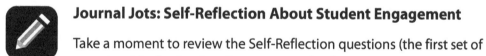

Journal Jots: Self-Reflection About Student Engagement

Take a moment to review the Self-Reflection questions (the first set of questions) in the Student Engagement Guiding Questions (see Appendix 1, as well as on my website; see the next Downloadable Resource box). This will help give you a sense of where you are in implementing effective student engagement strategies in your classroom. This assessment is for you alone, so be honest in your answers; that's the only way you can identify the gaps in your performance. (There's no judgment here; we all have to start somewhere!)

Downloadable Resource: Student Engagement Guiding Questions

Visit www.alwaysalesson.com/teacher-essentials to download your free resource!

CHAPTER 14

MASTERING STUDENT ENGAGEMENT

You control the pace, momentum, and the flow.

As a professional, you make the judgment call as to how much your students need to process learning and deepen understanding. When you're ready (and the students, too, of course), think about your lesson in 15-minute increments. Student attention begins to wane at this point, and it does not help student mastery to push through and keep delivering information to students.

A Pronto blog post entitled "Student Attention Span and How to Capture and Maintain It" states, "It's natural for a student's attention levels to vary according to motivation, mood, perceived relevance to material, and other factors. For teachers, developing a successful class period can depend upon how effectively it is structured to fit your student's attention span. A typical student's attention span is about 10 to 15 minutes long, yet most classes can last for 30 minutes to an hour" (Pronto 2022).

Knowing this, we need to allow students a break before consuming new knowledge. Chunking a lesson into bite-sized amounts helps student brains take in knowledge, sort it with other related information, and store it in their memory. Similar to a running faucet, if we give too much information at one time, the brain gets too saturated and unable to store information to retrieve later. You are flooding the system with too much, too fast. This does a disservice to students. We must control the flow of information. Engagement opportunities are a way to pause the flow, organize incoming information, and make room for more to come.

Strengthening Student Engagement

There are five ways to strengthen your student engagement opportunities (see Figure 14.1).

1. **Intentionality:** Be thoughtful in what engagement opportunities you select and how you implement them. Technology apps and websites can be tempting, but high engagement can come from simple not-techy opportunities, too. Think about these questions:

    •   What way should students engage to make this make more sense?

    •   What engagement strategy have we used/not used recently (e.g., written, oral, kinesthetic, etc.)?

    •   Should students engage in pairs, small groups, or a whole group?

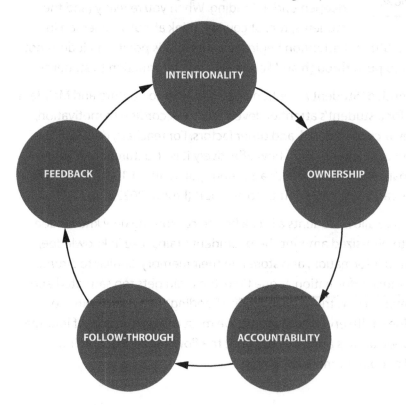

Figure 14.1   Five ways to strengthen student engagement.

Intentionality ensures you keep learning fresh and appropriate, selecting engagement strategies that would make the biggest impact on student learning.

2. **Ownership:** Allow students to lead the engagement, stepping back to watch and intervene only when necessary. This builds motivation and interest to engage. In order to ensure it is an effective student-led engagement experience, do the following:

   - Assign jobs for students to lead in the activity (behavior monitor, reader, discussion director, recorder, etc.). These jobs should be used in various other content lessons so that they are familiar to students. Having posters with these roles and a description of their duties ensure students can meet expectations.

   - Share exemplars during the learning process so students can see how others are making sense of the new information. Be sure to highlight a variety of ways so students do not feel pressure to conform to how one learner processes new information. Highlighting student work empowers them and takes the focus on the end product, shedding light on the learning process itself. Interrupting students during learning for a quick example or share helps students remain on track and course corrects if they aren't meeting expectations. This avoids waiting until the end of an assignment to clear up confusion.

   - Turn students into experts by allowing students to go off into groups to learn new information, synthesize it with peers, and then return to their seats to swap information with those sitting nearby who attended other learning stations. When students share the information they just learned, it helps them process it further, but it's also a higher investment engagement move because students are in charge of what they're learning and disseminating that to their peers. It is also a back-to-back engagement strategy—first in a learning content group and second reporting back to their seat group.

3. **Accountability:** Move from compliance to outcome by having students produce something from the engagement activity. This encourages full participation, resulting in knowledge processing. For example, students might create a visual representation of content learned in a lesson. Or verbal discussions can also offer a data artifact for how well students are understanding information and hold them accountable for the entire discussion. An example of this is a teacher leading a rapid-fire discussion, asking numerous questions in a row. A student may disengage when a student is called on in another part of the classroom farther away

from their seat. Or if they themselves are called on, they might tune out afterwards. It's important to use an unpredictable questioning pattern to keep all students paying attention and ready to answer when called on. Accountability enables all students to learn and grow while providing the teacher insight into the effectiveness of their instruction.

4. **Follow-Through:** Whatever you ask of students, be sure you receive it. Collect informal data by scanning the room, leaning in and listening to student discussions, and peering onto student's work to see how they're progressing in their understanding of content. Do not use the engagement activity to look for missing lesson material, talk to a colleague, or use the restroom. (There are times when you need to handle a behavior situation or speak with a guest who arrives at your classroom door, and using an engagement strategy to keep students focused on content for a few minutes is acceptable.)

5. **Feedback:** To keep engagement going, provide clear, consistent feedback to students. Specificity enables students to know what aspect of their engagement to alter, how, and why it's important. For example, you might say, "During your peer interview, don't forget to give eye contact when they are talking." This will help you hear what they are saying rather than focusing on what you want to say next. Then, when they are done speaking, you can decide if you want to reply using a question you preplanned or reply to something specific they said. Last, you can remind of engagement expectations by saying, "This is how we have stronger, deeper two-way communication with our peers." Then allow students a chance to implement your feedback. Acknowledge students for making the appropriate adjustments. Your feedback and affirmation motivate students to continue to engage during a lesson.

Engagement lends itself to be used as both informal and formal assessment. Students are discussing content and therefore their contributions can be used as intel into how well they are comprehending material. For informal assessment, grab a student roster and a pencil and walk around as students engage. Jot down notes as you listen in to discussions. This will help you know if you should slow instruction down to revisit sticking points in the content (speed bumps) or speed up (fast lane) because students are ready to move on. For formal assessment, have students produce evidence of the learning gained from the engagement. This could be a journal entry, exit ticket prompt, or a created product. You might even do a pre/post engagement assessment to show student growth in understanding after collaborating with peers during the engagement activity. This rewards students for contributions and continues content processing by engaging in reflection after learning.

I should also mention, carving out time in your lesson for engagement requires purposeful planning (hello, Brick 1!). If you only have 10 minutes to work with to keep the pace of the lesson and meet the lesson objectives, do not plan an engagement activity that takes the full 10 minutes. It's helpful to build time for pre- and post-engagement into the engagement opportunity.

For example, let's say you planned for students to engage in "Four Corners," where you make a statement and they must walk to a corner of the room that reflects their answer to your statement (e.g., strongly agree, agree, disagree, strongly disagree). Prior to diving into the activity, provide students time to review their notes on a recent topic they learned. Priming their brains for the activity ensures they can engage at high levels, recalling information and forming their opinion.

Just as important is the post-engagement time. After students engage in "Four Corners," allow them time to journal or revise their notes, adding in information they gained from the engagement activity. They will have gained new information from hearing peer discussion or made new connections during the activity. This continues to solidify learning, deepen understanding, and students feel successful, which motivates them to engage at high levels again. Sometimes the pre- and post-engagement time is more important than the engagement activity itself. You'll notice more students engaging in meaningful ways when you make time to prepare and reflect. See Table 14.1 for an example.

Table 14.1   Ten-Minute Engagement Activity Pacing Example

Time Allotment	Task
1 min	Explain "Four Corners" engagement activity.
2 min	Review notes and prime the brain.
5 min	"Four Corners"
2 min	Journal reflection

Student Engagement Strategies

If you need some ideas for engagement strategies to try out in your classroom, check out my Student Engagement Strategies sheet (in Appendix 1, as well as on my website; see the next Downloadable Resource box). It shares some common options with corresponding descriptions to help you successfully implement them into your lessons.

As you look over these strategies, think about what you are learning in this chapter:

- How might you tweak them to fit the needs of your students?
- Which strategies would work better at the beginning versus the end of your lesson?
- What strategies work best with low-level information versus high-cognitive load processing?
- What strategies could easily be used in multiple subject areas?
- Are there engagement strategies that prevent access or equity for all students currently in your classroom? (Refer to IEP or 504 plans to confirm.)

Downloadable Resource: Student Engagement Strategies

Visit www.alwaysalesson.com/teacher-essentials to download your free resource!

Journal Jots: Engagement Brainstorming

As you chat with friends, family, and colleagues, jot down additional engagement strategy ideas.

Engaging Students Virtually

Student engagement will look different on a virtual platform because you are not live in front of each other. Using video helps everyone see each other and participate with low-level interaction such as hand signals, head shakes, and so on. Some students do not have access to a camera or prefer not to show their surroundings, so you'll need to incorporate voice or chat as often as possible for their participation. A chat function will serve as the way student dialogue and interaction occurs, albeit everyone can see what everyone is typing.

If the platform has a breakout room function, small-group instruction can occur similar to how it does in a classroom. The teacher would assign groups of students to enter a private room by themselves where they would complete a discussion or create something together. Then the teacher enters and exits each room one at a time, similar to stopping by small groups in the classroom to observe students. Strong classroom management systems need to be in place so that when students are in their private rooms they are on task because the teacher is unable to see or be in all breakout rooms at once.

Overall, engagement virtually has to be even more intentional to ensure it aids student understanding of material. For example, students can read material ahead of the lesson on their own time. When they come together during class time, it is spent in small groups and whole-group discussion to compare knowledge gained, takeaways, connections, and so on. The flipped classroom model is what works best for virtual instruction, meaning all knowledge is gained ahead of class time through reading and researching. When students come together, they complete the activity or engage in discussions. This avoids silent, solo work time when together and enables students to complete information-intake procedures in a way that best fits their learning needs.

Students need to take breaks more often in a virtual setting because of screen fatigue, which can be described as eye and head pain due to the blue light from the computer, as well as restlessness from the lack of movement because of sitting still at a device. Knowing this, assign reading and writing away from the device so students are fresh when having to be in a face-to-screen meeting with you the teacher or their peers.

Journal Jots: Scenario Practice

Let's take a look at a common student engagement scenario:

Randy is a popular teacher among the students. They all show up on time to his class, high-fiving him and sharing about their day. Randy is full of energy and demonstrates a strong rapport with his students. He loves the latest tech options and uses 5–10 throughout his lessons daily. Students spend a lot of time moving around the room, troubleshooting technology, and chatting about things unrelated to the lesson. Student scores on the last assessment show 60% of students are not proficient. The students seem to be learning and having a great time in his class. He can't understand why his teaching methods aren't producing stronger results.

If you were Randy's mentor—and a strong engager yourself—how would you help him develop more effective engagement strategies to support student learning?

Script out what you would say before reading further.

Don't peek if you haven't yet completed your scenario practice! Do not read further until you've spent time reflecting and writing your response to the scenario. This will ensure you process your new learning before receiving feedback to solidify your application. Consider the following:

Key Points

- Randy has strong relationships with students resulting in their desire to learn from him.
- Technology is something Randy highly appreciates and therefore includes in his daily lessons.
- Lessons lack clarity in student actions and expectations.
- Student performance data is low.

Overall, Randy is in a position where he can positively affect student achievement because he has spent the time building relationships with students. He is up-to-date on technology and exposes students to new tools often. However, he is lacking foundational bricks of instruction and that is negatively affecting the success of his students, albeit they enjoy his class tremendously. Rewinding to the lesson design phase will enable Randy to know what and how he wants students to engage in his lessons and prevent misbehavior and tech troubleshooting that distract from the lesson. Due to having strong relationships with students, managing the classroom once he solidifies the design of his lesson will enable him to speed right back to student engagement. Planning for multiple opportunities throughout the lessons for students to engage with him, the content, and each other, all while having clarity in what and how they are to engage, will ensure he experiences success. Students will enjoy his class even more now, and the data will reflect the positive changes!

Before you move on to the next brick, let's assess where you are right now with this brick for classroom and career success by taking the Student Engagement Self-Survey (see Appendix 1, as well as on my website; see the next Downloadable Resource box).

Downloadable Resource: Student Engagement Self-Survey

Visit www.alwaysalesson.com/teacher-essentials to access your free resource!

The goal for this book is to help you grow your craft one brick at a time. Digesting and integrating this chapter makes your instructional foundation as a teacher three bricks thick! Following the sequence of the Teacher Success Pathway—from lesson design to classroom management to student engagement—will ensure you build the strongest instructional practices possible.

Before moving on to the next section, it would be good to take a moment to reflect on the journey so far. With this new knowledge your perspective is likely shifting. You might be excited to try new things in the classroom. You might be nervous to take risks. But trust that the learning process is messy—that's how you know you are doing it right!

Journal Jots: Brick 3: Check-In

Jot down whatever comes to mind, no holds barred.

After that, revisit the goals you set for yourself at the start of the book:

- Who do you want to become after implementing the principles in this book?
- Are you on the right track to make that a reality?
- What steps can you take right now to move closer to becoming the person you dreamed of becoming?

When you're ready, move on to Chapter 15 so we can keep building strong teacher essentials for classroom and career success.

PART FIVE

BRICK 4: STUDENT CHOICE AND OWNERSHIP

When the teacher is out of the way, students have more to contribute

Let's continue along the Teacher Success Pathway! You're making tremendous progress toward your goal of growing your craft one brick at a time. You have mastered lesson design, classroom management, and student engagement. Let's work toward our final brick, Brick 4: Student Choice and Ownership.

CHAPTER 15

UNDERSTANDING STUDENT CHOICE AND OWNERSHIP

The learning process is all about the students. Sometimes the teacher can be over-involved, causing students to put in less effort, have less contribution, and thus end up with a lower level of skill acquisition. Teachers must balance between directing learning and facilitating learning. Let's discuss the difference between those two terms:

- To **direct** learning means the teacher is the main character in the lesson, explaining content and modeling skills. The teacher is entirely responsible for delivering information. This usually occurs during direct instruction when there's limited involvement from students. They watch, listen, and write to help process new information. Teachers should direct learning only a portion of a lesson. (Remember when we discussed how to design lessons? I mentioned direct instruction is the smallest portion of a lesson. It is essential and necessary, but it must not overpower facilitation.)

- When teachers **facilitate** learning, students start to take on more involvement in the learning process. The teacher has presented new information and passes the learning baton on to students during guided and independent practice. The teacher is there to answer questions, clear up confusion and misconceptions, as well as review content as necessary. The transition from director to facilitator means students are now leading the learning instead of the teacher. This results in increased involvement and motivation to grow in skill acquisition.

One way to build in even more student involvement in a lesson or classroom environment is through choice and ownership. This should be attempted only when students

---

are familiar with a format, task, or skill to which they would be able to successfully do it on their own and/or lead it with their peers.

Student **choice** is creating learning opportunities with options so students have a say in how they demonstrate their knowledge. There are four considerations to make when building in choice in your classroom (see Figure 15.1):

- **Alignment:** The teacher must be careful in selecting learning options because they all have to align to the standard and objective for the lesson while also demonstrating a student's depth of knowledge. (But, you know that because you mastered lesson design already! Alignment was a huge portion of being success-ful in designing incredibly impactful learning experiences that create academic gains for students.)

- **Interest:** It is helpful if teachers know their students' likes and interests so that they can provide a variety of assignment options students would be attracted to. When students can use their gifts and talents to showcase their learning, they are more focused and invested in producing a top-quality product.

- **Familiarity:** Choice options should be familiar to students so they can complete the assignment on their own with limited involvement from an adult. (Just like you learned in Brick 3: Student Engagement, reusing routines and procedures enables students to be able to focus on content instead of the activity directives.)

- **Limitation:** Limiting options decreases overwhelm and decision fatigue—three to seven options are recommended (Pignatiello, Martin, and Hickman 2018). Save your other great ideas for a future choice assignment.

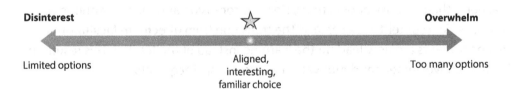

Figure 15.1   The assignment options continuum.

Student **ownership** means allowing children to become a leader in the process of learning, switching roles with the teacher—the teacher facilitates and students direct. This means the students have participated in similar activities before and the teacher has slowly transferred ownership over time. This is a careful, deliberate process, only passing ownership when students demonstrate mastery or responsibility. It is not sufficient for the teacher to lead an activity one time and then expect students to replicate it. For example, the teacher might lead a book club discussion among a small group of students. After meeting once a week for three months, students will be familiar with the flow of book discussion and expectation for participation. They can begin to lead book club meetings themselves with the end goal of it being student-led without teacher intervention or presence at all.

There is a reason student choice and ownership come as Brick 4. You cannot pass over the baton to students to begin running the classroom learning activities if you haven't planned thoroughly, consistently managed a classroom for more independence, or cultivated high-level engagement among students. The three previous bricks are an absolute necessity before successfully adjusting culture and climate for added choice and ownership.

Why Student Choice and Ownership Matters

Many of us have a desire to do things our own way. Having choice in how we do things is referred to autonomy. Dictionary.com defines *autonomy* as "freedom from external control or influence" (https://www.dictionary.com/browse/autonomy). This means students are able to complete assignments without teacher control or influence. They are able to choose how to complete the assignment in a way that uses their gifts and talents with limited to no intervention from the teacher. For students to experience autonomy is motivating because they are in charge of their own learning. When no one is telling them what to do and how to do it, suddenly they enjoy the process a bit more. This newfound freedom brings a sense of joy and pride in their work output. Students not only want to be the leader in their learning but also they want to feel the endorphin release of freedom.

Student choice and ownership provide autonomy to the learning experience. When you no longer have to showcase your learning in one way, but can pick how to demonstrate it, you are more motivated and engaged in the learning process. Creativity and innovation come to light.

This can feel uncomfortable for teachers. It's scary to give students freedom and flexibility in the classroom, worrying about losing control. The truth is, you *will* lose control and that is part of the process. Both the teacher and student have to learn to work together in a respectful way that meets expectations for learning and classroom climate.

Alfie Kohn (1993) shares, "The truth is that, if we want children to take responsibility for their own behavior, we must first give them responsibility, and plenty of it. The way a child learns how to make decisions is by making decisions, not by following directions." He cites how a study conducted by Ann K. Boggiano and others (1992, 278–80) "found that children given more 'opportunity to participate in decisions about schoolwork' score higher on standardized tests." This supports the idea that if we can get student choice and ownership right in our classrooms, we will see the academic gains in students. It's a win-win for all stakeholders—students, teachers, parents, administration, and the community at large. (We'll return to this topic later on.)

By implementing choice and ownership in assignments and how the classroom operates, students begin to build investment in their learning. They become more committed to the process because of the benefit they receive (choice and ownership). If teachers want students to be more involved and motivated in their learning, increase their investment and commitment levels through choice and ownership opportunities. For example, if a student is constantly late to class because they think it's boring, the teacher can create morning work choice boards so that students can showcase their understanding of a topic in a way that fits their daily mood, personality, or learning style (e.g., draw a comic strip, deliver a speech, write a story, etc.). Over time, the child will feel rewarded with choice and ownership and their tardies will decrease while their attitude and engagement in class increase.

Most important, when students are successfully executing choice and ownership options in the classroom, the teacher has now gained additional time because they are not leading classroom operation. This leaves more time for the teacher to spend supporting student learning. For example, when students are collecting papers, the teacher can check in on a student 1:1 to clear up misunderstandings or catch mistakes in their work. Or when students are leading their own book club, the teacher can pull another small group of students that need additional practice with a new skill. By allowing students to lead in the classroom, the teacher can focus on their most important task—student learning. More time spent on learning means more opportunities for students to strengthen their skills and knowledge. Academic gains are the top benefit to student choice and ownership.

An Edutopia post on Instagram offers an important tip to ensure autonomy is successful in your classroom. Tyler Rablin shares, "When I was a new teacher, everyone was like 'Give students autonomy! They'll love it and be motivated!' What no one mentioned was that autonomy only builds motivation when students have a sense of self-efficacy first, requiring evidence to believe success is possible" (Rablin 2023).

A belief in self drives choice. If students believe they can achieve, make friends, be successful, and so on, they will, because of the rule of self-fulfilling prophecy—whatever you think, it will become. As teachers are creating classroom culture, building relationships and student self-image are top priority. When students know you care about them, and when you share what you see as their potential, they'll begin to respond in kind. They'll see themselves how you tell them you see them. As they experience success, they'll begin to believe they can continue to experience success. Then, you'll see more and more students step up and lead themselves and their peers in new ways.

Lessons from the Trenches: Book Club

In my classroom, I had a handful of students performing above grade level in reading. They were responsible students who showed a desire to do more than expected in their assignments. They were self-regulating, confident, and excited learners. I had a meeting with them introducing the idea of a self-led book club instead of meeting with me weekly to discuss the common text they were reading independently. They were so excited to meet together as peers without me to discuss the text they were reading.

We discussed expectations:

- *Come to book club prepared with materials and the appropriate chapters read.*
- *Share ideas equally in discussion.*
- *Establish roles within the group (discussion leader, time keeper, summarizer, etc.).*
- *Ask questions of their peers when confused on what was happening in the story.*
- *Self-assess their peers and their productivity at the end of each meeting.*

These expectations were noted on a Book Club Reflection (in Appendix I, as well as on my website; see the next Downloadable Resources box). This was then turned in to me for accountability and so I could be alerted when productivity reduced.

I met with this group at the start of the week for a quick check-in for the week's goals:

- *Common text*
- *Reading requirement (e.g., pages or chapters read)*
- *Literacy concepts to cover (e.g., main idea, cause/effect, growth of a character, etc.)*

I would pull small groups for reading skills and the book club students would meet in a corner of the classroom by themselves where I could see and hear them. It was rare that I had to redirect their focus, and it was rarer that a student in the group didn't pull their weight in the group. I was beyond proud of their dedication to the book club, their growth as readers, their connection as a group, and their maturity in self-managing their learning. These students to this day speak about the self-run book club and how much fun it was.

I know the ownership and choice took time initially to set it up, but in the long run it saved me time so I could work with students who needed my expertise while the excelling students got to continue learning at their pace and level together. You might have students who grow into a book club, meaning their reading level or self-regulation skill level initially weren't a good match to join a student-led book club, but over time they progressed and became a good fit later in the year. Use your discretion; start small to set the tone; filter kids in and out as necessary.

If you'd like to see how I implemented book clubs, check out the Book Club Guide: Teacher and Book Club Guide: Students in Appendix 1, as well as on my website; see the next Downloadable Resources box.

Downloadable Resources: Book Club Reflection, Book Club Guide: Teacher, and Book Club Guide: Students

Visit www.alwaysalesson.com/teacher-essentials to download your free resource!

Building In Student Choice and Ownership

My classroom wasn't the only place that saw the positive effects of building in student choice and ownership. For her master's thesis, Sarah Theesfeld researched the "Effects of Student Choice on Student Motivation and Engagement Within an Elementary Classroom." She quotes Alfie Kohn (mentioned previously) stating that "students do better when they are given choice" (Kohn, 30) because "being able to make choices positively affects the educational development of children" (citing Blair and Johnson 2003, 184). Theesfeld continues: "The most important goal for any educator is to help our students become successful. Creating a learning environment that offers choice and fosters student engagement and motivation is how we can help our students become successful learners. When students are motivated to succeed, they are not the only ones who will benefit. Our students take what they gain from their education and bring it into the real world. They can carry the motivation they received from their teachers over into their own work environments, motivating even more people to want to succeed" (2021, 8–9).

When teachers build in strategic moments of choice, students get to lean into their strengths and interests to show off all that they learned. This is empowering. And then when teachers allow students to run learning moments, students truly experience the

EXPEDITIONARY
LEARNING

freedom of owning their learning. Being responsible for their peers and their own learning tends to add pressure to the situation. Students step up to the plate to ensure they meet classroom expectations. The newfound responsibility is a privilege most kids honor and respect. They crave more learning that allows for choice and ownership.

How we teach students, not just content but how to behave in cooperation with others, will enable them to be successful decision-makers when out in the world. In their book *An Educator's Guide to Effective Classroom Management,* Susan A. Coetzee, E. J. van Niekerk, John L. Wydeman, and Sello P. Mokoena (2008) describe why it's important to build ownership and choice into the classroom environment:

> The most important leadership task of the educator lies in the classroom. Here the educator must lead learners to become responsible adults. This means, among other things, that learners must be led to become independent in their learning and take an increasing measure of responsibility for their own learning. Once they are adults, these learners will have to plan their own development and careers and the foundation for this is laid at school. Learners have to learn to become life-long learners and the school is the place where they will learn to take up the challenge of being adults in the 21st century. (65)

Therefore, it's our duty as educators to provide real-world experiences in the classroom to prepare them for their future outside the school system. Building in choice and ownership is one way to do that.

The benefits of building in student choice and ownership in the classroom are enormous:

- Students learn to goal set realistically while tracking their growth and celebrating the progress.
- They practice responsible decision-making as they learn to manage, regulate, and direct their own learning.
- Students can be creative and enthusiastic in their pursuit of knowledge while persevering when the process is hard.

- The personal accountability is high as they take initiative and grow their self-belief and confidence.

- As a result, their enthusiasm for learning is expressed as they take pride in their work and feel an immense sense of belonging in their classroom.

- These feelings and experiences as a learner will translate to how they view themselves, how they treat others, and how they show up to pursue their passions out in the world.

By simply building in choice and ownership into the classroom, teachers are transforming the lives of children who will soon grow up to leave their imprint in the world. What a way to pay it forward!

CHAPTER 16

GETTING STARTED WITH STUDENT CHOICE AND OWNERSHIP

Anytime you begin something new, it's wise to slowly phase in the change into your routine. As you selectively introduce choice and ownership into the classroom, you'll also need to scaffold student learning so students receive support while navigating the new experience.

Being intentional with what you pass over to students and how you do it will increase the likelihood it is a successful process. Start with a simple task to shift ownership to students, and over time you'll be able to increase the complexity of the tasks you pass on.

For example, teachers may brainstorm a list of opportunities to build in choice and pass ownership to students. They then can prioritize the list in the order in which they will implement it, knowing simple is best at first and build in complexity over time. It might look something like this:

- **Assignments:** Students are able to choose to answer two out of three similar word problems in math or select a topic card for an opinion writing paper.

- **Routines/procedures:** Students can take on roles such as paper passer/collector or take attendance.

- **Discussion:** One student has the responsibility of operating the talking stick during a class discussion, selecting peers to speak next, or running a morning meeting by leading the discussion routine.

- **Self-led stations:** Student who once engaged in a teacher facilitated activity (e.g., book club) can now meet on their own as a group, following the same format and routine without the teacher present.

- **Learning review:** Students can engage in a learning review to peer teach other students a topic that has already been taught. They can design and present an anchor chart that provides a synopsis of the essential points.

As you can see, this list is helpful for the teacher to know what options they have to build in choice and ownership into their classroom. They also have been intentional with how they pass the leadership baton to students by starting with simpler tasks like passing papers and increasing in complexity of discussion, stations, and peer teaching. By knowing what options will be extended to students, prioritizing the difficulty of the tasks, and scheduling them out by month or quarter the teacher has developed a strong pathway for choice and ownership to roll out to students.

> **Quick Note:** It might take all year to get to a place where students are responsible enough to engage in group activities without a teacher facilitating or even teaching each other. Only provide the next choice or ownership option when students have shown they are successful under the current structure of being led by a teacher and have handled previous choice and ownership tasks successfully. The freedom is the reward. Allow students to earn it individually and organically over time.

Characteristics of Student Choice

To incorporate choice successfully, teachers must include three parts when designing their choice options:

- **Alignment:** Whatever choice option you offer must relate to the standard and objective of the lesson. If it doesn't measure what the standard and objective state, then it is busy work that will not help the student master their learning. (Are you getting tired of Brick 1: Lesson Design being woven into all other bricks of teacher essentials? That's why it is foundational; you can't escape it.)

- **Rigor:** Each choice option, albeit different and unique, should require the student to think and work at high levels. Be strategic in the options you create so that students don't work solely with too difficult tasks and get burned out, or too easy options and breeze through them. Mixing up low-level to high-level options ensures students demonstrate learning through a range of difficulty levels. For example, if you were working on vocabulary building, you would not want to provide only two options such as write the vocabulary word or write a word with a similar meaning. One is low level (copying the spelling of the word) and one is high level (writing a synonym). Students would choose the less arduous task that limits their growth. When choices options have components that vary in difficulty, no matter what combination of options a student selects, they will be thinking at high levels. (To illustrate this idea, see Table 16.1 later in this chapter.)

> **Quick Note:** If you want to provide low-level options, ensure students complete several of them to equal a single high-level option. For example, students could write a vocabulary word in a sentence or they could define a vocabulary word and draw its picture. This ensures students can't pick the easy way out. In the end, they'll work and think hard even if they choose multiple low-level options.

- **Demonstration of proficiency:** The choice options need to provide a data point as to where the student is performing to meet the expectation mentioned in the objective. With the previously mentioned example, the second choice option showcases the level of student learning. This data point tells the teacher that the student understands the definition of the vocabulary word and can access their long-term memory of previously learned vocabulary words to find a similar meaning word.

Scaffolding (providing varying levels of support) ensures students will be successful. Follow the three-part scaffolding process: model, show exemplars, and provide uninterrupted assistance during the learning process:

- Model completion of the options so students visually understand the outcome expected.

- Showcase exemplars when reviewing the assignment options. Start with minimal options (2–3) and build up to 8–10. This means you'll introduce the three options, show exemplars, and then help students complete these assignments.

- Watch, wait, and assist. You will not do anything else during the time students are working the first few times because you'll need to be available to answer questions, troubleshoot problems, and assist students in demonstrating their knowledge. Once students are familiar with the choice options, you can begin pulling small groups or working 1:1 with students as necessary while the other students work independently.

Again, as students demonstrate proficiency with limited options, you can slowly begin to expand choice options and follow the same scaffolding procedure (model, show exemplars, provide uninterrupted assistance during the learning process). These choice options can be reused in multiple subject areas and cover numerous topics, so it is important students get the hang of how to thoroughly demonstrate their learning.

For example, if students are learning about force and motion in science, some activity choices could be as follows:

- Write a poem with vocabulary words describing the relationship between two objects.

- Illustrate what happens during a roller coaster ride in a comic strip.

- Present a news segment to peers explaining a mishap incorporating force and motion.

All of these activities can be used again even when content changes—poem, comic strip, and news segment. This way students are familiar with the choice options and be more successful as they add on new options in the future.

When creating choice assignments for a single lesson, ensure it is on a smaller scale so students can finish in the allotted time frame. Here are some examples:

- Create a time line of important events.

- Cite a quote from an important figure related to the topic and explain what it means.

- Design a graphic organizer outlining the topic's essential points.

There are varied ways in which students could complete choice options:

- Complete odds or evens.
- Choose the order in which you wish to complete three assignments.
- Visit each workstation in the order you choose.

Table 16.1 provides an example of what an end-of-unit choice board could look like. Students would select choices (each being worth 25 points) to add up to 100 points and submit each piece as a portion of the overall grade. This also helps avoid a student completely failing an assignment if they did not do a particular assignment well, because they will have other options more aligned to their learning style where they could shine and earn full points. It is also helpful if you provide a rubric for each assignment so students know how they will be assessed and can self-assess before turning it in. Self-assessment or peer review of an assignment might not be realistic for

Table 16.1   Sample End-of-Unit Choice Board

Write a poem incorporating important vocabulary.	Illustrate a comic strip explaining the topic.	Perform a newscast to a peer explaining what happens when there's a problem with the main topic.
Create a diorama highlighting important con-cepts, vocabulary, essential people.	Write a journal entry to a pen pal in another country sharing all that you learned and why it's important for them to learn it, too.	Design a website that outlines the important points of the topic, including vocabulary and illustrations.
Map out a time line of events or essen-tial information.	Make an illustrated movie highlighting the main points of the topic using the app of your choice.	Visit three reputable web-sites, gather information related to the topic you didn't learn during the lesson, take notes, and cite your sources.

every assignment because it adds more time to quick deadlines, so these additional supports are usually built in for larger assignments or more important projects or assignments.

It is also helpful if you provide a rubric for each assignment so students know how they will be assessed—and can self-assess before turning it in. For example, a rubric for the pen pal letter might look like that shown in Table 16.2.

Take a moment to review the Student Choice and Ownership Guiding Questions (see Appendix 1, as well as on my website; see the next Downloadable Resource box). This will help you determine a starting point for where you are in implementing effective choice in your classroom. Be honest in your answers so that you can find the gaps in your own performance.

Table 16.2 Sample Pen Pal Letter Rubric

Component	Details	Point Totals	Points Earned
Written	The letter format is followed with a greeting, body, and salutation.	10	
Content	The letter is written to a pen pal in another country and shares important information on the newly learned topic, while emphasizing the importance of understanding this topic.	75	
Spelling/ Grammar	All spelling and grammar rules are followed.	10	
Clarity	Information is shared in a clear manner and the letter is easy to read.	5	

**Downloadable Resource: Student Choice and Ownership
Guiding Questions**

Visit www.alwaysalesson.com/teacher-essentials to download your
free resource!

CHAPTER 17

MASTERING STUDENT CHOICE AND OWNERSHIP

Now that you know what student choice and ownership are and how to begin implementing these concepts into your classroom, you're probably ready to incorporate more complex opportunities into your learning routine.

> **Quick Note:** As a reminder, increasing ownership and choice on a continuum scale of complexity ensures students get the hang of being in charge of learning or operating the classroom in small increments with support so that they can reach proficiency before more, or harder, options are available. Students will use what they learned with the easier task to also be successful with a more complex one.

In this chapter we consider components of student choice and ownership: communication, decision-making, environment, and equity and equality.

Communication

Create a variety of ways for students to communicate with you, whether through questions, comments, or concerns. You might survey students often about teaching strategies, assignment choice options, or how to best help them as learners. This can be implemented in an anonymous question/comment box in the classroom, an online link, or part of an entry/exit activity. Clear communication is vital for student voice to be acknowledged and valued.

Lessons from the Trenches: Question Box

When I taught fifth-grade science, I realized the group of students wasn't as forth-coming about questions they had during class. They were embarrassed to raise their hands or admit something was difficult. Many students did not perform well on homework or class assignments. I needed a way that they could communicate honestly with me but not in front of their peers. I brought in an old shoe box from home and cut a hole out of the top of the box. I cut index cards in half and placed them next to the box. I explained that students could talk to me secretly through the box. It could be anonymous or they could add their name. I wanted students to tell me what part of the lesson was confusing or an activity that they loved or really disliked—anything, really. At the end of each day, I reviewed the box and was able to tweak my next day's lesson based on what students had told me. Some feedback was very helpful (e.g., vocabulary being too difficult to remember so I made a vocab wall with pictures, words, and definitions) and others were unhelpful (e.g., jokes, inappro-priate comments, or silly drawings). I addressed the unhelpful feedback to students and reestablished expectations and reminded them of the purpose of the box. This method worked well with this age of student, especially when I held them account-able for using it correctly. They felt heard and I was able to meet their needs without embarrassing them in front of their peers. If I had to implement this again, I would have created a form instead of index cards so that it was more guided in asking for specific feedback. With technology being readily available to most students, a simple Google form could suffice. This would also avoid students being seen interacting with the box (walking over to it, dropping a note in, etc.).

Decision-Making

When it comes time to make a decision regarding students and their learning, allow students into the process. For example, you might need to decide field trip locations, revamping the classroom schedule, student seating arrangements, and so on. Set the expectation whether or not the final decision is majority vote or teacher final decision with input from students.

Lessons from the Trenches: Assigned Seats with a Twist

When I was in fourth grade, my favorite teacher Miss Lofy let us pick our own seats. After an entire year of our seats being switched after school and coming in early to be confused and spend five minutes locating our new desk spots, she allowed us to give input. It was a way to reward us for our hard work that year. She explained the process. We were to write down three names of people we would like to sit next to, with the person's name in the first spot being our most hoped-for request. She told us she could not promise everyone would get their first choice but she would promise we would get someone we had on our list. We all excitedly filled out our lists and turned them in. The next day we walked in and squealed with joy finding our desk next to our closest friends.

I knew when I became a teacher I wanted to do the same thing for my students. I followed suit and waited until the bitter end of the school year after students had worked hard and behaved well. I rolled out the same rules and protocol, but I did add the caveat that if students misbehaved, they would lose privileges and become islands without partners. (I learned this when my class of peers acted up and Miss Lofy hadn't thought about what would happen if students couldn't learn well next to their closest friends. She had to separate a few people who lost out on being learning buddies with their friends. I wanted to set this expectation up front as I had seen it firsthand.) I am not sure how long it took Miss Lofy to plan partners, but it was a very messy calculation trying to get everyone someone from their list. Of course, some peers were easy and others who appeared on many lists were harder to pair. After a late night, I finally figured out a game plan. Students were so excited to learn next to their friends. I only had to break up one pair! That was one of my students' favorite weeks at school!

Environment

Reflect on your current operations within the classroom. Where can students lead more so that you can support students in a different way? Think about entry and exit routines, common procedures, directions or announcements, and so on. The more that your students run the classroom, the more time you have to pull small groups or work 1:1 with students to spiral previously learned skills and increase student achievement.

- Make a list of all the ways in which you could step back and students could step up.

- Prioritize the list based on which options would excite students the most to begin taking on.

- Transfer ownership one option at a time, giving students plenty of time to watch you model it, discuss expectations, and guide students through a shared ownership before finally allowing students to run it on their own with feedback.

- Allow multiple opportunities for students to lead learning before introducing the next opportunity to transfer ownership. You don't want to put so much on their plates that it distracts from learning—a delicate balance.

Lessons from the Trenches: Classroom Jobs

Early in my career, all classrooms were outfitted with smartboard technology. The first administrative task I passed on to students was taking attendance. I took their picture and created an attendance slide to project on the smartboard. Every morning, they would enter the classroom and before sitting down or emptying their back pack, they'd walk to the front of the room and slide their photo from the "absent" side of the T-chart to the "present" side. By the time I was done with morning hallway duty welcoming students into the classroom, I looked up at the board and saw whose picture was still not moved to "present." While students were completing their morning work (specific steps listed on the front board), I walked to my computer and

---

completed online attendance for the front office. It took seconds and saved minutes that I could use for instruction.

Classroom jobs were another way to share administrative duties with students. I had paper passers/collectors, front office runners, guest greeters, new student buddies, technology helpers, line leader, and library book returners. One of my favorite class-room jobs was the pencil sharpener helper. I had two cups at the supply table in the back of the classroom labeled "sharp" and "dull." Students exchanged pencils, trading their dull pencil for an already sharpened one. This enabled students to get right back to learning. During dismissal procedures, my pencil sharpener helper would sharpen all the dull pencils and place them in the sharp container for the next day. If we were in need of more pencils, they knew where to locate brand new pencils in my cabinet and sharpen those to add to the "sharp" cup.

You already have heard about passing ownership on to students with book club. This was the largest instructional piece I passed on to students. It took a long time for students to qualify and then only a handful continuously participated. If I were to do this again, I would expose all students to it with shorter text, sentence stems, and mixed ability levels to help conversation flow (similar to the method I used for student desk placement and peer pairs based on ability and personality).

Equity and Equality

A classroom is made up of a variety of student backgrounds, abilities, and interests. Infusing a multiculturalism component into your lessons begins to help students experience belonging and awareness. However, choice and ownership bring equity and equality into the space. Classroom instruction needs to include everyone, regardless of academic performance, ability, language spoken, or needs. Even though you provide choice options or ownership opportunities, they still need to be differentiated so all students can participate successfully. Ensure all students have access to learning options and have an equal opportunity to lead.

Lessons from the Trenches: Equity and Equality in Action

In my classroom, I had a coffee cup where I placed 20+ popsicle sticks. I numbered them one to however many students I had in the class at the time. Students knew their number based on where they landed on the student roster alphabetically. This was used for numerous data collections and written on each students' papers. (Our administrators preferred numbers on student work rather than names so that when guests visited the buildings they would not know this identifying information.) I used these number sticks often, like when doing rapid-fire questioning during a lesson, I'd pick a number stick at random and that student would have to answer. (I would place the stick back in so that students had to pay attention the entire discussion in case they were called on again.) I'd also use these sticks if I had an impromptu task that needed completed. I would pull a stick at random and select a student to help me. This enabled equal opportunity to participate.

I would also print out a student roster and mark positive, encouraging notes written for students. At the end of each day, I would write two sticky notes and place them in the corner of the students' desks. When they came into class the next morning, their faces lit up seeing a special note on their desk. They loved reading great attributes about themselves as learners and people. Many students kept every note they ever got in notebook in their desk. By using a roster and marking the date of when I wrote a note ensured all students received one and never in the same order.

A quick note about equity versus equality—I had a handful of students who needed specific math manipulatives during lessons (e.g., cubes, counting bears, unifix cubes, etc.). These students had individual baskets they would retrieve during math and keep at their desk for the duration of the lesson. This method was not equal because not everyone got one. But, it was equitable because everyone was able to be successful and have access to a quality education. Be careful mixing up the terms and ensure all students receive the support they need to be successful, which will not be identical across the board.

EXPEDITIONARY
LEARNING

Journal Jots: Choice and Ownership

Take a moment to brainstorm ways below to build in choice and ownership into your classroom through communication, decision-making, environment, and equity or equality.

An easy place to begin to build in choice and ownership is in reading instruction. Although there are times when students need to read specific books of a particular topic or mastery level, there are times where students can choose their own books for enjoyment. This is why reading instruction lends itself nicely to building in more choice and ownership for students.

In a *Reading Horizons* journal article entitled "Student Choices: Book Selection Strategies of Fourth Graders," Sherry Kragler and Christine Nolley (1996) outline a study on how students self-selected books during their instructional reading program. (A quick note—knowing this study was conducted with fourth graders leads us to believe that these students most likely had strong foundational reading skills by this time in their educational career; thus, this particular teacher is most likely working with proficient readers. All that to say, this approach might not be a fit for beginning readers such as early elementary-aged children.) The authors (355) cite Willard Olson's theory of child development, mentioning how "children are self-seeking, self-selecting, self-pacing organisms" (Olson 1959, 402). This tells us that children can be successful in making choices that are in their best interest. Kragler and Nolley conclude, "Students who are encouraged to self-select their own reading materials are more motivated and enthusiastic as readers. The process puts the learning responsibility on the reader thus providing early lessons in decision making and life-long learning. If taught effectively, most students are quite competent when it comes to selecting their instructional reading books suitable to their individual levels" (364). This is most successful when students are choosing texts for independent reading—a freedom in its own right. Selecting books for instructional purposes (e.g., working on a reading skill) should be left to the teacher only. However, students can still practice the skill taught by the teacher with their independent reading choice of text. The layer of choice and ownership (especially when explicitly taught how) is the motivation students need to practice what they learn in a strategic group led by the teacher. If self-selecting a book to read brings about feelings of enthusiasm and motivation to grow as a reader, then teachers need to figure out how to cultivate this best practice into their reading instruction.

> **Quick Note:** This is a little nod to Brick 1: Lesson Design to plan that implementation out, followed by Brick 2: Classroom Management in holding students accountable for doing it successfully and habitually, and of course closing out with Brick 3: Student Engagement, because students are invested deeply in the learning task at hand.

Overall, this study showcases the importance of helping students grow as individuals and scholars as being an essential duty of the classroom teacher. Implementing ownership and choice in reading instruction is a great way to help children grow as people and learners. The skills students learn through choice and ownership follow them into subsequent grade levels and into the career field.

The next sections will discuss a few other ways to push student choice and ownership to new levels.

Co-create Norms

As you start to pass the ownership baton to students, allow them to help design the new protocol and procedures. Before they even begin to lead their learning, they are leading the process for how they will lead their learning. Cocreating expectations and norms for different sections of the classroom or different learning activities will increase student motivation to participate and result in behavior and learning expectations to be met. Plus, the high-level cognition required to problem-solve future obstacles in order to implement their ideas expands the mind, further benefitting students' academic success.

Data Collection and Reflection

Not all data needs to be formally recorded in a teacher's grade book. It can be even more effective to allow students to collect and review their own performance data. Making performance review a part of your weekly or monthly schedule will create the habit of self-assessment and reflection. Students can have their own data notebooks to record informal and formal data points. They then can analyze trends among the data, review any outlier numbers, reflect on their overall performance, and plan next steps. Now students are no longer learning new material and taking tests; rather, they are learning and thinking about their learning to do it more successfully in the future. The goal of the data collection routine is to help students grow at faster rates because of the increased awareness of how they are performing and the personal motivation to continue to grow.

Lessons from the Trenches: Student Data Collectors

When I taught math, I created a bar graph template and students pasted it into their math notebooks. These math notebooks were where students solved "Problem of the Day" warm-ups to kick off math instruction. This was also a place where students collected vocabulary or important concepts to reference later. When students would take a test, I would write their test score in the upper-right-hand corner of their test paper. I then would fold the right-hand corner over that number. This allowed for privacy as papers were passed back to students. It also allowed students to focus more on errors they made then the final score. The first order of business was for students to flip their math notebooks open to the bar graph. They would record the date of the test, the name on top of the test (e.g., fractions unit), and then shade a bar from 0–100, stopping at the number of their test score. This visual representation helped students see their growth. We drew light lines in pencil across the 70% mark so students knew our goal as a class was to get above this percentage each test, and we also drew a light line in pencil across the 40% mark to remind us that this concept has limited understanding and needs intervention. Students loved to color over those two

---

light lines, surpassing an imaginary goal post. The accomplishment knowing they were out of the "danger zone" and maybe even hit the "proficient" top part of the graph released endorphins. Understanding numbers and how they relate to one another (e.g., 40% is closer to 0% requiring more instruction to better understand a concept and 70% is closer to 100% meaning proficiency or mastery has been accomplished) had a big impact on student performance. Their test score was no longer red numbers on top of their paper that would later land in the bottom of the trash can. Now those numbers had meaning and carried weight. Students knew they could move on to the next topic, needed additional practice, or had to study and learn the concept again from the start. That ownership in the process for what they achieved encouraged them to look at their errors and uncover misunderstandings. They'd ask questions, we would review common problems most of the class got wrong, and we would even reiterate essential information for that test. This process was more than reviewing a test or jotting down test data. It was building understanding in how much ownership students had in their own academic journey. Every student improved in math that year. I know having students collect and analyze their own performance data was a major reason why they improved collectively.

Flexible Seating

Provide students options for their workstations. You can create special spaces in your classroom with pillows and lamps or purchase unique seating options such as medicine balls, swivel chairs, or standing desks. Choosing where and how to work is a powerful way to exercise ownership as a learner. (No need to spend a lot of your own money on flex seating options. You can apply for a grant, ask your school for classroom supply funding, or even accept donations from parents and community members.) The most important thing is to explain to students why flexible seating can help them learn. Here are some reasons:

- **Comfort:** Surfaces are cozier and cushier than a desk chair.
- **Change up the scenery:** A new learning space sparks interest in continuing learning.

- **Longer attention span:** Focus can wane if uncomfortable or bored, so changing up seating options to more comfortable, interesting choices allows for a longer attention span to continue learning.

- **Health considerations:** Increase blood flow by using a standing desk, avoid spinal discomfort with the medicine ball, or allow fidgeting with a swivel chair to get out anxious energy.

Once students understand why flexible seating options are helpful, they begin to care for them as learning tools instead of toys. They use them appropriately and care for them gently so that they last all year long. Teachers are welcome to remove these tools if students cannot use them properly.

Peer Evaluations

Allowing students to review each other's work helps them learn to communicate respectfully, use a rubric to compare work samples, and exposes them to different ways of thinking. Although the peer evaluation rating might not be the final grade a student receives, it sure can weigh in as part of the process. The learning gained from the evaluation process is more important than the final rating. They are learning about communication, reviewing their final product with a new set of eyes, and gathering information to grow their knowledge of a concept. Add in some fun pen colors, stamps, and stickers to make the process even more magical for peer evaluators!

Project-Based Learning (PBL)

Allowing students to drive the learning route is the ultimate way to provide choice and enable them to obtain immense ownership in getting to the learning destination. Designing projects that align to the content standards and individual lesson objectives ensures students deepen learning while experiencing flexibility in what and how they learn. Include students in the decision-making for the project, such as whom they work with, what they work on, when its due, and how they show mastery.

> **Quick Note:** These often take a long time to put together to ensure they are rigorous and aligned, so add this into your quarterly planning day, leaving weeks to gather materials and design quality projects.

Speaking of PBL: As a way of building in voice and choice, an entire school was designed on this premise. In the book *"The Coolest School in America": How Small Learning Communities Are Changing Everything*, authors Doug Thomas, Walter Enloe, and Ron Newell (2005) outline how educators and community came together to design a new and unique high school that later became the New Country School. Over a planning year, they discussed all the necessary components to make the school successful. They learned that "the authenticity and use of choice creates conditions for the development of intrinsic motivation rather than the constant use of extrinsic motivation often utilized in traditional high schools" (33). And specifically, "the project-based model allows student choice rather than teacher choice of curriculum and learning is not time-based. This allows for a less boring atmosphere and challenges the adolescent mind. Interest-driven projects and choice allow for the brain to be engaged, which increases motivation and attention. This in turn triggers actual changes in brain chemistry, with the brain producing endorphins, chemicals that allow for attitudes of 'I can' and 'I will'" (24).

The design of this high school and what these educators were able to conclude about PBL solidifies the importance of choice and ownership in the learning process. It has a chemical reaction in our body that promotes success as we experience the freedom of choice and ownership as a learner. Students will then crave this feeling of success and desire it in all of their learning experiences, in the classroom and in life.

If a particular curriculum does not include choice and ownership in the structure of a lesson, teachers are encouraged to go beyond what's provided to ensure they meet their students' needs. Use what is provided to build your lesson and then sprinkle in moments throughout the lesson where students can share their thoughts and opinions while also making choices about how to showcase their learning. A little goes a long way. Reference this chapter and include a handful of ways to add choice and ownership into your lesson. Over time, you will learn what your students respond to best, what works best with your teaching style and management protocols, and so on.

Quick Note: Remember what we said in lesson design? We must go beyond the curriculum to ensure we deepen our own understanding and that of students. The same is true with building in ownership and choice into a lesson, especially when a curriculum doesn't incorporate it on its own. See how all signs continually point back to that foundation? It is essential to get that piece right!

Journal Jots: Scenario Practice

Let's take a look at a common student choice and ownership scenario.

Sayeed is a well-behaved student who meets grade-level performance standards. He is very interested in technology and often is found helping his peers log in to their learning app accounts. His teacher, Mrs. Hawk, noticed his involvement—especially how happy it makes him to assist others and how positively his peers respond. So she offers Sayeed the role of being "tech support" for the entire class.

During a class observation, the school principal saw that Sayeed spent the majority of class time assisting peers logging in, navigating app sites, and troubleshooting common errors. Unfortunately, he wasn't able to help all who needed assistance, and he was unable to complete his own assignments. He also seemed frustrated and anxious. Mrs. Hawk did not intercede during the lesson.

If you were Mrs. Hawk's mentor—and a strong student choice and ownership facilitator—how would you help her develop more effective student leadership strategies to support learning? Script out what you would say before returning to this chapter.

Don't peek if you haven't yet completed your scenario practice! Do not read further until you've spent time reflecting and writing your response to the scenario. This will ensure you process your new learning before receiving feedback to solidify your application. Consider the following:

Key Points

- Sayeed met academic expectations.
- He had a love for technology and earned the privilege of becoming a peer tech support.
- After the increased responsibility, his academic performance decreased and anxiety heightened.

Overall, Sayeed lacks the time to complete his academics due to helping his peers log in on their devices. Even though he is passionate about technology and responsible enough to help in the classroom, it is too much responsibility and not enough time to do both simultaneously. Sayeed's tech help may help take the load off the teacher's plate, but it began to affect his emotional stability. Students need to grow their skill set with technology because it is such a big part of the learning process these days. As a result, the teacher should set aside time to help all students become proficient. Sayeed can play tech support if he is finished with his academics and they are meeting expectations. He can also be a tech leader in other ways such as working the projector during a lesson or presenting his learning in a digital portfolio. We want Sayeed to be a successful student, who enjoys technology all while not experiencing stress or anxiety.

* * *

Before you move on to the next brick, let's assess where you are right now with this brick for classroom and career success by taking the Student Choice and Ownership Self-Survey (see Appendix 1, as well as on my website; see the next Downloadable Resource box).

The goal for this book is to help you grow your craft one brick at a time. After reading this chapter, your instructional foundation as a teacher is now four bricks thick!

Downloadable Resource: Student Choice and Ownership Self-Survey

Visit www.alwaysalesson.com/teacher-essentials to download your free resource!

Following the sequence of the Teacher Success Pathway (lesson design, classroom management, student engagement, and student choice and ownership) will ensure you build the strongest instructional practices possible.

When you're ready, move on to Chapter 18 so we can keep building strong teacher essentials for classroom and career success.

Journal Jots: Reflection

Capture your thoughts and feelings after reading this chapter. You've been learning so much already in this book and your brain might be on overload trying to sort everything out.

- What stands out to you?
- What reservations do you have?
- How might you begin to implement some changes in your classroom?

Don't focus on writing a perfect journal entry. Just begin writing without rules or distraction and let your mind guide your journal entry.

Then, revisit the goals you continue to refine as you read this book:

- Who do you want to become after implementing the principles in this book?
- Are you on the right track to make that a reality?
- What steps can you take right now to move closer to becoming the person you dreamed of becoming?

PART SIX

IMPLEMENTING YOUR NEW LEARNING

CHAPTER 18

TEACHER SUCCESS NEXT STEPS

The goal of this book is to grow your craft one brick at a time. Ideally you feel you now have a solid understanding of the four major bricks: lesson design, classroom management, student engagement, and student choice and ownership. I hope you also now have clarity as to the importance of attacking these instructional areas in a particular sequence in order to transform teaching and learning in your entire school building. And I'm guessing that, most important, you've been reflecting on your new learning—and begun applying it in your classroom. If so, well done!

> **Quick Note:** There are discussion questions by chapter for this book included in Appendix 2. Even if you have read this book once already, you can still engage in a book study or book chat with a colleague. The questions are designed to highlight essential information per brick but also stretch your thinking for how this applies to your role. This helps bridge the gap from reading the information, to processing it, and then finally to applying it. Get talking!

The Teacher Success Pathway is linear, given that it's a pathway, but it's also vertical, because each brick builds on each other. However, oftentimes, these bricks are in fact interwoven together. This requires educators to implement the principles at the same time. Experienced and successful teachers are capable of managing how these bricks interact with each other and leveraging them to create powerful learning experiences for students.

> **Quick Note:** Don't worry if you're not ready to weave these bricks together. Start at the most foundational brick where you need to strengthen and build from there one at a time. Eventually, you'll be ready to weave them together. Go at your pace for best results.

When these bricks intertwine, it creates the perfect recipe for success. In their 2019 article "A Review into Effective Classroom Management and Strategies for Student Engagement: Teacher and Student Roles in Today's Classrooms," authors Hayley Franklin and Ingrid Harrington, citing the Organisation for Economic Co-operation and Development, state, "Successful classrooms foster enthusiasm and motivation for learning, active participation, and high levels of engagement, with teachers not only knowing the content to be taught, but also knowing the impact their teaching has on their student's ability to become self-directed lifelong learners" (Franklin and Harrington 2019, 1). Luckily, not only are you aware of the essentials for classroom and career success, but you understand the sequence in which to deploy the strategies and the importance of having all four bricks present in your instructional arsenal. It is bigger than just teacher capacity; it's about student learning habits and gains. That impact is far more important and beneficial long term for our society as a whole.

This knowledge, however, will not get you far if you do not implement it. In his book *Trust-Based Observations: Maximizing Teaching and Learning Growth,* Craig Randall quotes Charlotte Danielson (2013) in saying, "A commitment to professional learning is important, not because teaching is of poor quality and must be *fixed*, rather because teaching is so difficult that we can always improve it" (Randall 2020, 171). Let's take her advice and stop binge reading for the sake of decreasing our stack of books and actually put our learning into practice. To ensure this new learning translates into a change in your instructional practice, it's essential you begin to plan your execution. It's not enough to just read this book, but you must reflect, plan, and adjust your implementation. The way you attack your growth will look different for each individual teacher because of your unique strengths and areas of focus for improvement. Everyone is starting at a different place (or brick I should say), and the pace at which you progress is different depending on your students, school, district, and so on.

To help you know what to do next, use the Teacher Success Execution Plan Template (see Appendix 1, as well as on my website; see the next Downloadable Resource box). This will help you design a practical, successful execution plan that is aligned to your goals and focus area.

Downloadable Resource: Teacher Success Execution Plan Template

Visit www.alwaysalesson.com/teacher-essentials to download your free resource!

Once you've completed the Teacher Success Execution Plan, you'll likely have gained clarity on what next steps you need to take to continue to grow as an educator.

Use the information from the Teacher Success Execution Plan to sequence your next steps, perhaps in the Next Steps Checklist (see Appendix 1, as well as on my website; see the next Downloadable Resource box). This includes the name of the task, a time frame to hold you accountable for completing the task, details in order to complete it thoroughly, and notes to yourself as you move through the process.

It is okay if the checklist is messy and changes over time. The important part of the process is that you design a plan to enable yourself to achieve success.

Quick Note: Having an accountability partner or mentor to hold you to the promise you made yourself to execute your plan will ensure you stay on track when you don't want to, don't see results, or feel frustrated. Accountability partners and mentors can also see you from a distance and appreciate your progress, effort, and transformation—often, well before you can see it yourself.

Decide who this person might be and shoot them a text message right now sharing your intention and hopes for the partnership. This holds you accountable to implement your new learning.

EXPEDITIONARY
LEARNING

Downloadable Resource: Next Steps Log

Visit www.alwaysalesson.com/teacher-essentials to download your
free resource!

CHAPTER 19

ONGOING LEARNING

We grow instructional capacity with passion and intention.

It is important educators hone their craft on a continual basis. As best practices in the field of education change, it's essential to keep up-to-date. Schools are required to provide ongoing professional development to their staff members monthly. However, teachers rarely have input on the topics and the delivery is often one-size-fits-all. This leaves teachers' learning desires unfulfilled. This means teachers need to take their learning into their own hands and not rely on what the school provides. This way they can learn about the topics they are interested in and interact in the learning experience in a way that they desire.

If we educators stagnate, we risk losing our edge. Our edge is our X factor—the thing that sets us apart from all other educators. It's the reason students want to learn from us. It's the reason colleagues want to collaborate with us. We radiate our uniqueness. But when we stagnate, we lose that spark. We stop attracting others into our sphere of influence. We lessen the positive impact we are making at our schools. Our motivation wanes when we are no longer energized by what we are doing. Learning sparks that motivation and re-energizes our spirit.

When we evolve our teaching practices, it benefits our students. We are more knowledgeable and capable to teach content deeply and at high levels. This enables students to gain clearer understanding of concepts and receive more targeted support to achieve success in the classroom. When we learn and grow, it enables our students to learn and grow at higher levels.

Lessons from the Trenches: Ongoing Learning

For as long as I can remember, I have participated in ongoing learning opportunities such as these:

- *Virtual book studies*
- *Social media chats*
- *Edcamp-style PD*
- *Conferences for elementary educators*

My formula for interacting in these ongoing learning opportunities was always the same. I went into each experience with a goal in mind. For example, I might join a free webinar for teachers online to develop a system for recording student data. Or I might go to our local elementary educator conference to meet and collaborate with three people who have expertise I don't have. When I go into learning experiences with a goal, I am clear in how I show up. I am not hemming and hawing over which conference session to attend because I know exactly the skills I need so it narrows down my options. I don't sign up for every online book study. I only purchase the books that align with my goals and engage deeply in those conversations with others who are reading and growing in that same area. When you have a goal in mind before taking action, your results will reap your intention and might even exceed your original goal.

Being intentional with ongoing learning ensured I made the most of every opportunity, engaged in learning topics that I needed to grow my skill set, built relationships with those who could mentor me as I strengthened my approach, and so on. If there is anything you have learned in this book it is that intentionality is the difference maker between success and average performance. You have all the knowledge contained in this book to be an elite educator, and now it is time to be intentional with how to put it into action in your role.

I truly believe learning is an ongoing process. I have a stack of books on my nightstand that I take my time reading so I ensure I am actually implementing learning and not just reading to check it off a list. Every day, I use various social media apps (e.g., Voxer, Marco Polo, Facebook groups, Clubhouse, etc.) to network with other educators to share ideas and grow my knowledge base. When I stop learning, I will stop being able to help others. The same is true for you—learn and grow daily and be intentional with how you engage in those opportunities.

Quick Note: When I interview educators on my podcast, the last question I ask everyone is, "How do you reignite your passion and potential as an educator?" The reason I do this is because I know there are times when you feel stuck, unmotivated, and ready to quit. I was there, too. Ongoing learning is one way to create a spark, develop a new interest, and fall back in love with a profession you once adored.

Just as students thrive in an environment where they have choice and ownership in what and how they learn, adults do, too. Spend time thinking about what topics you need to learn more about. Reflect on the modes of learning that fit your style and preference the best. Then, advocate for those very specific learning requests to administrators and district decision-makers. Waiting for a professional development opportunity that you will like and enjoy is unrealistic and counterproductive.

Just know that even if you ask for specific learning opportunities and maybe even engage in them, change takes time. We have bad habits to overcome and new habits to develop. Our mental muscles need rounds of practice to turn learning into comfortable daily habits. And, let's be honest, the teaching profession has added lots of "extras" to our plates, making it hard to even think about going above and beyond requirements to continue our learning. However, just applying the strategies in this book in the suggested sequence is going to have a strong effect on your impact in the classroom. Remember, it's not how fast you can move through the book, rather, it's how well you can build a strong foundation brick by brick.

If you need to hold off on ongoing learning for a minute until your brain has room for new incoming knowledge, that is fine. Don't wait too long or you might never get back into the learning swing of things. When your plate is less full and your energy tank is topped off, put ongoing learning on your to-do list and follow the tips listed in this chapter to set yourself up for more success as an accomplished teacher.

To get started in growing to your potential, complete the Teacher Success Learning Inventory Questionnaire (see Appendix 1, as well as on my website; see the next Downloadable Resource box). This will help you narrow your focus for what learning opportunities you should seek out. When you are specific about what you do not know or cannot yet do, you put yourself in position to grow in a way that will have a positive effect on your teaching. Intentional investment ensures you grow at rapid speed.

 Downloadable Resource: Teacher Success Learning Inventory Questionnaire

Visit www.alwaysalesson.com/teacher-essentials to download your free resource!

Ongoing Learning Opportunities

Now that you know your specific focus for learning, it's time to seek out ways to grow in that area. There are various ways to access ongoing learning that is personalized to your current level of performance and interests. Bookmark this page so that as your learning goals change, you can remind yourself of the opportunities that are most aligned to those goals.

- Attend in-person or virtual educational conferences in or around your area.
- Follow educational blogs by Googling your area of focus, reading search results, and subscribing on their landing page to receive updates from their blog. (Check out mine at www.alwaysalesson.com.)
- Join social media groups specifically for your role in education.
- Listen to educational podcasts by searching your area of focus on iTunes (or your preferred podcast platform) and subscribe so you'll be notified when recent episodes are released. (Check out mine at www.alwaysalesson.com/episodes.)

- Meet with a mentor to plan specific actions to increase performance.

- Observe colleagues teaching, take notes on what effective teaching strategies are used, and plan how to implement them into your own classroom.

- Partake in a book study (virtual or in-person) so that you can process what you're reading, plan how you will implement your leading, get strategies and tips from other educators, all while building a professional network of colleagues to collaborate with on an ongoing basis.

- Participate in optional, personalized professional development (e.g., office hours, PD in a box, book checkouts) provided by an instructional coach or teacher leader.

- Read educational books by searching for your area of focus on Amazon (or your preferred book platform), reading book reviews, and choose to dive into one at a time.

- Share your passion and future plans with colleagues and school leaders so that when opportunities arise, they recommend you to participate.

- Subscribe to educational magazines (e.g., *NEA*, *Education Week*, *ASCD*, *Edutopia*, etc.).

- Watch professional development videos from an accredited program and receive credits toward keeping your teaching license active.

It's a good idea to keep track of your learning. Feel free to use the Professional Development Log (in Appendix 1, as well as on my website; see the next Downloadable Resources box) to track the details (such as date, topic or title of the learning experience, how many hours to complete, and whether you received licensure credit, etc.) of each opportunity you engage in to grow your craft.

If you wish to keep another journal jotting down notes from your learning experience, that is encouraged, too. But the learning log is not a note catcher. It is simply to hold a list of professional development you have attended. This can be represented during your summative evaluation to show your principal how you participate in ongoing learning opportunities outside of what the school offers. This shows initiative and dedication, often resulting in a higher rating on your performance evaluation.

The best way to maximize the effects of your learning is to put it into action right away. Avoid overconsuming knowledge without implementation. If you read all the books and attend all the conferences but never try out what you've learned, you'll never get better in practice. Start small and decide what you will implement, and provide a time line for doing so.

Table 19.1 provides an example of what your implementation plan could look like.

This New Learning Implementation Plan outlines the new learning gained and clear next steps to put it into action. The deadline is realistic, giving the learner time to plan and implement without too much time where implementation will be foregone. The notes section enables the learner to track how it went in order to make adjustments for next time. Simply repeat this process with each new learning idea, but be sure to focus on only one implementation at a time to ensure success!

Table 19.1   New Learning Implementation Plan

New Learning	Plan of Action	Deadline	Notes
Use Nearpod technology in a lesson.	1. Design presentation in Nearpod. 2. Embed a beginning, middle, and end engagement opportunity. 3. Practice with a colleague. 4. Explain Nearpod to students. 5. Try out in a lesson.	One week	• Keep engagement simple. • Only explain related components of Nearpod to students to avoid overwhelm. • Students loved it! • Repeat similar beg., mid, and end engagement in next lesson for familiarity. • Add other types of Nearpod engagement options throughout the month.

Downloadable Resources: Professional Development Log and New Learning Implementation Plan

Visit www.alwaysalesson.com/teacher-essentials to download your free resource!

Not only is this a helpful planning and reflection tool for teachers but also it can be submitted to your administrator during your summative evaluation to showcase ongoing learning outside of what the school provides. (You can find the New Learning Implementation Plan template in Appendix 1, as well as on my website; see the next Downloadable Resources box.)

Continuous Collaboration

Regardless of how you engage in professional development, one thing I know to be true is that if you continuously collaborate with colleagues you will grow your skill set.

Great teaching happens in collaboration.

Sounds easy, but it's a bit more complicated than it sounds. Collaboration is often confused with talking at or about a topic. Just like students interact during a turn-and-talk with a peer, talking at someone without talking with them inhibits growth. We push students to listen and respond before sharing their ideas with their peers during a turn-and-talk, so adults need to do the same.

True collaboration requires adults to listen and respond in a way that adds value to the conversation or clarifies a point. When multiple minds come together to enhance a single idea, that how is how everyone grows their knowledge and skills. That only happens when collaboration occurs. And if that collaboration occurs on a continuous basis, then we amplify the effect it has on our own practice.

We are the sum of the parts. Education is not a profession of islands. It's a collaborative effort. We are as strong as the minds and talents among us. We must use the power created by the whole group and not rely only on ourselves.

The most naturally occurring opportunity for continuous collaboration is during a formal professional learning community (PLC) meeting. This collective mind approach acts like a think tank of sorts, where educators can calibrate instructional pacing and content topics among their peers while also problem-solving current obstacles. This is an ideal time to dissect student data and create a plan of action for how to best support students moving forward or designing an upcoming assessment aligned to the standards and content topics to be covered in the upcoming semester.

There is a wealth of knowledge shared among colleagues.

PLCs should consist of a group of educators teaching the same grade level or subject area. (A cross-subject or grade-level PLC can still be helpful if there's not enough teachers in a single grade level or subject area to meet.) These meetings should occur on a specified date and time on a reoccurring basis (e.g., Mondays at 11:30 in the conference room).

The benefits of continuous collaboration in a PLC include (but are not limited to) the following:

- Hear what other teachers are doing in their classroom.
- Gain new ideas for ways to reach students more effectively.
- Receive support in areas of weakness.
- Develop a short- and long-term game plan for instruction.
- Home in on what is happening in the classroom and why.
- Locate student achievement trends among grade levels or content areas.
- Build camaraderie and relationships among peers.

When educators consistently meet to strengthen their instructional practice (the four essential bricks: design a lesson, manage behavior, plan for varied engagement, as well as increase student ownership and accountability), each subsequent learning experience increases in effectiveness. Teachers aren't meeting to problem-solve a single issue. They are meeting again and again to refine a strategy, to check the data to see what is working, to make adjustments to the original plan based on feedback and execution in a variety of classroom settings, and so on. It is essential collaboration, not a single event, rather an ongoing commitment to each other as colleagues and the students in the school building.

Speaking of data, a PLC should decide ahead of time what type of data they plan to discuss at a future meeting (e.g., Thursday's formative math assessment). Teachers need to come to the PLC meeting with planning materials in addition to the actual data, such as highlights, sticky notes, chart paper, and so on. This will enable brainstorming to occur centered on the data.

There are three tips to ensure the data chat is productive.

- **Moving:** It can be tempting to dive into one section of data for a lengthy period of time, but keeping your eye on the clock and managing time will ensure you are able to holistically dissect data and create a plan in the allotted time frame. (Note: A pre-agreed-on agenda would be helpful to reference during the PLC data chat; see Appendix 1 for my PLC Agenda Example, PLC Meeting Minutes Template, and PLC Guiding Questions (as well as on my website; see the next Downloadable Resources box).
- **Focused:** Be ready to prompt colleagues back on task if discussion goes away from the dedicated topic at hand; going down endless rabbit holes is one major reason data dig discussions fail.
- **Positive:** Data can feel personal, so keeping the discussion positive without blame or shame can motivate colleagues to take action.

However, you do not have to wait for the next PLC meeting to actively engage with your colleagues in a dialogue about your practice. Informal collaborations can be just as effective, especially if they are occurring on a consistent basis.

For example, collaboration can happen at the copy machine, in the hallway, in the classroom, on the playground and even at bus duty. It doesn't matter where, it matters how.

Downloadable Resources: PLC Agenda Example, PLC Meeting Minutes Template, and PLC Guiding Questions

Visit www.alwaysalesson.com/teacher-essentials to download your free resource!

How are you engaging in a collaboration? These questions can prompt you to steer the conversation into a productive collaboration:

- Are you seeking an idea?
- Are you wanting access to resources?
- Can you elaborate on an idea to make it better?
- Do specific students need unique support options?
- How do past and future learning connect to a student's life and the world at large?

The list of questions could go on. The point is you are intentional with how you show up to discourse with colleagues. Together you should model best teaching practices as well as research and share ideas. Collaboration isn't just in word, but in action. Demonstrating a teaching technique can transform teaching ability just as much as verbal discussion about it. Taking risks in the classroom and telling colleagues about it so that they can try it will positively affect learning across the school building so that all students benefit.

If a formal collaboration is occurring, it's important to be clear where this continuous meeting will occur. For example, a PLC room that has access to materials and space to spread out and plan would be helpful. Tracking the content of the meeting by taking meeting minutes ensures teachers can go back to refresh themselves on all important information shared. It acts as a reference document that teachers can place in a PD binder or folder where they gather all of their notes from various learning opportunities. There should be a protocol, expectations, and a vision for how collaborations will occur. Otherwise, it is easy to get off topic, show up unprepared, and waste everyone's time, none of which build comradery or teaching skills. Last, everyone is accountable during a collaboration, whether you take notes, facilitate the discussion, manipulate technology, gather materials, or something else. Just like students are often assigned roles in the classroom (as discussed in Brick 4: Student Choice and Ownership), adults need specific duties to focus on to make the collaboration successful and efficient. Knowing that everyone has something to contribute and everyone is showing up as their best self enables the collaboration to operate at a high level with outstanding outcomes.

In a continuous collaboration, everyone is a leader. Together, we give and receive. We also lead and we follow. It's an interactive dance as the conversation ebbs and flows. No one has all the power or all the answers. The value of the collective partnership is in all of the members working together on a continuous basis to improve instruction. The more each member knows and is able to do, the better off the group is.

Continuous collaboration can also happen in a natural way. Two colleagues casually discussing upcoming lessons, and, in a few moments, a powerful learning opportunity was created. That's authentic professional learning—impromptu, timely brainstorming. Each colleague's viewpoints, past experiences, knowledge, and skill level all play a role in how to better the other person in the collaboration. We can't underestimate the power among ourselves as professionals.

Lead from within.

A collective mind is essential to our professional growth. That means we need to surround ourselves with others who can push our thinking and positively affect our actions. Growing a professional learning network (PLN) is the greatest form of natural professional development. There's no limit to how many members or even a location. A virtual PLN is just as helpful as an in-person one. What matters most is how the collaboration occurs in the PLN.

Continuous collaboration enables colleagues to feel success before they implement their learning. They experiment in a safe place among a supportive crowd. Their ideas are validated and upgraded. So by the time teachers implement changes in their instruction, teachers already experienced success and the results positively affect student achievement in the classroom.

Lessons from the Trenches: Collaboration and Accountability

I used to walk the block with my dog during the transitional years from teacher to instructional coach. Oftentimes my teacher neighbor would take her dog and walk along with me. She was just as passionate for improving education one day at a time as I was. Our conversations ebbed and flowed from silly stories of our day to the big dreams we had for ourselves in education. We supported each other as colleagues would—listening, brainstorming, holding accountable, celebrating, and continually supporting one another. We were collaboration partners. It was informal and practical and, most important, consistent. We both grew as educators and people during those casual doggie walks.

When I wasn't elevating my teaching practice during these accountability walk-and-talks, I would stop by my literacy facilitator's office on the way out of school a couple of times a week. After spending time in my classroom during walk-throughs and engaging with me at staff professional development sessions, we got to know each other professionally and personally. I started speaking my dreams of teacher leadership out loud to her. She would help me focus on state and district requirements so my teaching stayed model classroom worthy, while also helping me brainstorm ways to branch out in teacher leadership. She enabled me to present with her at staff meetings and in turn she tapped into my training of classroom management strategies from a national nonprofit organization so that I could help her reform the schoolwide mentorship program. This ying-and-yang relationship of using our expertise to help the other grow became a foundational piece in my growth as an educator. The consistency in which we collaborated in conjunction with the level to which we elevated our knowledge and skill was (and still is to this day) transformational for each of us. Proof is in the fact that years later we use social media apps to keep in touch with each other while also collaborating on current projects in our roles. She has gone on to affect the district and now state in helping schools transition instructionally to literacy best practices.

If it weren't for these everyday collaborations that didn't require a formal PLC, I would not have grown leaps and bounds professionally and personally. This means all educators should heavily engage in their PLC discourse to build the collaborative habit so that they can implement continuous collaboration at high levels with chosen PLN members. Use the PLC Data Chat Guide and Hone In: Question Prompts in Appendix 1 (as well as on my website; see the next Downloadable Resources box) to help guide these conversations.

**Downloadable Resources: PLC Data Chat Guide
and Hone In: Question Prompts**

Visit www.alwaysalesson.com/teacher-essentials to download your
free resource!

Regardless if you engage in formal or informal professional development experiences, it is important to ensure it is an ongoing occurrence. The repetition of learning and collaborating with colleagues is just as essential as the topic teachers are learning about. The behavior of learning is indicative of the potential an educator has in the classroom. If they build habits of learning and it becomes part of how they grow their craft, they will continue to see gains in student learning in the classroom. Continuous, high-quality, personalized learning should be your goal!

CHAPTER 20

CONCLUSION

I love to think of how much you've likely learned so much working through this book. I also hope that you've grown in your practice.

When you first started reading, you set goals for yourself. Hopefully, as you read and implemented your learning you started to become closer to the person you envisioned yourself becoming.

If you find yourself not quite where you'd hope to be, work backwards. Which brick of the Teacher Success Pathway do you need to revisit? Reread the section(s) if necessary. Draft out simple next steps for implementation. Track your progress and celebrate success. *Progress* is the key word here: it's a work in progress. (Along those lines, don't forget that your accountability partner is a great resource to support and encourage you as you refine your practice.)

I'd like to reiterate some of the essential points shared in each of the four bricks of the Teacher Success Pathway.

Brick 1: Lesson Design

- Create value and meaning in all of your lessons so that they hold long-term meaning for students.
- Use backwards planning (especially in quarterly planning) to create an instructional road map.
- Implement gradual release when rolling out content to students to support processing and mastery of the new information.

- Reference the five design aspects for each lesson: pacing, checks for understanding, transition routes, teacher and student actions, materials needed, and differentiation.
- Replicate core moves (reusable structures in all subjects areas) such as turn-and-talks and stop-and-jots so the focus is on content and not the learning activity.

Brick 2: Classroom Management

- Behavior management is not the same as classroom management.
- Create a philosophy of management, plan and prepare a system, and then set up the learning environment to reflect the philosophy and plan.
- The three Rs (relationships, routines, and rope students in) were created to prevent misbehaviors from occurring, bring clarity to expectations, and create engaging lessons to help students master content.

Brick 3: Student Engagement

- Engage students with the content, each other, and the teacher to deepen understanding.
- There are three engagement types to consider: behavioral, emotional, and cognitive. These all elicit connection, motivation, and understanding in the minds and hearts of students.
- When strengthening engagement, think about intentionality, ownership, accountability, and follow-through.
- Try out some of the 12 engagement strategies shared in Chapter 14.

Brick 4: Student Choice and Ownership

- Both directing and facilitating learning have a place in each lesson.
- Begin by focusing on alignment, rigor, and demonstration of learning.
- Build in additional layers of freedom through communication, decision-making, environment, and equity/equality.
- Some favorite choice and ownership options are to cocreate norms, data collection paired with reflection, flexible seating options, peer evaluations of student work, project-based learning, choice boards, and performance rubrics.

I've shared stories and examples to help you see how the four bricks can look in your classroom. I hope you have been taking advantage of the reflection exercises throughout the book to process your own learning and bridge the gap of what currently is happening in your classroom compared to what you can intentionally create. (Don't forget to implement your Teacher Success Execution Plan Template, discussed in Chapter 18!)

If you make adjustments to your instruction brick by brick—paying close attention to the sequence of what you tweak and when (lesson design first, followed by classroom management, then student engagement, and finally student choice and ownership)— you will reap tremendous rewards in both your and your students' performance in the classroom.

And don't forget: order matters. Don't underestimate the power of going back to the beginning to uncover tiny fissures in the foundation. The quicker you mend your support bricks, the stronger your instruction will become.

Wishing you the best as you implement these teacher essentials for classroom and career success!

GO BE GREAT!

APPENDIX 1: REPRODUCIBLES

Over the years I've tinkered with various structures to contain the different charts and lists that enabled my pathway, and now I offer them to you—both here and at my website, where you can download them in two formats: to use as they are or to tinker with them yourself. Feel free to make them your own to best meet the needs of your students.

 (www.alwaysalesson.com/teacher-essentials)

From Chapter 3: Lesson Design Phase Overview
- Backwards Planning Template
- Backwards Planning Guide

From Chapter 4: Effective Design
- Student Learner Survey

From Chapter 5: Getting Started with Lesson Design
- Lesson Plan Checklist
- Lesson Plan Template

From Chapter 7: Mastering Lesson Design, Part 2
- Lesson Design Guiding Questions
- Lesson Design Self-Survey

From Chapter 9: Getting Started with Classroom Management

- End-of-Year Student Reflection Sheet
- End-of-Year Parent Reflection Sheet

From Chapter 10: Addressing Misbehaviors

- Classroom Management Guiding Questions

From Chapter 11: Mastering Classroom Management

- Classroom Management Self-Survey

From Chapter 13: Getting Started with Student Engagement

- Student Pairing Sheet
- Student Engagement Guiding Questions

From Chapter 14: Mastering Student Engagement

- Student Engagement Strategies
- Student Engagement Self-Survey

From Chapter 15: Understanding Student Choice and Ownership

- Book Club Guide: Teacher
- Book Club Guide: Students
- Book Club Reflection

From Chapter 16: Getting Started with Student Choice and Ownership

- Student Choice and Ownership Guiding Questions

From Chapter 17: Mastering Student Choice and Ownership

- Student Choice and Ownership Self-Survey

From Chapter 18: Teacher Success Next Steps

- Teacher Success Execution Plan Template
- Next Steps Log

From Chapter 19: Ongoing Learning

- Teacher Success Learning Inventory Questionnaire
- Professional Development Log
- New Learning Implementation Plan
- PLC Agenda Example
- PLC Meeting Minutes Template
- PLC Guiding Questions
- PLC Data Chat Guide
- Hone In: Question Prompts

Backwards Planning Template

Standard	
Objective	
Assessment	
Lesson	Direct Instruction:
	Guided Practice:
	Independent Practice:

Backwards Planning Guide

Directions: Create a pacing calendar here by planning out your units/topics by month before flushing out a lesson in full. This ensures you plan to have enough time to teach essential content.

Month: _____

Monday	Tuesday	Wednesday	Thursday	Friday

Directions: Collect all your information for a unit in the following space.

Unit Theme: _____

UNIT TOPICS

KEY POINTS

VOCABULARY

END-OF-UNIT OUTCOME

Student Learner Survey

1. Describe yourself as a learner (strengths and weaknesses).

   _____

   _____

   _____

   _____

2. When you learn something new and it seems easy, it is because . . .

   _____

   _____

   _____

   _____

3. When you learn something new and it seems hard, it is because . . .

   _____

   _____

   _____

   _____

4. What are your favorite subjects/topics to learn about in school?

   _____

   _____

   _____

   _____

5. What can the teacher do to help you learn better?

   _____

   _____

   _____

   _____

6. When you struggle while learning something new, what kind of encouragement do you like to receive?

_____

_____

_____

_____

7. In order for you to participate in class (e.g., ask questions, talk with peers, or answer questions), what do you need from the teacher/environment to feel safe to do so?

_____

_____

_____

_____

8. If you make a mistake, how do you prefer to be told so that you can correct it?

_____

_____

_____

_____

9. What can your teacher do to make you feel listened to and or heard?

_____

_____

_____

_____

10. When you are frustrated while learning, what helps you bounce back?

_____

_____

_____

_____

Lesson Plan Checklist

DIRECTIONS: When planning a lesson, use this checklist to ensure you have included all key components for a successful learning experience for all students.

1. **Proper Alignment:** All parts of the lesson are aligned to give evidence in support of learning mastery:
   - Standard
   - Objective
   - Entry/Exit Assignment
   - Activities

2. **Specific and Clear Student Directions:** All directions for student actions and transitions are scripted in advance for clarity purposes.

3. **Specific and Clear Teacher Questioning and Directives:** All teacher deliverables are scripted in advance for clarity purposes.

4. **Student Discussion and Demonstration of Mastery Opportunities:** Moments are planned throughout the lesson for students to discuss what they are learning and demonstrate the level of their mastery:
   - Is this the majority of the class time?
   - Is it the majority of the students?

5. **Specific Time Increments:** Each section of the lesson plan is labeled with time stamps to keep on track and to ensure the lesson can be delivered in the time allotted, countdowns included.

6. **Appropriate Pacing:** The I Do/We Do/You Do portions of a lesson should mimic a triangle where the top is the smallest piece (I Do), middle is larger than the top (We Do), and the bottom is the largest piece (You Do). The size of the piece represents the portion of an entire lesson devoted to that section (e.g., smaller the piece, shorter the time).

7. **Rigorous Text:** Students gain information from a text (e.g., annotate a reading passage) versus a teacher-centered delivery so when meeting 1:1 or in a small group with the teacher, the reading has already been completed and the teacher can provide ability-appropriate instruction.

8. **Appropriate Checks for Understanding:** Informal data is gathered from students about their level of understanding frequently throughout the lesson (more than "yes/no" or "thumbs up/down").

9. **Materials Listed:** What materials will be used, how they will be used, and where they will be stored or accessed is made available.

10. **Engaging Approach to Content:** A varied approach is used to deliver content (e.g., learning styles) to capture student interest and increase their motivation.

11. **Differentiation Opportunities:** Use planned scaffolds for a variety of student learning needs (based on informal and formal data collection) that occur throughout the lesson.

Lesson Plan Template

Standard		
Objective		
Materials		
Direct Instruction (I DO)	Teacher Actions:	Student Actions:
Guided Practice (WE DO)	Teacher Actions:	Student Actions:
Independent Practice (YOU DO)	Teacher Actions:	Student Actions:
	Differentiation:	
Assessment		
Homework		

Lesson Design Guiding Questions

Standards/Objectives

- What resources did you reference to plan your lesson?
- How did you pick the standard?
- Describe your thought process for developing the lesson's objective.
- How did you know the standard/objective was developmentally appropriate for your students?
- What action verb were students to engage in to meet the lesson objective? How were they to do this?
- After you picked your standard and objective, what did you plan next? Why?
- How are you unpacking your standards so that you teach them thoroughly?

Assessment

- Does your lesson end with some sort of data collection to show which students met the objective and to what degree? If so, what process did you choose and why?
- After you designed your lesson assessment, what did you plan next? Why?
- Did your assessment collect accurate data of student performance? How do you know?
- What new information did you learn about your students from the assessment?
- If you were to redesign the assessment, what would you change? Why?
- What will you do with the data collected? When?

Alignment

- Were the standard, objective, assessment, and activities aligned? How do you know?
- Why is it important that each portion of your lesson is aligned?
- How does alignment help students progress in their learning?
- How can you ensure your future lessons include strong alignment?

Differentiation

- Were specific students in mind when you planned this lesson? Who were they?
- What support options did you offer students to help them achieve the goal of the lesson?
- Did you offer support to high and low learners? If so, how?
- Did you offer different supports during the lesson that you didn't plan to offer? If so, what were they and why did you offer them?
- How do you know that your support options were effective?
- How could you have supported students more effectively if teaching this lesson again?
- What learning supports will students need to be successful with tomorrow's objective?
- Do you notice you tend to reuse the same learning supports for your lessons? If so, what are they? What new learning support can you offer?
- How do you support all students to answer higher-order thinking questions?
- How do you ensure you differentiate the content, process, and product as necessary for students?
- How do you accommodate student learning styles?

Release of Responsibility

- Did you follow a guided release of responsibility? How so?
- How did students take ownership of their learning throughout the lesson?
- How might you encourage more students to develop independence and comfortableness with content/skills?
- Did you experience students who were ready to try on their own and others who needed more guidance? If so, how did you respond?
- What patterns of behavior are you noticing in your students in terms of their readiness for more ownership in their learning?

Pacing

- How did you determine how long each portion of your lesson would be?
- Did you meet your planned pacing expectations? Why/why not?
- How does planning the pacing of your lesson ensure students meet the standard and objective?
- What will you do differently with pacing in future lessons?

Activities

- How did you find/create the activities used in the lesson?
- Were they effective in helping students practice the skill listed in your objective?
- Do you wish you used different activities in hindsight? If so, why?
- How could you reuse these activities in future lessons?
- What was the biggest obstacle with the lesson activities for students?
- How do you provide support to students in terms of meeting varying assignment deadlines?

Impact

- Will the uniquely designed student experience help solidify the newly learned knowledge or skills?
- Is the lesson material presented so that students do the heavy lifting in thinking and applying?
- Are students making connections without the teacher explicitly presenting them?
- Can the knowledge and skills obtained help students in other disciplines or outside the classroom?
- Will the lesson help students grow as individuals and collectives?
- How do you connect new learning to the real world?

General

- Did you use the backwards planning method to design your lesson? Why/why not?

- How did you envision the lesson unfolding? Did the reality meet your expectations?

- If you taught this lesson again, what would you do differently? Why?

- How do you ensure all the content you are presenting to students is accurate?

- How are you making your lessons memorable for students? How will you ensure students retain the essential information?

- How do you hold students accountable for meeting deadlines?

- How often do you showcase exemplars of student outcomes? Do you think this is sufficient and often enough?

- What support do you provide to your hands-on learners who are learning online?

Lesson Design Self-Survey

On a scale of 1 to 3 (1 = never, 2 = sometimes, 3 = always), rate the following statements by placing a checkmark in the appropriate column. Afterwards, review your results and choose one or two areas to improve in. Track your progress in a journal. Not only is this motivating to see your growth on paper but also it is evidence of professional learning that can be shared during your annual performance evaluation—and maybe even earn some extra brownie points!

Statement	1 Never	2 Sometimes	3 Always
I make content relevant to students by letting them know how it applies to their life.			
I succumb to the lesson plan vortex, focusing more on filling in the boxes on a lesson plan than designing an effective lesson start to finish.			
I use the backwards design method (standard, objective, assessment, activity) to ensure my lesson components are aligned.			
I put pacing markers in my lesson to keep me on schedule to finish all that is planned by the predetermined time.			
I script questions to ask students to check for understanding throughout the lesson (beginning, middle, and end).			
Student transition routes are planned, explored, and tweaked for efficiency.			

Statement	1 Never	2 Sometimes	3 Always
I map out both teacher and student actions throughout the lesson for accountability on who should be doing what by when.			
I make notes to myself about what materials are needed, how they will be organized and distributed.			
I know where to find my state standards and incorporate them into daily lessons.			
The lesson objectives I write refer to skills students must master during the lesson instead of the activity they will complete during the lesson.			
Student small groups are planned in advance with a clear skill focus, practice element, and assigned roster of students.			
Activities are engaging, rigorous, and deepen student understanding of the lesson topic.			
A formal or informal assessment is included at the end of every lesson and measures the level of student mastery of the skill taught.			
I am consistent in how I design daily lessons.			

Statement	1 Never	2 Sometimes	3 Always
I receive positive feedback from leaders on the effectiveness of my lesson design process or lesson plan.			
While teaching, I know what part of the lesson comes next without having to reference my plan.			
My students are excelling academically because of my thorough lesson design process.			
I have a deep understanding of the content I teach due to my lesson preparation habits.			

End-of-Year Student Reflection Sheet

A. Answer the questions based on your STRONGEST subject area:

Subject: _____

I am successful in this subject because _____

_____

_____

I was able to help other students perform better in this subject by _____

_____

_____

_____

Something I can try next year to help my peers is _____

_____

_____

B. Answer the questions based on your WEAKEST subject area:

Subject: _____

I struggle in this subject because _____

_____

_____

The teacher helped me in this subject by _____

_____

_____

_____

The teacher can continue to help me in this subject by _____

_____

_____

_____

Over the summer, I can become stronger in this subject by _____

_____

_____

_____

C. Share your opinion:

My favorite part about this year was _____

because _____

Three things I enjoyed about this school year are

_____

_____

_____

Other comments I want to share are:

_____

_____

_____

End-of-Year Parent Reflection Sheet

1. I would describe my child's learning experience this year to be

    _____

2. I am most proud that my child [accomplishment] this year.

    _____

3. Academic Strength:

    3a. My child was successful in [subject area] because

    _____

    3b. I was able to help my child perform better in [subject area] because

    _____

4. Academic Weakness:

    4a. My child struggled in [subject area] because

    _____

    4b. The teacher helped my child in [subject area] by

    _____

    4c. I was able to help my child perform better in [subject area] by

    _____

5. My overall opinion of this school year for my child is

    _____

Other comments I want to share:

_____

_____

Classroom Management Guiding Questions

Self-Reflection

- What is it you hope to provide for children as the teacher in their classroom?
- What are your beliefs and attitudes toward managing a classroom of students?
- What prior experience do you have managing a classroom? If it was a positive experience, what do you want to replicate? If it was a negative experience, what do you want to eliminate?
- Think back to times when you were a student yourself. What do you remember about teachers managing classrooms? What feelings does this bring up for you? How might your students react to how you manage the classroom?
- What management strategies (whether you experienced them or read about them) feel most aligned to your values and beliefs?
- What three words describe your classroom management performance as of right now?
- When did your classroom feel most in control? When did it feel least in control? What contributed to whether it went smoothly or not?
- What challenges are you struggling to find a solution for?
- How are misbehaviors addressed? Does this prevent future misbehaviors of self or others? Why/why not?
- How might you use student self-reflection to improve student behavior in your classroom?
- What themes do you notice during your most challenging and rewarding days?
- If you are unable to strengthen your classroom management performance, what might be at stake for yourself and your students?
- How are you teaching procedures to students? Does this translate to students meeting procedure expectations daily? Why/why not?
- How often are you updating routines and procedures based on student compliance? Does this reset serve as a reminder or a motivation to meet expectations?

- Are you consistently planning student and teacher actions in your lessons as a way to prevent misbehaviors during the execution of a lesson?
- What system of parent-teacher communication is used to encourage a partnership with the student, parent, and teacher? Is it working or does this need to be revised? How do you know?
- Are efficient transitions used to increase on-task time and decrease off-task time? What needs to be reworked to reach optimum efficiency?
- What challenges are you facing with classroom setup that negatively affect managing the classroom? How might you mitigate this?
- Is there a discrepancy between your in-person management style and systems and virtual classroom protocol? What adjustments could be made here to better support student learning?

Procedures and Routines

- Do you tend to use more subject-specific or common routines? Why?
- What common routines are you using in your classroom? Are they effective? Why/why not?
- What procedures do you have set up in your classroom?
- Do you believe procedures are necessary for students to be successful in the classroom? Why/why not?
- Why is it important to routine a procedure?
- What common routines would you like to see in your classroom?
- Which procedure/routine is your strongest? Why? Which procedure/routine is your weakest? Why?
- How do you develop a procedure into a routine?
- How do you create your procedures?
- How do you teach your procedures to students?
- What subject-specific procedures have you found to be helpful? Why?
- How many routines and procedures should you have in the classroom? Why?
- How did you prioritize which procedures to teach students first?

- How do you give students feedback on their ability to meet procedural expectations?

- When (and how often) are you needing to reset expectations with procedures?

- What do you do when you notice a routine is no longer necessary or is not working?

- What are the essential structures you have in your classroom?

Teacher/Student Actions

- What are common teacher/student actions used in your lessons?

- Are there moments where you the teacher or your students are left with nothing meaningful to do? If so, how might you resolve that?

- Are there moments where you the teacher or your students have too much to do in the time allotted? If so, how might you resolve that?

- Why might it be important to plan for a student action for each teacher action and vice versa?

- How do you hold yourself and students accountable for meeting the actions you planned in your lesson?

- On a scale of 1 to 10, how clear do you believe you are when giving directives? How do you know?

Student Behavior

- What are your expectations of students in terms of their behavior?

- What do you consider "acceptable" and "unacceptable" behaviors?

- How do you address misbehaviors?

- How can you redirect misbehaviors without drawing attention to the offending student?

- What reward and consequence system do you use? Why?

- How might you use reflection to improve student behavior in your classroom?

- Do you believe you mostly use reactionary or preventive classroom management systems?

- How have you built in student autonomy and independence into your classroom?

- What student leadership roles have you used?

- How do students hold each other accountable for meeting behavior expectations?
- When you notice a pattern of misbehaviors, what do you do first?
- How do you know that the behavior expectations you set are age appropriate and realistic?
- How often do you reset student behavior expectations?
- Did you set norms with students or for students? Why?
- What is your most challenging student behavior right now? Why?
- What additional support do you need to help students consistently meet behavior expectations?

Other

- How are you tracking student behavior?
- How are students tracking their own behavior?
- How are you communicating with parents about their children's behavior?
- How can you increase student time management skills?
- Are there a set of commonly asked questions that you could create a system for so that lessons move along swiftly?
- How do students access learning materials during the lesson? Is this system equitable?

Transitions

- How many transitions did you have in your lesson? On a scale of 1 to 10, how efficient were they?
- How did you teach each transition to students?
- How might students have more ownership in the transition?
- Are there any transitions that could be eliminated without having a negative effect on the lesson?
- What are the requirements of students during a transition?
- What are you doing during student transitions? Why?
- What supports can you put in place to ensure all students are successful during the transition?

- Are there any transitions that need a facelift? Why?

- Which transition is eating up a large chunk of your lesson? How might you resolve this issue?

- What transitions do you still need to plan and/or teach to your students?

- What common transitions do you use that are routine for students and make classroom management easier?

Classroom Setup

- What furniture placement keeps student misbehaviors at bay?

- What challenges are you facing with your classroom setup in terms of student behavior?

- How might you rearrange classroom furniture to prevent misbehaviors and gain additional learning time in the classroom?

- How does classroom setup help or hinder your classroom management strategies?

- Where are your student behavior hot spots in the classroom?

- Do your management strategies differ depending on where students are located in the classroom? Why/why not?

Virtual Environments

- How do you adjust when a lesson takes longer due to technical difficulties?

- What procedures/routines do you use on your virtual classroom platform?

- What are your class norms for student interactions?

- How do you encourage students to collaborate when they are virtual and may not be present online at the same time?

- What does your reward/consequence system look like online?

- Do you provide a platform tour or site map to help students successfully navigate the website?

- Do you offer a commonly asked question area for students to reference?

- How do you communicate important reminders to students?

- Do you moderate/approve all communication? Why/why not?

- How do you support student voice?

Classroom Management Self-Survey

On a scale of 1–3 (1 = never, 2 = sometimes, 3 = always), rate the following statements by placing a checkmark in the appropriate column. Afterward, review your results and choose one or two areas to improve in.

Statement	1 Never	2 Sometimes	3 Always
Students know classroom expectations and follow them.			
Classroom instruction begins and ends on time (bell to bell).			
Students know how to turn in daily assignments and follow these procedures.			
Common routines and procedures are posted in the classroom for students to reference.			
I have designed clear procedures for common classroom routines.			
I have taught students classroom procedures and remind them of them when expectations are not met.			
Students who do not follow classroom expectations receive consequences for their choices.			
Students are aware of consequences when classroom rules are not followed.			
Common classroom routines are used in the same fashion for a variety of subject areas and/or lessons.			

Statement	1 Never	2 Sometimes	3 Always
Student misbehaviors are dealt with quickly before escalating.			
Directions are clearly stated and posted for all activities to limit student confusion and questions.			
I use a timer to keep the pace of the lesson on track.			
A timer is displayed to help students self-monitor their progress during a lesson.			
Students respect the voice of others and speak one at a time.			
Students transition around the room in an orderly, efficient fashion.			
Materials are passed out and collected in an orderly, efficient fashion.			
I control the classroom environment, not student behavior.			
Students understand the purpose behind classroom routines and procedures.			
I am consistent in enforcing classroom expectations and fair in holding all students to the standard.			
Virtual classroom expectations are in place for students to be successful online.			

Statement	1 Never	2 Sometimes	3 Always
Students know how to operate in a virtual classroom (e.g., access materials, turn in assignments, and collaborate with peers).			
Separate learning areas in the classroom are labeled with specific directions and expectations per location.			
Students are aware of their responsibilities as learners and meet expectations.			
My classroom routines are simple and easy to follow.			
I know my students as people and build relationships daily.			
Students know what to do when they finish a task early and begin working without disrupting others.			
I am clear on my philosophy for managing a classroom and consistently uphold my actions to make my philosophy a reality.			
I have a formal and informal data collection system and implement it consistently.			
I can manage my classroom while differentiating for students with small-group instruction.			
Students adhere to classroom expectations while working in centers or various learning areas.			

Student Pairing Sheet

Student Name	Notes	Student Name	Notes

Partner A	Partner B	Partner A	Partner B	Partner A	Partner B

Student Engagement Guiding Questions

Self-Reflection

- What does *student engagement* mean to you?
- What does authentic engagement look like in your classroom?
- How are your students performing in terms of engagement right now? Where do you want them to be?
- What is your strength with student engagement?
- What obstacles do you face with student engagement?
- What subjects lend themselves to high engagement? Why do you think that is?
- What subjects lend themselves to low engagement? Why do you think that is?
- What next steps might help make all subjects operate at high engagement levels?

Communication and Collaboration

- How do you foster collaboration among students?
- What student behaviors signal they are present and engaged?
- How do you help students develop interpersonal and intrapersonal skills?
- How do you set and uphold expectations for how students are to engage with one another?
- How do you help students hold each other accountable to pull their own weight in a group setting?
- What supports do you provide to help all students communicate their ideas to their peers?
- When student communication and/or collaboration stops short, what do you do first? Why?
- How often are you modeling appropriate and rigorous discourse? Do you think that is happening enough in your classroom? How could you make student engagement behaviors/expectations more visible so students can learn to self-correct?

- When do you ask students to interact during the lesson and what does that look like?
- How can you best explain to students the importance and benefit of engaging with you, the content, and each other?

Activities

- What are your students' favorite engagement activities? How do you know?
- How do you incorporate relationship-building activities into the curriculum?
- What calls to action do you provide in your virtual lessons to encourage students to implement their new learning?
- How do you navigate the thin line between entertainment and engagement?
- Do students have a say in what activities, projects, or assignments they complete to showcase their learning?
- What is the shortest amount of time students remain engaged in one single activity? Why do you think that is? What is the longest amount of time students remain engaged in one single activity? Why do you think that is? How can you expand their engagement stamina?

Strategies

- What strategies do you use in your lessons to engage students?
- How effective are those strategies? How do you know?
- How often do you implement an engagement strategy during a lesson?
- How do your engagement strategies differ as you progress through a lesson (e.g., direct instruction, guided practice, independent practice)?
- How do you follow up and follow through during engagement opportunities?
- How do you motivate students to concentrate for long periods of time?
- When student interest in a lesson begins to wane, how do you help them regroup?
- What technology tools do you use to engage students during a lesson? Does it have an impact on student engagement? Does the use of technology add or take away from the learning experience?

- How do you praise or draw attention to students properly engaging with content and each other? Do you think that the way you're rewarding engagement is working? Might it be deterring or encouraging to others?
- How do you increase student participation?
- Who has strong student engagement practices that you can learn from?
- How do you pass the ownership baton to students to manage their own engagement?

Student Engagement Strategies

Engagement Strategy	Description
3–2–1	Students write down 3 facts they learned, 2 questions they still have, and 1 opinion they formulated after learning. (You can change up what the 3, 2,1 stands for if you wish!)
Find Your Match	Create pair cards with newly learned content. Students silently hold their card on their forehead and walk around the room locating their partner. Once they find their match, they must share out how they know they found their correct match.
Gallery Walk	Provide learning prompts around the room on large chart paper. Students visit the prompts and write their responses on sticky notes and leave on the chart paper before moving to the next station. After each station is visited, students remain at the last chart paper, review all answers, and share out findings.
High Five Hustle	Teacher provides a prompt. Students stand, put their hand high in the air, walk toward a partner, high five, and discuss the prompt. At the High Five! signal, students thank their partner and repeat the process with new partners. Five to seven rounds should suffice, or change up the prompt and continue with additional rounds.
Interview	Allow students to create a short list of interview questions to ask a peer as a pre-engagement activity. These questions should relate to the new content being taught and works best at the end of a unit so there's enough material to design questions around. Students then pair up, and one at a time take turns being the interviewer and recording their peer's answer. These papers can be graded or not.

Engagement Strategy	Description
Jigsaw	Students become experts on a piece of content by visiting a center in the classroom and reading information. Students at the center can collaborate as they are reading and learning. After students learn their piece of content, they come back to their group and report out. Students jot down notes from their peers so that they put the puzzle pieces of knowledge together. A discussion should follow to explain how each piece sequentially completes the whole topic. Q/A should also be available to eliminate misunderstandings and clarify confusing points.
Mini Whiteboards	Provide a quick task (e.g., math problem) and students work it out on mini whiteboards, covering their responses until the teacher says "Reveal!" By a quick scan of the whiteboards, teachers can informally assess student understanding.
Quick Write	Provide a short prompt and allow students to write without stopping for two minutes. They do not need to use punctuation or ensure grammar rules are followed. The goal is to keep their pencil moving, jotting down all related thoughts to the prompt. Think of this as a mental dump of information. Then have students pair up and share essential components to add more information to their paper. This can be referenced later when studying for end-of-unit assessments.
Snowball	Provide a prompt and students jot down their answer on a piece of paper. Students ball up the paper in their hand. When the teacher says "Let it snow!" students throw the paper to a peer who opens it and responds to that student's answer—agreeing or disagreeing. Repeat for as many rounds as applicable.

Engagement Strategy	Description
Think, Partner, Discuss	Provide a prompt. Students think about the prompt, pair up with a peer, and share their thoughts. It is important that students also respond to their peer's comments so that it is not just talking at each other.
Waterfall	Have students line up in a single line. Provide a topic or prompt, and like a waterfall, students respond quickly one right after the other without repeating a fact or response. If a student repeats a response from another student, they go to the end of the waterfall to take their turn again.
Workshop/ Centers	Create mini activities around the room and have four to five students work collaboratively at each center. Students can rotate to the other stations every 10–15 minutes. This work can be collected for informal data check or grade.

Student Engagement Self-Survey

On a scale of 1–3 (1 = never, 2 = sometimes, 3 = always), rate the following statements by placing a checkmark in the appropriate column. Afterwards, review your results and choose one or two areas to improve in.

Statement	1 Never	2 Sometimes	3 Always
Students ask and answer questions that are appropriate to the content being taught and discussed.			
Opportunities exist for students to engage with content (e.g., text) throughout the lesson.			
Opportunities exist for students to engage with each other throughout the lesson to share ideas and process new knowledge.			
Opportunities exist for students to engage with the teacher throughout the lesson to gain clarity or share ideas.			
I am intentional with which engagement strategies I use.			
Students engage rather than interact with the content.			
I facilitate learning, passing the ownership to students to lead the learning.			
Technology enhances the learning instead of being a place filler.			

Statement	1 Never	2 Sometimes	3 Always
Checks for understanding are implemented throughout the lesson to gather information on the level of student understanding.			
Engagement opportunities are simple to implement and are replicable across other subject areas.			
Students are held accountable for engaging fully throughout the lesson.			
I follow through on what I request of my students.			

Book Club Guide: Teacher

- Create reading groups of four to six students.
- Students in a group must be reading on or very near the same reading level.
- Discuss book club purpose and expectations with the class.
- Meet with each group for their first official book club meeting (one per day) to ensure they follow procedures correctly.
- Have book club groups meet within eye sight/ear shot of your guided reading group to maintain productivity.
- Check in with each group weekly to deliver praise, make announcements, reestablish expectations, and so on.
- Move students in and out of book club groupings based on their growth and performance as a reader.

Book Club Guide: Students

- Meet with your book club on your designated day.
- Sit in a circle so that everyone can see and hear one another.
- Bring all necessary materials: pencil, notebook, and book club book.
- Establish roles within the group (discussion leader, time keeper, summarizer, etc.).
- Be sure you have read the required reading for the discussion.
- Participate actively by listening to other students' comments, sharing your own comments, adding on to someone's comment, nodding in agreement, and so on.
- When your timekeeper ends the meeting, establish what the next reading assignment will be and fill out the "Student Book Club Reflection."
- Give your completed sheet to your teacher.

Book Club Reflection

Our main goal to discuss today was . . .	
Three things I learned from my peers were . . .	1. 2. 3.
Our assignment to be prepared for our next meeting is . . .	

We made good use of our time	YES NO
I listened to my group members.	☺ ☺ ☹
I shared my ideas.	☺ ☺ ☹
I was prepared with my reading.	☺ ☺ ☹
I encouraged my group members to share.	☺ ☺ ☹

Other comments for the teacher (use other side of page if needed):

_____

_____

Student Choice and Ownership Guiding Questions

Choice

- What type of choice options do you provide students?

- Do you know your students' interests/preferences? If not, what can you do to get to know them better? If yes, which ones do you implement most and why?

- Are students able to choose where to sit to learn (e.g., flexible seating) or how they can learn (e.g., manipulatives or choice boards)? If not, how might you incorporate this? If yes, how is it going and what support do you need?

- How can PBL (project-based learning) enhance choice in your classroom? What subject(s) lends itself more easily than others?

- Would students feel like they have a sense of autonomy learning in your classroom? Why/why not?

- When you use choice options for learning are they aligned to the standards? Rigorous in application? Demonstrate learning?

- Are there a variety of ways in which students can communicate with you (verbal, written, technology, etc.)? How can you expand these options?

Ownership

- What are some ownership opportunities you can think of to pass off to students right away?

- Have you cocreated norms with students for areas of your classroom or certain subjects? If not, what might this look like for you? If yes, how is it going?

- How are students collecting their own data and reflecting on the results? What support do you need for this practice to be more consistent and/or effective?

- How might you facilitate more learning instead of direct it?

- Are students able to be part of the decision-making process in your classroom? If not, how might you begin to do this? If yes, what positive/negative effects have you seen because of this?

Other

- What do you need to do with the culture of the classroom before rolling out more student choice and ownership?

- Are students ready and looking forward to having more choice and ownership in the classroom?

- Are your colleagues already implementing effective ideas for more choice and ownership? If so, how might you collaborate with them to implement those ideas in your own classroom?

- What are your own experiences with choice and ownership as a student? How does this play into your role as a teacher now?

- How might you communicate with parents to inform them of potential changes in the classroom and how their child is adjusting to the changes?

- What other preparation might you need before rolling out choice and ownership options to students?

- If students respond negatively or cannot handle additional choice and ownership options, how might you scale back? When would you try again?

Student Choice and Ownership Self-Survey

On a scale of 1–3 (1 = never, 2 = sometimes, 3 = always), rate the following statements by placing a checkmark in the appropriate column. Afterwards, review your results and choose one or two areas to improve in.

Statement	1 Never	2 Sometimes	3 Always
I direct learning for 30% or less of the lesson.			
I facilitate learning for 70% or more of the lesson.			
I provide choice on assignment completion.			
Students lead their own learning where and when appropriate.			
I know my students' likes and/or interests.			
Students receive the right amount of choice options to avoid overwhelm or disinterest.			
Students have a sense of autonomy in the classroom.			
Choice options are in alignment with lesson standards and objectives.			
Choice options are rigorous where students have to think and work at high levels.			
Choice options enable students to demonstrate their content and skill proficiency.			

Teacher Success Execution Plan Template

1. On a scale of 1 (ineffective) to 10 (masterful), rate your consistent performance in the following four brick categories:

   a. Lesson Design 1 2 3 4 5 6 7 8 9 10

   b. Classroom Management 1 2 3 4 5 6 7 8 9 10

   c. Student Engagement 1 2 3 4 5 6 7 8 9 10

   d. Student Ownership and Choice 1 2 3 4 5 6 7 8 9 10

2. Prioritize your area of focus by reviewing your ratings. Find the lowest level brick category (not rating) where you did not score an 8 or above. This is your area of focus. (Example: If you score a 6 in Lesson Design and a 2 in Classroom Management, you would still prioritize Lesson Design even though it has a higher score because the category requires foundational mastery before moving on.)

   a. If you score an 8 or above, consider yourself proficient enough to move on to the next category to master.

   b. Rerate yourself monthly to determine if you can move on to the next category to master.

3. Reread the corresponding chapter of your area of focus brick category. Jot notes down for aspects of that category that you are not consistently implementing. Do not try to create your action steps yet, just collect ideas.

4. Organize your notes by joining together similar ideas that would be easy to implement at the same time (e.g., If my area of focus was Lesson Design, I could plan to implement similar ideas like "reread standard course of study" and "practice writing daily objectives").

5. Sequence your ideas into a checklist of actions:

   a. Task = simple actions you can take to implement missing aspects of your instruction.

   b. Time frame = when will you start? Space out your action steps to give you plenty of time to build a new habit. Some tasks are easier to implement and master (e.g., collecting informal data during a lesson), where others are nuanced and require ongoing practice and feedback (e.g., writing check for understanding questions into lesson plans).

    c.   Details of Implementation = How will you do this? As if you are writing a lesson plan for a substitute teacher to follow, write a very detailed execution.

    d.   Reflection Notes = How are things going? Jot down your ahas and progress. This will help you notice patterns in your learning or behavior, as well as track your growth and implementation (a great artifact for your performance review with your principal!).

6.   Update the checklist with notes of progress. This can be submitted to your administrator as proof that you are a professional learner, tracking your growth and adjusting instruction as needed.

7.   Continue the checklist as you grow through the performance bricks categories 1–4.

8.   Encourage a colleague to join you in the learning journey. You can plan together, meet monthly to discuss progress, and problem-solve obstacles. This will provide you with an accountability partner so that your growth goes from an idea to action.

9.   Share this book and your personal growth story with colleagues and encourage them to complete the same process for themselves so that all teachers are growing to their potential for the benefit of their students.

Next Steps Log

Task	Time Frame	Details of Implementation	Reflection Notes

Teacher Success Learning Inventory Questionnaire

- What are current best instructional practices? Are you using these on a daily basis? Why/why not?
- What are you capable of doing in the classroom (instructional strategies) in comparison to what you are expected to be able to do? (Reference your district or school performance rubric.)
- What is the latest research stating educators should be doing in the classroom by subject area? Are you currently doing this? Why/why not?
- What sounds interesting that you want to learn more about?
- What are you passionate about and want to become an expert in?
- How do students, parents, or colleagues describe your teaching ability?
- What themes or commonalities come up in feedback from administrators about your teaching?

For Reflection

- What teaching skills are your strengths? Why is this?
- What teaching strategies do you want to acquire and why?
- Is teaching what you envisioned it to be when you started? Why/why not?
- What do you fear the most about achieving goals/reaching expectations? Why?
- What additional support do you need?
- What exciting things are happening in your classroom?
- How do you plan to be more intentional with your instruction? How can I hold you accountable in that area?
- Is there an area of your instruction (that's in your control) that it would be helpful to implement a strategic plan for?
- Is there a barrier that keeps you from putting your learning into action?
- What kinds of data do you use to make decisions about your past, current, and future lessons?
- Where are you in your teaching proficiency compared to where you want to be?

Professional Development Log

Date	Topic	Hours	Credit (Y/N)

New Learning Implementation Plan

New Learning	Plan of Action	Deadline	Notes

PLC Agenda Example

- [ ] Greeting
- [ ] Wins of the Week
- [ ] Opening Announcements
- [ ] Review Group Norms
  - [ ] All Members Acknowledge and Agree
  - [ ] Add/Delete norms (if needed)
- [ ] Review of Agenda
  - [ ] Outlined at last meeting
  - [ ] Add/Delete items
- [ ] Data Dig
  - [ ] Share data pieces (student work, score rosters, etc.)
  - [ ] Discuss trends
  - [ ] Problem-solve areas for improvement
- [ ] Lesson Plan
  - [ ] Review district calendar for upcoming important dates
  - [ ] Review school calendar for upcoming events
  - [ ] Review quarterly plan and assessment
  - [ ] Make necessary adjustments to get all team members on track
  - [ ] Write weekly lesson plan outline
  - [ ] Ensure alignment (quarterly assessment → lesson assessment → lesson objective → lesson activities)
- [ ] Update PLC Notes
  - [ ] Add details for today's meeting
  - [ ] Script plan for next meeting
  - [ ] Agree upon what data pieces to bring to next meeting
  - [ ] Email or save notes for admin
- [ ] Closing Announcements
- [ ] Group Cheer/Chant/Encouragement

PLC Meeting Minutes Template

Date:	Team Members Present:
Grade Level:	
Subject Area:	

Meeting Goal:

Agenda:

Notes:

Next Meeting Date:

Next Meeting Time:

Next Meeting Location:

Items to Bring to Next Meeting:

Next Steps:

Person(s) Responsible:

PLC Guiding Questions

Data Dig

Student Work Samples

- What stands out about the sample? Why?
- Is the sample a high, medium, or low performer? How do you know?
- Is the sample indicative of other student performers or is it an outlier?
- Where does the sample fall in alignment with the (1) standards, (2) course of study/pacing guide, (3) end-of-unit assessment, and (4) prior and post assignments?
- What does the sample tell us about the type of follow-up support this student needs? How do you know?

Student Grades

- What trends do you see in the grade data? Why might this be?
- Does the data support that students are on or off track for meeting grade-level expectations?
- Are there any concerning outliers? Why? How can we support these students?
- What communication needs to occur with parents?
- Are there any upcoming assessments or projects that could contribute to this data trend positively or negatively? What plan of action is necessary in the moment?

Lesson Planning

- What standards, objectives, and topics need to be addressed this quarter, month, or week?
- What does the instructional pacing look like on a calendar? Is this realistic and doable? If not, whom do we need to contact for help?
- Are students ready for upcoming lessons? If so, how can we extend learning? If not, how can we support prior learning?

- What does the end-of-unit assessment look like? How can we design lessons that set students up for success?
- Are the standards aligned to grade-level requirements? Are daily lesson objectives aligned to standards? Are daily lesson assessments aligned to standards and objectives? Are daily lesson activities aligned to objectives and standards? If not, what tweaks need to be made?

PLC Data Chat Guide

Use the following question prompts to successfully lead a PLC discussion on student achievement by referencing data.

Protocol

1. Each teacher should have a data set in front of them.
2. Ask the question prompt.
3. Allow each teacher to review their own data set.
4. Open the discussion to the group.
5. Allow teachers to reflect/take notes before moving on.

OVERVIEW: Question Prompts

Look at the data from a bird's-eye view and answer the following questions.

1. What outliers do you notice? (e.g., nonclustered data points: high or low)
   - Are the data points positive or negative outliers?
   - Why might these data points have landed where they did?
   - Was there an instruction focus contribution?
   - Was there a student characteristic contribution?
   - Was there an outside factor contribution?
   - How might we target the negative outliers for better support?
   - How might we leverage positive outliers to support the growth of other students?
2. What trends do you notice?
   - What commonalities or patterns among data points do you notice?
   - Why might there be clusters of data points at certain performance levels?
   - Are these trends positive or negative?
   - What type of support might be most beneficial for each trend?

3. Are there any data points that initially shocked you? Why/why not?
4. What data points are worth celebrating? Why?
5. What does the data NOT tell us?

Notes

_____

_____

_____

_____

_____

Hone In: Question Prompts

Look at a subset of data to dive deep into discussion:

1. Why did you prioritize this subset of data?
2. What initial questions do you have?
3. How might digging deeper in this subset increase data points as a whole?
4. What students are/aren't showing mastery here?
5. What teaching strategies or interventions proved impactful on student performance?
6. What enrichment is needed and where? Why?
7. What reteaching support is needed and where? Why?
8. Is growth present even if proficiency is not yet met? If so, how can we expedite the growth?
9. Is the subset data consistent with classroom performance or other data sets?
10. How does each teacher's data subset compare to the grade level/subject area, school, or district as a whole?
11. What might have positively and negatively contributed to this subset of data?
12. What conclusions can you make based on the data discussion?

Notes

_____

_____

_____

APPENDIX 2: USING THIS BOOK TO MENTOR OTHERS

- Start by showing an image of the Teacher Success Pathway while sharing the philosophy of the sequence. This allows future and new teachers to thoroughly understand why the sequence matters and can continue to hone their craft even when not under your tutelage.

- Choose the chapters or sections that fit your instructional focus for mentorship and coaching. Each teacher will have unique needs, so allow their performance to dictate the plan.

- Design professional development exercises in which the skill is introduced followed by time to practice for effective implementation. You'll want to watch teachers execute these skills multiple times in practice and in real time in front of students. This will help you get a sense for how effective and consistent the implementation is for each particular skill.

- A book study is a great way to enable new and future teachers time to read and process their learning before coming together to discuss how to implement the skill into their teaching.

- Think about how these teachers can see a live demonstration of the skills being discussed, like a modeled example or going on a learning walk to see other teachers in the building implementing the skill live in front of students. When new and future teachers can see a skill showcased by multiple skillful teachers with different styles, they can begin to envision how they might execute the skill in a way that fits their personality and teaching style as well.

Book Study Questions

Part One | The Beginning, the Pathway, and the Formula

Prologue: Where It All Began

- What resonated with you most about my story? How is our teacher journey similar? Different?
- What lessons did I learn in order to be an effective teacher?

Introduction: The Teacher Success Pathway

- Why is teaching an intricate mental and physical dance?
- Why might the rules of teaching change every few years?
- What changes have you personally seen in the field? How has this affected your practice as an educator?
- How can teaching trends help and hinder your growth as an educator?
- What experience level do you consider yourself? How might that change your approach to reading and learning the principles covered in this book?
- What do the terms *teacher proficiency* and *student learning outcomes* mean to you and your school?
- How are teacher proficiency and student outcomes related? Why is this relationship important to understand?
- What is the difference between new and future teachers being underprepared versus under-supported?
- Why might how you read this book affect how effective you apply what you learn?

Chapter 1: The Formula

- How can you become a great teacher more quickly?
- What similarities and/or differences do you have as an educator in comparison to the experiences described in the Lessons from the Trenches?

- How does knowing this story shape your understanding of the purpose/contents of the book?

- Why might a "bag of tricks" not be as helpful as intended?

- What does a kindergarten teacher and high school chemistry teacher have in common?

- How does Maslow's hierarchy of needs relate to how teachers should learn and grow their teaching practice?

- Explain the Teacher Success Pathway and the importance of its sequence.

- Who else do you know who should read this book (colleagues, friends, family)? Why?

- When components of your career change, why would reading this book (or sections of the book) again be helpful?

- What changes do you expect to see in your classroom after reading this book?

- What challenges do you expect to encounter?

Part Two | Brick 1: Lesson Design

Chapter 2: Obstacles to Lesson Design

- What are the four major obstacles teachers face to planning effective lessons? Why?

- Describe the lesson plan vortex.

- What obstacles are you facing when it comes to designing lessons? What support would be helpful in overcoming that obstacle?

- How did my painfully embarrassing objective writing lesson exemplify the need to build better planning habits as a teacher? What could have been the outcome if this habit continued?

Chapter 3: Lesson Design Phase Overview

- What is the first foundational brick in the Teacher Success Pathway? Why might this be?

- What is the difference between lesson planning and lesson design?

- Compare and contrast these two lesson plan aspects: value and meaning.
- How might backwards design increase a teacher's effectiveness? Why?
- Explain this statement: "How we plan matters more than what we're planning."
- Can you see your team planning during a quarterly planning day? Why/why not?
- How does gradual release improve teacher effectiveness in their daily lessons?
- If the flow of a lesson were to be shown in a visual of a triangle divided horizontally into three sections, what would you name the three sections? Why is their order relevant to the shape of the triangle?

Chapter 4: Effective Design

- Why are understanding the needs, wants, and interests of students helpful in designing a lesson?
- What are the six aspects of design in the lesson creation process?
- What is the benefit of pacing your lesson ahead of time?
- What are the three types of checks for understanding questions? Why should teachers script them into their lessons?
- If a teacher doesn't preplan transitions in the classroom, what happens as a result? What is the impact of that result?
- Why should teachers think about teacher and student actions throughout the entire lesson?
- How does accounting for material distribution in a lesson save time during the execution phase?
- What does *differentiation* mean to you? How can teachers get on the same page as to what it means and how to implement it in their lessons?
- What does "Teaching is 10% being on stage and 90% planning" mean to you?
- If a teacher has not planned well, what happens during the lesson? Why?

Chapter 5: Getting Started with Lesson Design

- How can all teachers be successful lesson plan designers when their state, district, or school require different planning templates?

- Why should teachers begin designing lessons with the standard? What happens when they don't? Why?

- How can teachers become stronger in writing lesson objectives related to the standard while also ensuring it is manageable to be taught in a single lesson?

- Why should teachers design formal or informal assessments before flushing out a lesson?

- How is planning on paper versus digitally similar and different? Which do you prefer? Why?

Chapter 6: Mastering Lesson Design, Part 1

- What are *core moves*? What core moves do you use yourself?

- How were the example boxes provided in the book helpful in your learning of how to design a thorough, effective lesson?

- Task sharing is a popular way to divide the workload among teachers. What are the benefits? Drawbacks?

- What is important to remember about a lesson's objective, standard, and assessment? Why?

Chapter 7: Mastering Lesson Design, Part 2

- Review the two example lesson plans. What do you notice? What can you apply to your lesson design process after seeing it outlined in the plan?

- How do you plan to use the Lesson Design Guiding Questions? Why is it helpful to reference them?

- What changes will you make to how you currently design lessons?

- Discuss the common lesson design scenario and share your answers from the follow-up question.

- What did you learn about yourself after filling out the Lesson Design Self-Survey? What do you plan to do next with the information you learned?

- What comparisons were you able to make between your planning process and how the Lesson Design chapters describe the process?

Part Three | Brick 2: Classroom Management

Chapter 8: Understanding Classroom Management

- Why is clarity so important when managing a classroom?
- What is the difference between *behavior management* and *classroom management*?
- What are the three Rs of classroom management? Why are these important?
- Do you believe you can control other people? Why/why not?
- How would you define *influence* in terms of classroom management?
- What do authors Jason E. Harlacher and Sarah A. Whitcomb say the three characteristics are that teachers should develop as part of their classroom management strategy? Why are these three the most important?
- Why does classroom management afford students a richer learning experience?

Chapter 9: Getting Started with Classroom Management

- What are the five common aspects of instruction to manage? What would happen if one aspect was not managed well?
- Why should teachers avoid over-teaching their management systems to students?
- Describe how automaticity in classroom management will positively affect student learning.
- Finish this sentence: "The key to effective classroom management is _____." Why might this be true?

Chapter 10: Addressing Misbehaviors

- Why do misbehaviors provide a clue into a student's well-being?
- Name the five ways to address student misbehaviors. Which one is most challenging for you?
- How did the visualization technique help you create a more effective and supportive plan in overcoming misbehaviors in the classroom?

Chapter 11: Mastering Classroom Management

- How does delivering engaging content to students relate to classroom management?

- If a teacher struggles in classroom management, should they build in numerous opportunities for student discourse and interaction into their lesson? Why/why not?

- Is a well-run classroom one that is orderly and quiet? Explain.

- How might differentiating instruction for your students add difficulty to effectively managing a classroom?

- Are classroom management strategies that are used live with students different than those used for virtual instruction? Give an example.

- Has learning about this brick changed any of your beliefs?

Part Four | Brick 3: Student Engagement

Chapter 12: Understanding Student Engagement

- Why might it be advantageous to layer engagement opportunities in a lesson taking student thinking from what is obvious to making an inference?

- Compare and contrast a classroom with high student engagement to low student engagement. What does it look like, sound like, and feel like?

- Complete this statement: "We cannot force students to learn, but we can create the conditions in which they _____ to learn." How can we do this?

- Explain the analogy about riding a bike in relation to student engagement.

- What is the difference among the three types of student engagement: behavioral, emotional, and cognitive?

- How does student engagement foster learning?

- How does equity play into the equation when it comes to planning and executing engagement strategies in the classroom?

- Complete this sentence: "Results from a recent study on student engagement stated that high engagement decreases _____ in the classroom leading to increased time on _____ and better overall student _____." Why might this be?

Chapter 13: Getting Started with Student Engagement

- What does "You don't need flair and fireworks to make a lesson engaging" mean to you?
- How can social media affect a teacher's perception of expected student engagement in the classroom?
- Why is engagement a three-pronged approach?
- What is the difference between interaction and engagement? And which do we want to see more of? Why?
- How does a Check for Understanding (CFU) affect student engagement?
- Why does executing wait time during a lesson increase student engagement?
- What part of a lesson should students be most engaged in?
- How do student pairings affect student engagement?

Chapter 14: Mastering Student Engagement

- What does this quote mean? "You control the pace, momentum, and the flow."
- What are the five ways to strengthen student engagement opportunities?
- How can teachers use student engagement as an informal or formal assessment?
- What is your favorite engagement strategy? Why?
- How does student engagement differ in a live classroom of students versus a virtual one?
- What is one way you can see your classroom engagement strategies changing after completing this brick?

Part Five | Brick 4: Student Choice and Ownership

Chapter 15: Understanding Student Choice and Ownership

- Explain the difference between directing learning and facilitating it. Which are you currently doing more of in your classroom?
- What does student choice look like? How do the four considerations help teachers build choice into the classroom?

- Why is ownership important in a classroom?
- How do you define autonomy? Why is it important for students to experience autonomy?

Chapter 16: Getting Started with Student Choice and Ownership

- What are the benefits of choice and ownership in the classroom?
- Why do alignment, rigor, and demonstration of proficiency help teachers incorporate choice successfully?
- Choose two to three examples of student choice from the chapter to discuss the impact those assignments could have on a class of students.
- How do rubrics help students meet (and exceed) expectations for assignments?

Chapter 17: Mastering Student Choice and Ownership

- In the four areas to master student ownership and choice (communication, decision-making, environment, equity and equality), which one is the most challenging to implement? Why?
- Why should students be able to select their own books for reading practice and/or assignments?
- There are ways to push student choice and ownership to new heights in the classroom (e.g., cocreate norms, data collection and reflection, flexible seating, peer evaluations, project-based learning). Which one could have the biggest impact on student learning? Why?
- What might happen if teachers do not successfully incorporate student choice and ownership into their classrooms?
- What can you add or take away from your instruction to enhance student choice and ownership?
- If you have already made changes in your classroom, what have you noticed? Have the changes in student choice and ownership made an impact? In what ways?

Part Six | Implementing Your New Learning

Chapter 18: Teacher Success Next Steps

- How are the Teacher Success bricks linear but also interwoven? Give an example.

- Why should teachers constantly improve their instructional approaches in the classroom? What would happen if they decided to stop being a learner themselves?

- Outline your next steps that include time stamps to hold you accountable for when you will complete, as well as any stakeholders you'll need to partner with to accomplish the step.

Chapter 19: Ongoing Learning

- How did this book and book study enable you to engage in ongoing learning?

- How did this experience empower you to engage in a future ongoing learning opportunity?

- Why might ongoing learning produce powerful change?

- What are professional habits you are interested in developing? Why?

- What did you learn after completing your learning inventory?

- After reviewing ongoing learning opportunities, which two would be easiest to implement for you?

- What ongoing learning opportunities would you add to the list?

- How do you plan to track your learning? Why might this be important?

- How can you share what you are learning with your colleagues to aid in their growth as well?

REFERENCES

Blair, Anne, and Denise Johnson. 2003. "The Importance and Use of Student Self-Selected Literature to Reading Engagement in an Elementary Reading Curriculum." *Reading Horizons: A Journal of Literacy and Language Arts* 43, no. 3 (February): 181–202. https://scholarworks.wmich.edu/reading_horizons/vol43/iss3/3.

Boggiano, Ann K., Ann Shields, Marty Barrett, Teddy Kellam, Erik Thompson, Jeffrey Simons, and Phyllis Katz. 1992. "Helplessness Deficits in Students: The Role of Motivational Orientation." *Motivation and Emotion* 16: 271–296. https://doi.org/10.1007/BF00991655.

Bowen, Ryan S. 2017. "Understanding by Design." Vanderbilt University Center for Teaching. https://cft.vanderbilt.edu/understanding-by-design/.

Brandwein, Sharon. 2021. "10 Thoughtfully Illustrated Children's Picture Books That Celebrate Diversity." *Forbes* (September 28). https://www.forbes.com/sites/forbes-personal-shopper/2021/09/28/multicultural-childrens-books/?sh=3d9ba838602e.

Briggs, Leslie J., Kent L. Gustafson, and Murray Tillman. 1991. *Instructional Design: Principles and Applications.* 2nd ed. Englewood Cliffs, NJ: Educational Technology Publications.

Brooks, Douglas M. 1985. "The First Day of School." *Educational Leadership* 42, no. 8 (May): 76–78. Accessible in *Jump Start for Success.* Department of Professional Learning, Washoe County School District. https://www.washoeschools.net/cms/lib/NV01912265/Centricity/Domain/189/Jumpstart%20Booklet.pdf, pp. 5–6.

Carey, Jenna, Howard Cameron, and Rebecca Leftwich. 2013. "Improving Elementary Students' Engagement During Independent Reading Through Teacher Conferencing, Teacher Modeling, and Student Choice." Saint Xavier University Action Research Project. https://files.eric.ed.gov/fulltext/ED541338.pdf.

Clear, James. 2018. *Atomic Habits: An Easy & Proven Way to Build Good Habits & Break Bad Ones*. New York: Penguin Random House.

Clear, James. n.d. "How Long Does it Actually Take to Form a New Habit?" https://jamesclear.com/new-habit.

CLI. n.d. "Classroom Culture." Children's Literacy Initiative. Accessed September 20, 2023. https://learn.cli.org/best-practices/classroom-culture-and-environment/culture.

Coetzee, Susan A., E. J. Van Niekerk, John L. Wydeman, and Sello P. Mokoena. 2008. *An Educator's Guide to Effective Classroom Management*. Pretoria: Van Schaik Publishers. http://ndl.ethernet.edu.et/bitstream/123456789/36053/1/164.SA%20Coetzee%2CEJ%20van%20Niekerk.pdf.

Core Standards. n.d. "English Language Arts Standards » Reading: Literature » Grade 3." Common Core State Standards Initiative. Accessed September 27, 2023. https://www.thecorestandards.org/ELA-Literacy/RL/3/#CCSS.ELA-Literacy.RL.3.2.

Danielson, Charlotte. 1996. *Enhancing Professional Practice: A Framework for Teaching*. Alexandria, VA: Association for Supervision and Curriculum Development. See also https://www.andrews.edu/~rjo/Artifacts/Danielson%27s%20Framework%20for%20Professional%20Practice%20web.pdf.

Danielson, Charlotte. 2013. *The Framework for Teaching Evaluation Instrument, 2013 Edition: The Newest Rubric Enhancing the Links to the Common Core State Standards, with Clarity of Language for Ease of Use and Scoring*. Self-published.

Doyle, Walter. 1980. *Classroom Management*. West Lafayette, IN: Kappa Delta Pi. https://files.eric.ed.gov/fulltext/ED206567.pdf.

Franklin, Hayley, and Ingrid Harrington. 2019. "A Review into Effective Classroom Management and Strategies for Student Engagement: Teacher and Student Roles in Today's Classrooms." *Journal of Education and Training Studies* 7, no 12 (December). https://doi.org/10.11114/jets.v7i12.4491.

Garrett, Tracey. 2014. *Effective Classroom Management: The Essentials*. New York: Teachers College Press.

Glossary of Education Reform. 2014. "Rigor." Great Schools Partnership. Last updated December 29, 2014. https://www.edglossary.org/rigor/.

Harlacher, Jason E., and Sara A. Whitcomb. 2022. *Bolstering Student Resilience: Creating a Classroom with Consistency, Connection, and Compassion*. Bloomington, IN: Marzano Resources. Free reproducibles from https://www.marzanoresources.com/reproducibles/bolstering-student-resilience.

Kagan Structures. 2023. "About Kagan Publishing & Professional Development." Accessed September 27, 2023. https://www.kaganonline.com/about_us.php.

Keams, Geri. 1997. *Grandmother Spider Brings the Sun*. New York: Cooper Square.

Kohn, Alfie. 1993. "Choices for Children: Why and How to Let Students Decide." *Phi Delta Kappan* (September). https://www.alfiekohn.org/article/choices-children/.

Kragler, Sherry, and Christine Nolley. 1996. "Student Choices: Book Selection Strategies of Fourth Graders." *Reading Horizons: A Journal of Literacy and Language Arts* 36, no. 4 (April 1): article 5. https://scholarworks.wmich.edu/cgi/viewcontent.cgi?article=1323&context=reading_horizons.

Kuninsky, Jack. 2022. "Why Are Teachers Struggling Executing the Lesson That They Planned?" Facebook (October 11).

Learning A–Z. n.d. "Effective Lesson Plans: The Backwards Design Way." Accessed September 27, 2023. https://www.learninga-z.com/site/resources/breakroom-blog/effective-lesson-plans.

Levin, James, and James Nolan. 2007. *Principles of Classroom Management: A Professional Decision-Making Model*. New York: Pearson Education.

LINCS. n.d. "TEAL Center Fact Sheet No. 8: Effective Lesson Planning." Literacy Information and Communication System. Accessed September 27, 2023. https://lincs.ed.gov/state-resources/federal-initiatives/teal/guide/lessonplanning.

Maden, Jack. 2021. "Socratic Method: What Is It and How Can You Use It?" Philosophy Break. https://philosophybreak.com/articles/socratic-method-what-is-it-how-can-you-use-it/.

Merrett, Frank, and Kevin Wheldall. 1990. *Positive Teaching in the Primary School*. London: Paul Chapman Publishing.

Milkova, Stiliana. n.d. "Strategies for Effective Lesson Planning." Center for Research on Learning and Teaching. Accessed September 27, 2023. https://venktesh22.github.io/Strategies_for_Effective_Lesson_Planning.pdf.

Nyong'o, Lupita. 2019. *Sulwe*. New York: Simon & Schuster Books for Young Readers.

Olsen, Shannon. 2020. *Our Class Is a Family*. Self-published.

Olson, Willard. 1959. *Child Development*. Boston: D. C. Heath & Co.

P., Amy. 2002. "Years Ago, a Conversation with a Quieter Student Convinced Me to Change 'Class Participation' to 'Class Engagement.'" *Edutopia*. Instagram (November 8). https://www.instagram.com/p/CkuLtY1O1uA/?igshid=OTU1ZGJIYWQ%3D.

Pignatiello, G. A., R. J. Martin, and R. L. Hickman Jr. 2020. "Decision Fatigue: A Conceptual Analysis." *Journal of Health Psychology* 25, no. 1: 123–35.

Pronto. n.d. "Student Attention Span and How to Capture and Maintain It." Accessed September 27, 2023. https://pronto.io/student-attention-span-capture-maintain/.

Rablin, Tyler. 2023. Instagram post by *Edutopia* (May 30). https://x.com/Mr_Rablin/status/1663704053904461824?s=20.

Randall, Craig. 2020. *Trust-Based Observations: Maximizing Teaching and Learning Growth*. Lanham, MD: Rowman & Littlefield.

Riggs, Ernestine G., and Cheryl R. Gholar. 2009. *Strategies That Promote Student Engagement: Unleashing the Desire to Learn*. 2nd ed. Thousand Oaks, CA: Corwin Press.

Rutherford, Mike. 2009. "7 Tools for Developing Teachers and Teaching." Waxhaw, NC: Rutherford Learning Group. http://www.rutherfordlg.com/new/wp/wp-content/uploads/2014/04/7toolsfordevelopingteachersandteaching.pdf.

Sieberer-Nagler, Katharina. 2015. "Effective Classroom-Management & Positive Teaching." *English Language Teaching* 9, no. 1 (December 14). http://dx.doi.org/10.5539/elt.v9n1p163.

Singer, Emma. 2021. "18 Children's Books with Moral Lessons to Raise Empathetic Kids." PureWow (October 25). https://www.purewow.com/family/childrens-books-with-moral-lessons.

Skowron, Janice. 2006. *Powerful Lesson Planning Models: The Art of 1,000 Decisions*. Thousand Oaks, CA: Corwin. https://us.sagepub.com/sites/default/files/upm-assets/9325_book_item_9325.pdf.

Sullivan, Roisin. n.d. "Why Is It Usually the Boys Getting into Trouble at School?" https://thekidscoach.tv/2019/01/16/why-is-it-always-the-noys-getting-into-trouble-at-school/.

Tanner, Kimberly D. 2017. "Structure Matters: Twenty-One Teaching Strategies to Promote Student Engagement and Cultivate Classroom Equity." *CBE-Life Sciences Education* 12, no. 3 (October 13). https://doi.org/10.1187/cbe.13-06-0115.

Theesfeld, Sarah. 2021. "Effectives of Student Choice on Student Motivation and Engagement within an Elementary Classroom." Minnesota State University Moorehead Graduate Studies Dissertations, Theses, and Projects. https://red.mnstate.edu/thesis/500.

Thomas, Doug, Walter Enloe, and Ronald Newell. 2005. *"The Coolest School in America": How Small Learning Communities are Changing Everything*. Lanham, MD: Scarecrow Education.

Ullman, Ellen. 2011. "How to Plan Effective Lessons." *ASCD Publications* 53, no. 10. https://www.ascd.org/el/articles/how-to-plan-effective-lessons.

Unangst, Gabby. 2021. "Passive Learning vs. Active Learning." ASU Prep Digital (April 15). https://www.asuprepdigital.org/student_blog/passive-learning-vs-active-learning/.

Wilson, Greg. 2019. "Ten Quick Tips for Creating an Effective Lesson." *PLoS Computational Biology* (April 11). https://doi.org/10.1371/journal.pcbi.1006915.

Wong, Harry K., and Rosemary T. Wong. 2009. *The First Days of School: How to Be an Effective Teacher*. Mountain View, CA: Harry K. Wong Publications. www.EffectiveTeaching.com.

ACKNOWLEDGMENTS

Writing a book is therapeutic for me. I transport in time back to previous versions of myself, honing in on lessons learned from my unofficial mentors. It wouldn't feel right to publish these lessons without giving acknowledgment where it is due—to the people who helped me grow and transform into my potential. Without you, this book would be full of empty pages.

My husband, Adam, you've allowed me to dream big and take risks all while you took on the burden of provider for the beautiful family we created. Marrying you was (and still is) the best decision I ever made. I love you.

Mom and Dad, you both play pivotal roles in raising me to be who I am today. Dad, you always break out the "you are special today" red plate for the small and big moments in my life. You're my biggest fan and provide specific and detailed feedback that lets me know just how close you pay attention to me and my work in this world. Mom, you're a selfless leader who helps me navigate being the best mom I can be while chasing my dreams. Thank you for always being a phone call away!

My kiddos, Lily, Avery, and Elijah, thank you for choosing me to be your mom. I know writing this book took me away from you for a bit, but because of your sacrifice other teachers and leaders are going to be able to help lots of children in their schools become the best version of themselves. I want you to watch Mama dream big, take risks, and rely on a support system to leave an imprint in this world. You, too, will go on to do the same, and I will be right alongside you cheering you on. I love you all the mostest!

My former principals, Turner and Henderson, you spotted my teaching and leadership talent quickly and supported my growth in those areas. Turner, you reminded me of my value and the impact of my contribution, not just at Berewick Elementary but also in every role I would have in education. "The good ones never stay," you smirked at me. You knew in my first year of teaching I would spread my wings to help even more teachers and students. Henderson, shadowing you for a day unlocked a new path of leadership for me with instructional coaching. I learned leading as an administrator was too far removed from the classroom where I wanted to be with students and teachers. Thank you for our candid conversations and for providing opportunities for me to lead around campus to develop my craft. Both of these principals saw my potential and encouraged me to become what I desired.

The New Teacher Project (TNTP), I absolutely loved my time at TEACH Charlotte serving new teachers K–12 in our large, urban district. I made mistakes, I had moments of triumph, and I fell in love with coaching. I grew not only as a person but as an instructional coach, PD presenter, and collaborative colleague. I treasure that chapter of my life that enabled me to gain the perspective to write this book.

Linda (Schultz), you're my forever mentor. I did not know that when I met you at Berewick Elementary that I would carry you with me to every role I would have afterwards. You've become a trustworthy friend, knowledgeable mentor, and my favorite colleague to work with. You listen empathetically, connect me with relevant resources, are honest and transparent, and never hold back on showcasing your personality. I have so much yet to learn from you.

Nicole, we have been through it all, haven't we? Virtual besties taking the education world by storm! Voxer and the Simply Instructional Coaching Summit has solidified us as friends and colleagues for life. Thanks for listening to my dreams and goals, checking in on my progress, and shouting me out for my accomplishments. You're a dear friend, business buddy, and coaching colleague. I couldn't do this without you!

The team at Wiley, a department of Jossey-Bass, thank you for believing in my stories and strategies shared here in this book. I will never forget the day you reached out offering to partner together. We went through some iterations until we got it just right, but you never wavered in your belief that educators needed this book and that they needed to hear it from me. You instilled confidence in me all while holding my hand growing as an author.

To all my former students and teachers I have supported over the years, please know you are the biggest piece to this puzzle. You have challenged me to problem-solve differently, critically think without emotion, be flexible in the face of technology and bad weather, and develop skills I didn't even know I needed to lead well. Thank you for extending grace to me through my missteps as I grew into who I am today. This book is for you and because of you. May you all continue to grow into who you were meant to become, knowing I am rooting for you, reminding you that you are capable of more than you know. Go get 'em!

ABOUT THE AUTHOR

Gretchen is a two-time National Board–certified elementary school teacher. She currently resides in Charlotte, North Carolina, with her husband, three young children, and labradoodle named Belle.

In 2006, Gretchen received her bachelor's degree at Marist College in Poughkeepsie, New York. In 2010, she received her master's degree in curriculum and supervision from the University of North Carolina at Charlotte.

Gretchen taught grades 2, 3, and 5 before transitioning into the role of a new teacher development coach for The New Teacher Project (TNTP). During this time, she also published her first book for new teachers called *Elementary EDUC 101: What They Didn't Teach You in College* to help prepare future teachers for the realities of life in the classroom.

For more than a decade, Gretchen has passionately mentored and coached educators, led professional development experiences for school building staff members, and presented at district and national conferences as the owner of Always a Lesson. Her impact continues to amplify serving educators worldwide through her blog, Empowering Educators podcast, classroom resources, professional development courses, and personalized coaching opportunities. She has since coauthored a book with more than a dozen other elite educators called *Teachers Who Know What To Do: Experts In Education* to share proven strategies that transform classrooms and leaders around the world, as well as written this book.

Whether you're teaching a lesson or learning one yourself, there's Always a Lesson.

INDEX